FINLAND

Leningrad ●

BALTIC SEA

EN

ARMY GROUP NORTH

Moscow ●

Smolensk ●

RUSSIA

●Rastenburg HQ

ARMY GROUP CENTER

Warsaw ●

POLAND

● Kiev

rague

ZECHOSLOVAKIA

Vienna ●

Odessa ●

STRIA

● Budapest

HUNGARY

UKRAINIAN ARMIES

RUMANIA

BLACK SEA

Belgrade ●

● Bucharest

YUGOSLAVIA

BULGARIA

TURKEY

A. M. JAUSS

To Kill the Devil

To Kill The Devil

The Attempts on the Life of Adolf Hitler

Herbert Molloy Mason, Jr.

W·W·NORTON & COMPANY·INC·

New York

Copyright © 1978 by Herbert Molloy Mason, Jr.
Published simultaneously in Canada by George J. McLeod Limited,
Toronto. Printed in the United States of America.
All Rights Reserved
First Edition

Library of Congress Cataloging in Publication Data

Mason, Herbert Molloy.
  To kill the devil.

  Bibliography: p.
  Includes index.
  1. Hitler, Adolf, 1889–1945—Assassination.
2. Anti-Nazi movement—Biography. 3. Germany—Politics
and government—1933–1945. I. Title.
DD247.H5M2848 1978   364.1'524'0922   78–5070
ISBN 0-393-05682-1

1 2 3 4 5 6 7 8 9 0

For

CAREY GOODWYN
Stalag Luft I
1944–45

Contents

CONTENTS

Photographs appear following pages 78 and 174.

Foreword

In the winter of 1943 two German officers at a headquarters near Smolensk secretly experimented with plastic explosives to be used to assassinate the German head of state, Adolf Hitler. One of the plotters was a full colonel, the other a reserve lieutenant and respected peacetime jurist; their commanding officer considered them dedicated soldiers with brilliant wartime records. What would drive such men to choose the path of the assassin or, as some would later claim, to turn traitor at the height of a death struggle to determine the nation's survival?

It is not generally realized that mortal opposition to Hitler began long before German armies became bogged down in Russia. The public did not know that many high-ranking, conservative members of the General Staff and other army figures consistently opposed, within the limits of their means, Hitler's plan to launch a second world war, a war these generals and field marshals knew Germany could not win. Once the war began, the rest of the world assumed that the brutally efficient series of conquests had been engineered long in advance by eager "Prussian militarists" acting in collusion with their Führer. Exactly the opposite was the case.

Between 1919 and Hitler's rise to power in 1933, the German General Staff thought only in terms of defense against an attack from the east, where the Poles and the Czechs could mobilize 1.6

million troops between them. Limited by the Versailles treaty to a standing army of only 100,000 without tanks or heavy artillery (the air arm, eventually the Luftwaffe, was being trained secretly in Russia), the General Staff entertained no thoughts of starting a war of aggression.

Hitler's sudden appearance on the political scene in the 1920s at first raised no Prussian eyebrows. As one general, Georg von Sodenstern, said in postwar recollections, "In the Army the impression was encountered in all quarters that Hitler could not amount to much, otherwise he would have gotten further than a corporal during the war."

In 1932 the German officer class was an elite; 24 percent of those with the rank of lieutenant and above belonged to the aristocracy, and almost to a man they were disgusted with the makeup of the senior Party leaders and the men they commanded. Hitler was an Austrian nobody; Göring a bloated caricature of a 1918 air hero, now addicted to morphine; Goebbels a dwarfish demagogue; Julius Streicher a Jew-baiter and pornographer and the Nazis' martyred hero, Horst Wessel, had been a pimp. Hitler's original bodyguard, the brown-shirted storm troops, were street thugs to whom brawling and bloodletting were everyday occurrences, acceptable means of wielding power. In short, the majority of German officers looked upon the new régime much as the West Point Association would have looked upon an American government in the hands of Al Capone and Legs Diamond backed by men carrying tommy guns and brass knuckles. The comparison is not extreme.

But when Hitler started to woo the military with promises of a resurgent Reich based upon a modern rearmaments program, he struck a responsive chord throughout the armed forces. A disarmed Germany lacking martial pride was intolerable to every man who wore field gray. General von Sodenstern points out that after 1933, "many succumbed to the dangerous self-deception that Adolf Hitler was basically a decent man with high ideals who, in possession of the power of the state, would get rid of the ugly concomitant phenomena of his movement."

But the "ugly concomitant" was what had brought Hitler to

power and would keep him there by oppression and terror wherever the swastika flag was raised. Many officers realized this and continued to oppose Hitler even when National Socialism was at the zenith of its power and popularity. As early as 1938, detailed planning was carried out by ranking German commanders first to balk Hitler's plans, then to seize his person, then to kill him in order to halt the precipitate rush to conflagration. These plans were overhauled constantly during the following years as Germany's name was blackened by Hitler's mania for conquest and extermination. The conspirators, always few in number, never flagged in their determination to rid Germany of the scourge of National Socialism, and many of them paid with their lives for their daring. They came close to succeeding in their attempts to assassinate the Führer on two occasions, and only flukes kept Hitler alive until *Götterdammerüng* descended upon Germany in the spring of 1945.

The attitude toward those who staked all in their efforts to liquidate Adolf Hitler was summed up in a statement made to the U.S. army after the war by Sodenstern, who watched the rise and fall of the Reich's fortunes from the beginning. "It was the German soldiers who brought themselves through difficult conflicts of conscience to the realization that legal methods could have no effect against the National Socialist terror. The path taken by these men was long and thorny. Their story deserves the appreciation of posterity because their actions had been barred not only by traditions of German soldierdom, which were hundreds of years old, but also by the professional ethics of all soldiers of the world."

Here, then, is the story of those men who tried to kill the devil.

—H. M. M.

Acknowledgments

The author is especially indebted to Mr. Robert Wolfe and Mr. John Mendelsohn of the Modern Military Branch, Military Archives Division, National Archives and Records Service, Washington, D.C., and to Dr. Anton Hoch, Archive Director of the Institut für Zeitgeschichte in Munich, West Germany, for valuable guidance in gathering research material for this book. The National Archives holds thousands of rolls of microfilms of German records captured at the close of World War II, many of them dealing with German opposition to Hitler, and copies of these microfilms are available to the researcher.

Equally helpful were copies of interrogation reports of certain German officers who spoke freely to their U.S. Army captors. Obtained from the Office of the Chief of Military History and used here were the following transcripts in English: MS # B-272, *20 July 1944*, an interview with General Günther Blumentritt; MS # A-855, *History of the Attempt on Hitler's Life*, an account of Colonel Rudolf von Gersdorff's own failed assassination attempt, and MS # B-499, *Events Leading up to 20 July 1944*, by General Georg von Sodenstern, a perceptive examination of the inner conflicts individual German officers experienced between their oath to the Führer and the certain knowledge that Hitler was leading the nation to shame and destruction.

I wish to thank Mrs. Agnes F. Peterson of the Hoover Institu-

ACKNOWLEDGMENTS

tion on War, Revolution, and Peace in Stanford, California; Mrs. Frances Hay of Mystole Park, Kent, England, a wartime member of MI-5, and Dr. Frank H. Panton, Director of the Propellants, Explosives, and Rocket Motor Establishment at Waltham Abbey in Essex, for supplying details of the British explosives used in the attempts on Hitler's life. And I owe thanks to Mr. Leif Hansen, of Fredrikstad, Norway, for securing copies of the Gestapo interrogation of Georg Elser, expertly translated by Mrs. Hildegard Adams of San Antonio.

I extend my appreciation to Mr. Thomas Wheaton Coward for the extended loan of his file on Wilhelm Canaris, including personal letters from General Franz Halder, General Achim Oster, Herr Josef Müller, the Countess Elisabeth Freytag von Loringhoven and from other survivors and relatives of those who opposed Hitler.

Dr. Hubertus Strughold, once a ranking Luftwaffe scientist and pioneer flight surgeon—and wanted by the Gestapo in 1945—provided the author with insights into the character of Stauffenberg, whom he knew in Berlin.

Additional thanks are due to Mr. Claude R. Hall of Los Angeles, Mrs. Mary Deason, Mr. Alfonso Butcher, and Mr. Curtis Watson of the Fort Sam Houston Library; Mr. Craig Likness of the Trinity University Library; Mr. Rod Henshaw and Ms. Rose Blumenthal of the San Antonio Library System. And, as always, thanks to Rigmor and Berit for help in many ways.

For the reader interested in delving deeper into the Hitler phenomenon and learning more about the dedicated opposition to the Führer, a select bibliography is offered at the end of the text.

Cast of Characters

BARGATSKY, Walter: A German war ministry official based in Paris who was privy to the plot of July 20, 1944.

BAVAUD, Maurice: Swiss theological student who stalked the Führer in Munich and near Berchtesgaden shortly before the outbreak of the war.

BECK, General Ludwig: Chief of the Army General Staff from 1935 to 1938. He constantly opposed Hitler's plans for war and was active in the planning to liquidate Hitler from 1938 onward.

BLOMBERG, Field Marshal Werner von: Hitler's complaisant war minister (known behind his back as the "Rubber Lion") until 1938, when a mésalliance resulted in his ouster from office.

BLUMENTRITT, General Günther: Chief of staff to Field Marshal Gunther von Kluge (see below), commander-in-chief, West, during the battle for Normandy in 1944. Blumentritt was ignorant of the July 20 plot until after the fact.

BOESLAGER, Lieutenant Colonel Georg von: Extraordinary commando-type infantry commander on the Russian front who volunteered to machine gun Hitler and his entourage in 1943 during a Führer visit to advanced headquarters.

CAST OF CHARACTERS

BRAUCHITSCH, Field Marshal Walther von: Commander-in-chief of the German army from 1938 until December 1941, when he was sacked by Hitler for indifferent performance. Hitler assumed direct command of the army after Brauchitsch's dismissal.

BREDOW, General Kurt von: German defense minister, briefly, in 1932, he was assassinated during the so-called Blood Purge of 1934 for his opposition to the Nazi party.

BREITENBUCH, Captain Eberhard von: A general's aide, Breitenbuch volunteered to attempt to kill Hitler with a pistol at close range.

BUSSCHE, Captain Axel von dem: Frontline infantry officer who planned to sacrifice his own life in an attempt to blow up the Führer with a bomb.

CANARIS, Admiral Wilhelm: Chief of the Abwehr, the German counterintelligence organization. Canaris held Hitler in contempt and allowed Abwehr HQ to serve as the nerve center for military planning to overthrow the Führer.

DOHNANYI, Hans von: Peacetime jurist and wartime junior officer actively involved in the plots against Hitler's life.

ELSER, Johann Georg: Master cabinetmaker who single-handedly conceived and executed a plan to assassinate Hitler with explosives—a plan that very nearly succeeded.

FELLGIEBEL, General Erich: Chief signals officer at the Führer HQ near Rastenburg, East Prussia. Fellgiebel played a key role in the attempt of July 20, 1944.

FINCKH, Colonel Eberhard: Deputy chief of staff, Army Group B, during the battle for Normandy in 1944. Finckh revealed to Field Marshal Erwin Rommel (see below) plans for the assassination attempt of July 20, 1944.

FREISLER, Roland: President of the so-called People's Court, responsible for sending thousands of Germans to their deaths for anti-Nazi activities. Freisler was Hitler's favorite legal executioner.

FROMM, General Friedrich: Commander of the Home, or Replacement, Army in Berlin. Fromm was seized by the conspirators in Berlin on the afternoon of July 20.

GERSDORFF, Colonel Rudolph-Christoph von: Another frontline officer who volunteered to blow himself up along with Hitler to bring an end to the war and the Nazi régime.

GISEVIUS, Hans Bernd: A former minor Gestapo official actively involved in many of the plans to eliminate the Führer.

GOERDLER, Carl: One-time lord mayor of Leipzig and a staunch opponent of Hitler and the Nazis from the beginning, Goerdler planned to assume the chancellorship of Germany upon Hitler's removal from the scene.

HAEFTEN, Lieutenant Werner von: Aide to Colonel Claus von Stauffenberg (see below), involved in the plot of July 20.

HALDER, General Franz: Chief of the Army General Staff after Beck in 1948. Hitler fired him in late 1942. He survived Flossenburg and Dachau concentration camps.

HAMMERSTEIN-EQUORD, General Kurt von: Commander-in-chief, Army Group A, with headquarters in Cologne. Hammerstein hoped to lure Hitler to Cologne in September 1939 and there arrest or do away with him and so end the war.

HASE, General Paul von: Commandant, City of Berlin, and an active conspirator in the attempted takeover of the capital on the afternoon of July 20, 1944.

HEYDRICH, SS General Reinhard: Head of the infamous RSHA, the Reich Main Security Office, and later named protector of Bohemia-Moravia. He was assassinated in May 1942 by a Czech team flown in from England for the purpose.

HIMMLER, Heinrich: One-time chicken farmer who became Reichsführer SS. Himmler implemented Hitler's plans for

CAST OF CHARACTERS

the destruction of European Jewry. His SS Death's Head units ran the concentration camps inside and outside the Third Reich. He betrayed his Führer in Germany's final agony.

HOEPNER, General Erich: Assumed General Fromm's place as commander, Home Army, during the 1944 putsch.

HOFACKER, Lieutenant Colonel Cäser von: Aide to the military governor of France, and the only Luftwaffe officer to take an active part in the attempt to overthrow Hitler.

HUBER, Kurt: A Swiss-born, naturalized German citizen, Huber became head of the philosophy department at the University of Munich. His leaflet campaign against Hitler and the war in 1942 triggered a student revolt.

KEITEL, Field Marshal Wilhelm: Chief of the German High Command, the OKW, from 1938 until the end of the war. Keitel, known as Hitler's lackey, was hanged by the Allies after the Nuremberg trials.

KLUGE, Field Marshal Hans Günther von: After long service in Russia, Kluge succeeded Field Marshal Erwin Rommel as commander, Army Group B, in France on July 17, 1944. Kluge, an energetic combat commander, was wooed repeatedly by the conspirators.

KORDT, Erich: Foreign ministry official in Berlin who volunteered to assassinate Hitler with explosives or pistol in 1939.

MERTZ VON QUIRNHEIM, Colonel Albrecht: Chief of staff, after Stauffenberg, of the General Army Office in Berlin and active in the events of July 20, 1944, inside the capital.

OLBRICHT, General Friedrich: Commander, General Army Office, Berlin. Olbricht was minister of war–designate had Hitler's removal been effected and a new government formed.

OSTER, General Hans: The debonair mainspring of conspiracy within the Abwehr.

xviii

Cast of Characters

REMER, Major Otto Ernst: Commander of the Grossdeutschland Guard Battalion in Berlin. It was Remer more than any other officer who helped quell the rebellion inside the capital on July 20, 1944.

RIBBENTROP, Joachim von: A champagne salesman who became Hitler's foreign minister.

RÖHM, Ernst: Leader of the Sturmabteilung, the SA, Röhm was a crony of Hitler's whose ambitions led to his downfall in the Blood Purge of 1934. Röhm's Storm troopers helped club Hitler's way to power.

ROMMEL, Field Marshal Erwin: The famed "Desert Fox," Rommel, initially an ardent admirer of Hitler, earned a reputation as a brilliant armored warfare tactician first in France and later in North Africa. Rommel was ready to take an active part in the revolt against Hitler and the war when a chance misfortune on the battlefield removed him from the scene at a critical juncture.

RUNDSTEDT, Field Marshal Gerd von: Commander-in-chief, West. Rundstedt referred to Hitler as "that Bohemian corporal" but took no active part in the revolt of the generals.

SCHACHT, Hjalmar: Germany's astute economist and minister of finance, fired by Hitler for his pessimistic—and accurate— warnings that the Third Reich could never survive a major war from the economic standpoint alone. Acquitted at the trials at Nuremberg.

SCHELLENBERG, SS General Walter: As head of Department IV E, Schellenberg was responsible for counterespionage work for the Gestapo inside Germany and later reorganized the Gestapo's Foreign Intelligence Service. He survived the war to write his memoirs.

SCHLABRENDORFF, Fabian von: Peacetime lawyer and wartime reserve officer in the Wehrmacht. Schlabrendorff served in Russia and was actively involved in the assassination attempts. Eventually seized by the Gestapo, he endured brutal tortures and survived the war.

SCHLEICHER, General Kurt von: After a brilliant career as staff officer during World War I, Schleicher helped rebuild the German army and then turned to politics. Earned Hitler's hatred in 1932 when he became—for fifty-seven days—chancellor of Germany. Shot down in the purge of 1934.

SCHOLL, Hans: Wehrmacht sergeant and medical student at the University of Munich. Scholl, his sister, Sophie, and other undergraduates launched an anti-Hitler pamphlet campaign.

STAUFFENBERG, Lieutenant Colonel Claus Schenk von: Aristocratic and implacable foe of Hitler following the debacles in Russia and in North Africa, Stauffenberg became the trigger of the assassination attempts beginning in 1943. He overcame crippling and disfiguring wounds to pursue the goal of Hitler's death.

STIEFF, General Helmuth: Head of the Organization Section of the General Staff based in East Prussia, Stieff refused to attack Hitler directly but agreed to secrete the explosives to be used by others.

STÜLPNAGEL, General Karl Heinrich von: Military commander of occupied France. Stülpnagel was in charge of arresting and disarming the SS and the Gestapo during the takeover of Paris by the Wehrmacht on the evening of July 20, 1944.

THOMAS, General Georg: Head of the army's War Economy Section, Thomas tried in vain to persuade Hitler that the launching of a second world war would be economic and military suicide.

TRESKOW, General Henning von: Former stockbroker and world traveler, Treskow served in Russia with Army Group Center and worked unceasingly for Hitler's overthrow. Treskow and Schlabrendorff worked closely with the Abwehr circle in Berlin.

Cast of Characters

WITZLEBEN, Field Marshal Erwin von: Ended a forty-year career with the German army in 1942 and was active in plans for ridding Germany of National Socialism. He was to assume overall command of the Wehrmacht once Hitler was dead and the Nazi organization dismantled.

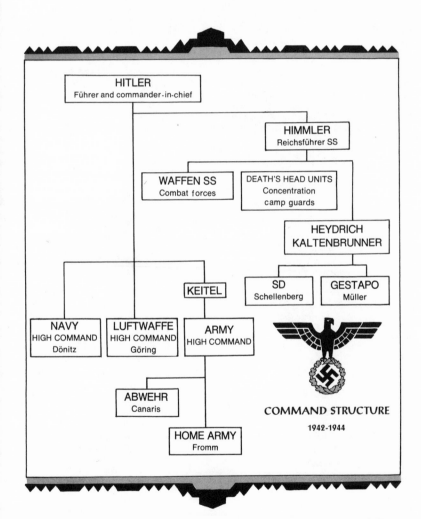

COMMAND STRUCTURE

1942-1944

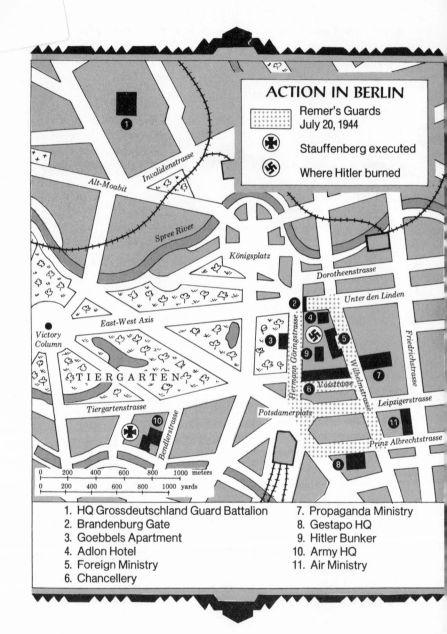

ACTION IN BERLIN

Remer's Guards
July 20, 1944

Stauffenberg executed

Where Hitler burned

1. HQ Grossdeutschland Guard Battalion
2. Brandenburg Gate
3. Goebbels Apartment
4. Adlon Hotel
5. Foreign Ministry
6. Chancellery
7. Propaganda Ministry
8. Gestapo HQ
9. Hitler Bunker
10. Army HQ
11. Air Ministry

If the governmental power is leading
a people to destruction, then for every
subject rebellion is not only a right
but a duty. Human rights always prevail
over state rights.

—ADOLF HITLER
Mein Kampf, 1925

Part 1

The Hunted

1

Executive Action

SATURDAY, JUNE 30, 1934, was an unusually warm day in Berlin. The temperature stood at eighty-five degrees by midmorning and threatened to go even higher. At Neubabelsberg, a fashionable district on the southeastern outskirts of the city, General Kurt von Schleicher retreated to his ground-floor study shortly after breakfast and seated himself at a polished desk that, like all the other furniture in the two-story villa, was heavy and expensive. Despite the heat, Schleicher was impeccably dressed, as though ready to be chauffeured at a moment's notice to the government buildings on the Wilhemstrasse. But in fact Schleicher had been unemployed ever since the Nazi upstart Adolf Hitler had taken his job as chancellor of Germany seventeen months earlier.

At fifty-two, Schleicher believed that his best days still lay ahead; his health was sound and the agile brain that had served his ambitions so well over the years was still capable of exercising a foxlike cunning.

Schleicher's career had been built on shrewdness and political instinct. Early on he saw that while the front lines might yield glory, real power was held in a narrow circle that spun around the upper echelons of command. As a first step to entering that circle, Schleicher secured an appointment to the War Academy and so impressed his superiors with brilliant theories on tactics and strategy that he soon joined the staff of an elite regiment, the 3rd Foot Guards. Along the way, he cultivated the friendship of Oskar von Hindenberg, son of the venerable and revered field marshal. After Germany's defeat in 1918, Schleicher, unlike most other officers, stayed on, displaying a flair for political manipulation and undercover work in rebuilding the German army and re-creating—largely with Russian help—an air force forbidden by the Versailles treaty. By 1931 Schleicher was a two-star general, intimate with President von Hindenburg and members of his cabinet, many of whom Schleicher had maneuvered into power. But he was not satisfied: his ambition had grown. He wished to exchange his now-superfluous general's uniform for the black silk hat and wing collar of the chancellorship; from there it was but one step upward, and Hindenburg was eighty-four.

Schleicher's golden opportunity came during the first week in December 1932, when Hindenburg appointed him chancellor. It was to be a short tenure. Able neither to split the Nazi party, which was bankrupt in funds but not in spirit, nor to woo parties Left and Center, Schleicher failed totally to create a majority in the Reichstag and was back out on the street fifty-seven days after taking office. But not before he had made a deadly enemy. Adolf Hitler would not soon forget Schleicher's attempt to divide his party, which he had carefully nurtured for more than ten years, and to bury it under the feeble wing of the Weimar Republic.

Seated at his desk inside the house at Neubabelsberg, Schleicher reflected on the events of the night before. Shortly after 7:00 P.M. an old friend, Arno Moysischewitz, had appeared at the door and was readily admitted. Moysischewitz, a confidant, was informed on the inner workings of the army's ministerial offices. Schleicher listened with indignation as his friend reported rumors to the effect that Schleicher was working behind the scenes for Hitler's ouster. Schleicher was said to be plotting with Ernst Röhm, the leader of the SA—the *Sturmabteilung* (storm troops)—for the violent seizure of the government. Röhm, a porcine homosexual in the habit of wearing cheap perfume, was hardly the type of man with whom the aristocratic Schleicher would associate. Schleicher told Moysischewitz that Röhm had indeed sent one of his deputies out to the villa, no doubt to strike a bargain, but that the housekeeper had been ordered to send him packing. Assuring his worried caller that he had not dabbled in politics since his resignation from high office, Schleicher declared that God had decided that he was no longer needed as His instrument after January 1933. The general confided to Moysischewitz, "Nothing could tempt me to get back into politics unless God should give me an unexpected call." Moysischewitz left the house around midnight, reassuring Schleicher that he would report back concerning his efforts to scotch the ugly rumors floating through the corridors of the army ministry.

Schleicher sat at his desk, waiting for the phone to ring; but when it did, the caller was not Moysischewitz with further news but a fellow general officer who wished only to engage in small talk. He chatted about Schleicher's recent holiday spent with his bride of eighteen months, who at that moment was in the next room arranging flowers in a vase.

While the general was on the phone, the door buzzer sounded in the entranceway. The maid, Marie Güntel, opened the door and was brushed aside by five men in long coats demanding to see Schleicher. She gestured toward the study. Two of the men stalked across the carpet and approached the desk.

"Are you General von Schleicher?" one of them demanded.

"Yes, I am," he replied.

The men pulled out Walther automatic pistols and opened fire, hitting Schleicher in the neck and chest; the sound carried to Schleicher's caller before the receiver was replaced in the cradle. Frau von Schleicher rushed into the room, and she, too, was shot down. Then the gunmen stuffed their automatics back in their trenchcoat pockets and ransacked the room for incriminating papers. There were of course none. As they stepped over the bodies and headed for the door, the maid stood paralyzed. "We won't kill you, miss," one of them said, and they walked out of the house, climbed into a sedan, and drove away. The maid fled,

5

leaving the bodies to be discovered by Schleicher's sixteen-year-old stepdaughter arriving home for lunch. Hitler had settled his first score, the first of many.

A dozen miles away, in the lobby of Berlin's plush Adlon Hotel, Major General Kurt von Bredow sat having tea. Outside, Saturday strollers walked past the tall windows overlooking the Unter den Linden. A string orchestra played operetta music in one corner of the baroque lobby, and white-jacketed waiters— many in the pay of the Gestapo—stood discreetly at strategic locations throughout the room awaiting the commands of the clientele, Berlin's elite and foreign diplomats.

General von Bredow, who had served as defense minister during his close friend Schleicher's brief term as chancellor, was now also out of work—but, like Schleicher, he still maintained contact inside the Reichswehr ministry. His teatime conversation with one of the foreign military attachés was interrupted by the appearance of one of these contacts, who bent over to whisper the news of Schleicher's murder in Bredow's ear. Bredon straightened and said in a voice loud enough for everybody to hear, "It's a wonder the swine haven't shot *me* before now." He then paid his bill, rose, and walked out of the Adlon lobby.

At about five that afternoon there was a clamor at Bredow's front door. The general got up to answer it himself and was greeted by a fusillade of pistol shots fired at point-blank range that sent him staggering backward to crash on the floor. The gunmen picked up the body, dragged it outside, and loaded it into a waiting car that sped off to deliver the "assignment" to the cadet barracks at Lichterfelde, on of the southern outskirts of Berlin. Bredow's crimes consisted of his friendship with Schleicher and having aroused a vague suspicion, never proved, that he was the author of a book printed in Paris entitled *Diary of a Reichswehr General*, which was critical of the Nazis.

Thus were destroyed the first two German generals who transgressed against the shifting policies of a new government intolerant of the slightest opposition, whether real or imagined.

6

Schleicher and Bredow were only two of many eliminated on June 30, 1934; the killing had been going on since early morning all across southern Germany, and would continue into the next day.

Some three hours before Bredow's murder, Adolf Hitler had boarded a trimotored, corrugated metal Ju.52 transport at an airfield outside Bonn in western Germany. He slumped in his seat for the ninety-minute flight southeast to Munich. With him was the diminutive intellectual Dr. Paul Joseph Goebbels (sometimes known behind his back as "Wotan's Mickey Mouse"); his current press chief, Otto Dietrich, and the rather dull-witted storm trooper officer Viktor Lutze, one of the few SA leaders Hitler felt was loyal to the bone. Hitler, seated forward in the crew compartment, remained detached from the others; he gazed silently through a port window at the darkness outside, which was lighted only by the orange flare of the engine exhaust stacks. Loss of sleep and thoughts of the unpleasant actions that were rapidly approaching had put him in a bad mood.

Hitler had been in the steel town of Essen the day and night before to attend the wedding of Josef Terboven, the *Gauleiter* (district party leader) of Westphalia. The festivities had had a Renaissance flavor, with the nighttime skies lighted by fireworks, floodlights, and more than 20,000 flaming torches carried through the streets. Hitler through it all had seemed oblivious to the pageantry, and his congratulatory speech to Terboven and his bride was perfunctory.

He was in fact preoccupied: throughout the festival and the days preceding it Hitler was struggling with himself to reach a decision—whether or not to order mass arrests and executions of men whom he had known for years and who had in many cases helped him along the road to power. Hitler's deputies had never known him to be so indecisive.

The targets of Hitler's fluctuating wrath were the leaders of the SA, a monster largely of Hitler's own making. Created in 1921 as a bodyguard for the handful of misfits organizing the National Socialist German Workers party, the ranks of the SA were filled

7

by war veterans, the shiftless, the jobless, even by ex-convicts. In their brown-shirts the toughs excelled in street brawls; cracked heads were considered a badge of honor. One seasoned storm trooper bragged of having faced a judge more than thirty times for such offenses as assault and battery, resisting arrest, and "other such misdemeanors that are natural for a Nazi." He was proud of the "knife scars on the back of my head, on my left shoulder, on my lower lip, on my right cheek, on the left side of my upper lip and on my right arm."

By 1933, the SA, twelve years old and numbering more than 400,000 men, was a paramilitary force that posed a serious threat to the supremacy of Germany's small standing army, the *Reichswehr*. It was Ernst Röhm's great dream to absorb the 100,000 regular troops into his SA to create a true National Socialist army, which he would command. Hitler, waiting in the wings for the aged President von Hindenburg to die, knew that the dictatorship of Germany could be his only with the backing of the Reichswehr. When he drifted away from the SA and began courting the establishment military clique, Röhm became furious. "Adolf is rotten!" he told a gathering of SA officers during one of their frequent drinking sprees. "He only goes around with reactionaries. His old pals aren't good enough for him, so he brings in those East Prussian generals . . . Adolf will always be a civilian, an artist, a dreamer. Right now all he wants to do is sit up in the mountains and play God while guys like us have to cool our heels when we're burning for action."

Many around Hitler saw the opportunity, and a plot to crush the SA's ambitions violently was concocted behind Hitler's back early in 1934, months before he was duped into taking action himself. The conspiracy was engineered by the head of the SS—the *Schutzstaffel*—Heinrich Himmler, a one time chicken farmer, and his chief of security, Reinhard Heydrich, a cashiered naval officer. As ranking officers of the elite SS, they wanted the SA, the parent organization, drained and impotent. There was no faster way to bring this about than by liquidating Röhm and those who backed his dreams of power. They were joined in the plot by Hermann Göring, minister of Prussia, who promised to add his own police force to the effort to bring down the SA power monolith. The Reichswehr would not dirty its hands in any active operations against the brown shirts, but Major General Walther von Reichenau, in charge of the army ministry, promised to provide barracks, transportation, and weapons to those who would.

While evidence was being manufactured to convince Hitler that Röhm was organizing a putsch against the government and the Reichswehr, Hitler himself was trying to reason with the corpulent SA leader to moderate his demands. After one of Hitler's impassioned speeches, Röhm stomped out of the room, snarling to his followers, "What that ridiculous corporal says means nothing to us . . . if we can't get there with him, we'll get there without him."

Heydrich, Himmler, and Göring drew up separate lists of names of those to be shot and compared notes. Hitler had one last meeting with Röhm and persuaded him and the entire SA to take a thirty-day leave, beginning on July 1, to let things cool off; Röhm's leave would begin earlier so that he could take a cure for a kidney ailment. This turn of events threatened to wreck the SS plans. How could Hitler, the army, and, for that matter, the rest of the nation be convinced that the SA was planning a putsch with the leaders on vacation and the rank and file disbanded? More evidence was needed, and Heydrich's forgers went to work fabricating letters with Röhm's signature wherein Röhm ordered the SA to arm itself secretly in order to overthrow the Reichswehr. When the forgery was shown to General von Reichenau, he exclaimed, "Now it is high time to act!" and Hitler declared that he would personally visit Röhm and "square accounts." But still he vacillated between sacking Röhm and trying once again to reconcile their differences; he was as yet unaware of the death lists already drawn up, and he did not speak of liquidation.

It wasn't until the evening of June 28, during Terboven's wedding festival, that Hitler's attitude hardened. The telephone in his suite at the Hotel Kaiserhof in Essen rang almost incessantly with alarming news from Berlin. A dramatic touch was provided with the arrival of Göring's crony Paul "Pilli" Körner, who flew

9

down from Berlin to tell Hitler in person that the armed SA rising was imminent. Göring, standing at Hitler's side, was ordered
back to Berlin to alert the SS *Leibstandardte* (Life Guards) regiment to prepare for action. "I've had enough!" Hitler shouted. "I
shall make an example of them!"

When Hitler reached Röhm by telephone at his lakeside retreat
at Bad Wiessee, south of Munich, he did not mention a putsch; he
only ordered Röhm to assemble the upper-echelon leaders of the
SA at Bad Wiessee and to be ready for a conference at 11 A.M. on
June 30. Röhm was agreeable, and after sending off telegrams to
his colonels and brigadiers, he and a companion went for a leisurely stroll through the woods.

Government offices in Berlin and in Munich swarmed with activity all the next day, Friday—activity that few at command
level of the Reichswehr could take seriously. Colonel Gotthard
Heinrici, a tough, bantam-sized officer with heavy combat experience, was at his desk at the Reichswehr ministry when a young
aide marched up to him and leaned a rifle against his desk.
"What's that for?" Heinrici asked.

"So the colonel can defend himself against the SA."

"Son," Heinrici said, "don't be silly."

Himmler and Göring continued to feed Hitler alarming reports
all day Friday and into the night: *Armed bands of SA are marching
through the streets of Berlin . . . the putsch will erupt all across Germany
at 4 P.M. sharp on Saturday . . . Röhm has set the machinery in motion
for Hitler's ouster.*

It was then that Hitler ordered the precipitate flight to Munich,
toward a confrontation so bloody it would stand out even in an
era when violence was commonplace.

Hitler's Ju.52 touched down at 3:45 A.M. in the predawn mist
that blanketed the airfield at Munich-Oberwiessenfeld. He
stamped past the ranks of waiting political and SA officials roused
from bed to form a reception committee, pausing only briefly to
comment that this Saturday had been "the blackest day of my
life." Then he entered one of the waiting cars and was swept off
to the center of Munich. The car stopped in front of the building
housing the Bavarian Ministry of the Interior, and Hitler got out
and walked quickly up the steps and inside.

He first encountered Obergruppenführer (Lieutenant General) August Schneidhuber, who had been waiting for the chancellor's arrival, wondering at the commotion. Schneidhuber sprang to attention, only to have Hitler bark, "Traitor!" and rip off his epaulettes and rank badges and throw them on the floor. Schneidhuber was grabbed and hustled out of the building and hurried to Stadelheim Prison. Gruppenführer (Major General) Wilhelm Schmid, who had been roused from bed at 4 A.M. and ordered to report to the ministry, arrived and was just as puzzled as Schneidhuber. Hitler ripped at his uniform and cried, "You're under arrest! You'll be shot!" Schmid was dragged off to Stadelheim.

Ordering the pickup of SA leaders in Munich to continue, Hitler stalked out of the building and got back in his open Mercedes, seating himself beside the driver. Hitler's Mercedes was supercharged and ran easily above 100 mph on the open road, to his delight. Pulling a leather aviator's helmet down over his head, he ordered the small caravan of official cars and commandeered taxis to head out of Munich for Bad Wiessee, thirty-five miles away, toward the Austrian frontier.

They reached Bad Wiessee at 6:30 A. M. and drove through the quiet streets to a promontory jutting into the Tegernsee lake. There sat the Pension Hanselbauer, a white and brown resort hotel, typically quaint in a Bavarian way, with its windowboxes sprouting flowers. They got out of the cars, stomped noisily up the wooden steps, and flung the doors open. Hitler marched down the corridor, followed by men with drawn pistols; reaching Röhm's door, he hammered on it, and a moment later Röhm stumbled out of bed to confront the trenchcoated figure of Adolf Hitler with a wild look in his eyes. "You're under arrest!" Hitler cried. Uncomprehending, surprised to see Hitler at this hour, Röhm could only reply, "Heil, mein Führer!"

Hitler launched into a tirade that snapped Röhm awake. He vigorously denied the charges of treason, but was nonetheless ordered to be seized and locked in the hotel basement.

Hitler, the SS, and the plainclothes detectives raged up and down the corridors, banging on doors and hauling SA leaders out of bed. In the room opposite Röhm's Obergruppenführer Edmund Heines was hauled out of the covers along with a male sleeping partner. Hitler made no comment, but Goebbels found the scene, "revolting, nauseating." Within twenty minutes the pension was emptied of SA leaders; all were on their way to Stadelheim in trucks provided by the Reichswehr. More SA leaders were bagged as they stepped off the train in Munich, and still others were flagged down and arrested on the roads leading to Bad Wiessee—all bound for the spurious 11 A.M. meeting with Hitler.

Hitler drove back to Munich, where he flashed a signal, *Hummingbird*, to Berlin. Now the SS unleashed its killer packs, not always with the results Hitler intended. Dr. Wilhelm Eduard Schmid, a well-known Munich music critic, was at home playing the cello when a gang of SS broke into the house and dragged him off in front of his wife and children. He was driven the few miles to the new concentration camp at Dachau and shot to death. Schmid was the wrong man: the SS had been sent to arrest Obergruppenführer Ludwig Wilhelm Schmitt; failing to find him, they had simply unearthed another "Dr. Smith" from the phone book and exterminated him instead. Frau Schmid received a coffin from Dachau with the order that it must not be opened before her husband's burial. She also received a check from the SS as compensation, which she contemptuously returned.

In Berlin, Dr. Erich Klausner had just returned to his office at the Ministry of Transport following lunch when a captain Kurt Gildisch of the SS, wearing a black uniform, barged into the anteroom and demanded an audience. Klausner, a heavy-set, balding man in his fifties, could not imagine what the captain wanted, but he asked him to enter his office. Told he was under arrest. Klausner turned to fetch his jacket, and Gildisch shot him in the back of the head. Klausner's crime was being president of the Catholic Action Society.

The orgy of arrests took macabre turns. When Gildisch reported back to Heydrich, he immediately received another assignment: fly to Bremen and arrest Gruppenführer Karl Ernst who, according to information fed to Hitler and the Reichswehr, was planning to lead the SA revolt in Berlin that very afternoon.

12

In fact, Ernst was planning to board ship with his new bride for an extended honeymoon in Tenerife. The impassive Gildisch located Ernst and told him he was under arrest. Ernst, in high spirits, thought that a typical honeymoon joke was in motion and decided to play along. Gildisch snapped handcuffs on Ernst's wrists, and they boarded a plane for Berlin, where the bridegroom was transferred to a car and driven to Lichterfelde Barracks. Ernst joked with the silent SS guards during the drive and was still in good humor when he was stood against a brick wall. The rifles cracked, and Ernst had only a split second to realize that he was indeed a victim, but not of a prank.

Hitler spent that afternoon at Party headquarters in Munich monitoring the progress of the purge. He was handed a list of SA leaders snared in Bavaria and thoughtfully penciled a mark against six of the names; he could not yet bring himself to condemn Ernst Röhm. An SS squad was despatched to Stadelheim at 5:30 P.M., and after a heated argument with the prison director over who had legal custody, the condemned were dragged from their cells, taken into the courtyard, and shot one after the other. Generals Schneidhuber and Schmid died still in a state of shock and bewilderment, and one-armed Hans Peter von Heydrebreck unaccountably stared at the rifle muzzles pointed at his chest and cried out, "Long live the Führer! Heil Hitler!" only seconds before he was blown into eternity.

Very few of the intended victims got away. One of them, a former minister under Schleicher named Gottfried Reinhold Treviranus, was not at home when the SS called; he was on the courts of the Wannsee Tennis Club in Berlin playing his usual Saturday afternoon game of singles. Treviranus looked up to see a quartet of SS questioning the steward and sensed what was up. Dropping his racquet on the grass, he took to his heels, dashing in his white flannels and rubber-soled shoes to a nearby park, and from there to the house of a friend who managed to spirit him to England.

Paul Schulz was surprised at his home in Berlin shortly after 8 P.M. by five "young toughs with pistols at the ready" who hauled him away from the dinner table. He was first thrown into a cell at

Gestapo headquarters at 8 Prinz Albrechtstrasse. After a tele-phone call was put through to Himmler, the plainclothesmen re-moved Schulz and manhandled him back to a car that roared out of central Berlin, headed west in the direction of Potsdam. Schulz knew they were searching for a deserted place to stop and gun him down—he was being taken for a ride, American-gangland-style.

The death car skirted the edge of the Grunewald, the forested park where Gottfried Treviranus sought refuge, but the Saturday night traffic was heavy, and the killers could find no secluded spot free of lights. The frustrated driver turned south on the highway to Leipzig, and after a while he slowed to a stop on a deserted stretch of road near a wood. Schulz was shoved out of the car and told to start walking. Instead he broke into a run and heard the cracking of pistols. A slug burned across his back and he fell, then rose and stumbled across a field to reach the trees. He kept going until he found a stream where he hid in the reeds, letting the cool water wash across his back. His pursuers gave up the hunt, and Schulz hitchhiked back to Berlin. There he found refuge with a retired naval officer who hid him until the flesh wound healed and he could make his way out of Germany.

On Sunday, July 1, the pace of the executions stepped up. At Lichterfelde Barracks, rifle barrels grew too hot to touch; the fir-ing squads dispatched a victim every fifteen minutes. The sounds were clearly audible to shocked householders living in the vicin-ity. One Reichswehr officer's wife became so unnerved at "the continual shooting and screaming" that her husband was forced to drive her into Berlin to stay with relatives.

Hitler had meanwhile enjoyed a sound sleep and was up late that morning getting ready for an afternoon tea party at the Chan-cellery. No sooner had Hitler dressed in black shoes, black trou-sers, tan, officer-style jacket, white shirt, and black tie than Himmler and Göring came to badger him to order Röhm's execu-tion. At first Hitler protested, pointing to Röhm's long and faith-ful service to the Party in the past. Göring and Himmler re-minded Hitler that Röhm alive would always remain a threat, and that a public trial was out of the question: Röhm knew too much and would tell all. Finally Hitler gave in and agreed that Röhm would have to go, but not in front of a common firing squad: he should be offered a chance to destroy himself.

Himmler called Dachau and told the commandant, SS General Theodor Eicke, to attend to the matter in person. Eicke and two of his SS officers left Dachau and drove to Stadelheim Prison at nearby Munich, reaching there at three that afternoon. They were escorted to cell 474; a jailer unlocked the heavy metal door. Röhm was stripped to the waist, his heavy torso glistening with sweat. He stood up to face Eicke, who told him why he was there, laid a heavy 7.65-mm Walther pistol containing one shell on the table in the cell, turned on his heel, and walked out. Ten minutes passed, then fifteen. Röhm's cell remained silent. Eicke and the others got up from their chairs, took out their own pistols, and marched back down the corridor. Whatever his faults, Röhm did not lack personal courage: he stood erect and looked his executioners in the eyes. Two shots roared in the close confines of the cell, making Eicke's ears ring. Röhm flew backward and crashed heavily to the floor. Hit twice in the chest, Röhm was still breathing, trying to say something. Eicke leaned down to listen. Röhm gasped out, "Mein Führer, mein Führer. . . ."

"You should have thought of that before," Eicke said, and another round was fired into Röhm, this time killing him.

Hitler's tea party lasted until late in the afternoon, and Hitler alternated between appearing before a drummed-up crowd outside a Chancellery window and chatting with the numerous guests milling around in the garden under the summer sky. The party broke up, but the executions went on in Berlin, in Munich, and elsewhere, until finally, at 4:00 A.M. on Monday, Hitler ordered the butchery to cease; most of his known enemies were now dead, and he had promised President von Hindenburg that the shooting would stop. At least eighty-three men had died in the bloodbath.

The reaction to Hitler's purge of the SA provided a heady tonic for the Führer. The defense minister, General Werner von Blomberg, sent congratulations on Hitler's "soldierly decision" required for the crushing of the "traitors and murderers." Hindenburg emerged from the dreamworld of senility long enough to dictate a telegram saying, "You have saved the German people from grave danger." The field marshal went on to express his "profound thanks and recognition."

The jubilation was not universal, however. General Ludwig Beck, chief of the General Staff, was shocked at the wanton, gangland-style killings and was especially outraged at the murders of General Schleicher and Bredow. Beck, like other of the more perceptive Reichswehr general officers, realized that the SA "revolt" was probably a fiction, and that the SS would doubtless replace the SA as a politically bound force competing for power with the regular army.

Thus were the seeds of opposition to Adolf Hitler sown during that bloody weekend of 1934. If his generals needed further warning, it was not long in coming. In a tirade delivered before the Reichstag on July 13, Hitler, his voice strident and threating, painted for the assembled deputies and ranking military leaders what opposition to the new totalitarian régime would mean:

> Mutinies are suppressed with laws of iron, which are immutable. If anyone reproaches me and asks why I did not turn to the regular courts of justice for conviction of the offenders, then all I can say to him is this: during this hour I was responsible for the fate of the German people, and so I became the supreme judge of the German people. . . . Let the nation know that its existence, which depends upon internal order and security, cannot be threatened with impunity by anyone! And let it be known for all time to come that if anyone raises his hand to strike down the state, then certain death is his lot.

Betrayal in Berlin

SHORTLY AFTER NINE on the morning of August 2, 1934, Hindenburg died quietly in his sleep at his estate at Neudeck outside of Berlin. Hitler was ready for this moment: five months earlier he had submitted to the Reichstag, the German law-making body, an enabling act that in effect would rob the Reichstag of its powers and its reason for existence, although Hitler promised that the act would be implemented "only to the extent required to carry out vitally important measures," and that the existence of the Reichstag was in no way threatened. The act, valid for four years, meant that the administration would have the power to make laws and to change the constitution arbitrarily, as well as to conclude treaties with foreign nations. Hitler pointed out that since his National Socialists already had a clear majority in the Reichstag, he would seldom have need to implement the enabling act. Then he spoke more harshly, saying that passage of the act "offers the parties of the Reichstag the chance for peaceful development in Germany, and the reconciliation which will spring from that development." He warned that he was "resolute and equally prepared to meet any announcement of refusal, and will take that as a statement of opposition. You, the Deputies, must decide for yourselves whether it is to be peace or war."

After more of Hitler's thundering rhetoric and after several agonizing hours of debate, the deputies retired to vote. They

17

emerged with a 441 to 94 majority in favor of passing the law, which effectively abolished the parliamentary system in Germany. Hitler invoked the act on the day before Hindenburg's death, pushing through a law that combined the offices of president and chancellor. Thus, Hitler, at forty-five, reached his goal as undisputed political overlord of nearly 80 million people and supreme commander of their armed forces.

Hitler's short-range goal—promulgated in his book, *Mein Kampf* (*My Battle*), and in countless political harangues—was to destroy the Versailles treaty and its limitations on German rearmament. His long-range goal—which he kept to himself—was to conquer Europe and Soviet Russia. He moved first to increase the size of the *Wehrmacht*, as the armed forces were now called, and to equip it with modern weaponry.

Among the first to hear Hitler's plans for expansion were his war minister, Blomberg, and his commander-in-chief, Fritsch. These two top generals upon whom Hitler initially depended had nothing in common except careers of long and dedicated service; but they were to share a common fate, both becoming victims of Nazi purges against the old army.

General Werner Eduard Fritz von Blomberg was fifty-six when Hitler seized the reins of Germany's destiny, and behind him stretched thirty-seven years of unbroken service. Brilliance as a staff officer during the First World War earned him the Pour le mérite, and boldness gained him an Iron Cross, First Class, and a wound stripe. Blomberg was enthusiastic, impetuous, romantic, and intense in his desire to see a greater Germany arise from the ashes of defeat. He espoused Hitler's ideas as to how the resurrection could be brought about through National Socialism; but he was soldier enough to know that politics do not mix with the military function, and he forbade any Wehrmacht officer to join the Nazi party. Blomberg fell early under Hitler's hypnotic spell; others at the ministry who were not so carried away called him the "Rubber Lion" behind his back.

General Werner Thomas Ludwig von Fritsch, fifty-four, had served only a year less than Blomberg and with equal distinction.

Fritsch, who never married, had only two passions: his military career and the pursuit of equestrian excellence. A half-dozen horses accompanied him on weekend leaves in the country, but aside from this extravagance Fritsch lived a frugal, almost spartan existence. Outsiders found him arrogant and distant; with these traits and his characteristic clipped speech, he seemed to embody the typical Prussian staff officer. Those who knew him better realized that he was introverted and actually tongue-tied when it came to talking about himself. Unlike Blomberg, Fritsch had no political acumen. "I lack everything necessary for politics," he once said. "The less I speak in public, the more speedily I can fulfill my military task."

Fritsch refused to hide his contempt for Hitler and his satraps. Forced to attend a review of SS and Wehrmacht troops at Saarbrucken on March 5, 1935, Fritsch astonished those sitting nearby with a withering running commentary directed against the Party, the SS, and their leaders when they appeared in the reviewing stand. A few weeks later, on April 20, Fritsch was in his office in Berlin trying to get through the morning's work in the face of distracting noise in the streets below. Irritated, he turned to Colonel Gotthard Heinrici and demanded to know the occasion for the revelry. "But it's the Führer's birthday," Heinrici replied.

Fritsch, raising his voice, replied, "Why celebrate that!"

Despite his private convictions, Fritsch, his face kept rigid with the help of a monocle "when I confront that man," was always militarily correct in Hitler's presence, and the Führer was largely unaware of his commander-in-chief's active dislike. Hitler believed Fritsch to be "incorruptible." Fritsch, for his part, often expressed his view that "Hitler is Germany's fate, for good and for bad."

Hitler's generals greeted with amazement the Führer's plans for expansion of the Wehrmacht. Blomberg, Ludwig Beck, Fritsch, and the others had long agreed that the seven divisions permitted by the Treaty of Versailles were woefully inadequate to defend the frontiers of the Reich, but when Hitler ordered a trebling of the Wehrmacht to twenty-one divisions even Beck protested that the order constituted "not a build-up of a peacetime army, but a mobilization." And a mobilization was of course exactly what Hitler had in mind.

On March 9, 1935, Hitler decided to test world opinion by revealing the existence of the hitherto-secret Luftwaffe, the German air force, which had been clandestinely created in Germany and in Russia. Herman Göring and Blomberg argued heatedly over whether or not the Luftwaffe should remain under control of the army, as it had been in the last war. Göring triumphed. He not only obtained independent status for the air arm but took the antiaircraft defenses for himself as well. Blomberg's stubborn opposition earned him Göring's lasting enmity; he was determined to destroy the power of the hostile members of the officer class that Blomberg represented.

When the world failed to react to the first breach of the Versailles treaty, Hitler moved to phase two a week later. He summoned Blomberg and Fritsch to a meeting of the Reichs Defense Council on Saturday, March 15, and told them he now wanted a thirty-six division army totaling 550,000 men, a fivefold increase. Moreover, he planned to reintroduce military conscription. In short, the military provisions of the Versailles treaty were to be scrapped unilaterally. Blomberg protested that France and Britain would now move against Germany. One of those present, a ranking Foreign Office member, Joachim von Ribbentrop, tried to sooth Blomberg by saying that there was nothing to fear from either nation. Blomberg lost his temper and shouted, "What you say is all stuff and nonsense!"

Fritsch stated his objections to Hitler's plans, pointing out that mobilization on a crash basis would put a strain not only on the armaments industry but on the economic structure of the nation. Both Hitler and Göring grew irritable at the recalcitrant generals, and the meeting broke up late that night in an atmosphere of strain and acrimony. But Hitler had his way.

The rearmament program slowly gathered momentum during the following two years, but by late 1937 the disputes between the three services over allocation of matériel had grown so serious that Blomberg, now a field marshal, asked for a showdown meeting with Hitler inside the Chancellery. Hitler set the meeting for the afternoon of November 5. It did not turn out as Blomberg expected.

Besides Fritsch and Blomberg, Hitler had summoned Hermann Göring to represent the Luftwaffe, Admiral Erich Raeder to represent the navy, and the aged Constantin von Neurath, then the minister of foreign affairs. Hitler's adjutant, Colonel Friedrich Hossbach, was present as an observer. No sooner had Blomberg broached the question of allocation than Hitler veered in another direction entirely and, as was his habit, spoke almost without interruption for two hours and thirty minutes. Hitler told them that what he had to say "should be looked upon in case of my death as my last will and testament."

He dwelled at length upon his obsession for more living space for the German people, then warned that "the problem can be solved only with force—and this is never without risk!" Declaring that it was no longer a question *if*, but *when* and *how* the force was to be exerted, he sketched out several scenarios that would trigger the German march of conquest. France and England could easily become embroiled in a war with Italy over complications arising from the Spanish civil war, then in its second year; in this case Hitler said he would move on Czechoslovakia, perhaps as early as 1938. Austria must be taken as well. On the other hand, France's internal problems could erupt into a full-blown crisis which would tie down the French army; then would be the time to seize Czech territory. In any event, Hitler concluded, all three armed services must be ready to solve Germany's space problems by 1943 to 1945 at the latest; if not, a certain decline awaited the Reich economically and militarily.

In short, Hitler was determined to launch another sanguinary European war within six years, if not sooner, no matter what. Blomberg, Fritsch, and Neurath were especially stunned. During the hour and a half that remained of the meeting they picked apart Hitler's various scenarios, then Blomberg and Fritsch turned on Göring with heavy criticism of his management of the

21

four-year plan for accelerated economic and industrial revival. Colonel Hossbach noted that "the sharpness of the opposition, both in content and in form, did not fail to make an impression on Hitler. Every detail of the conduct of Blomberg and Fritsch made plain to Hitler that his policies were met with plain, impersonal contradictions instead of applause and agreement . . . he knew very well that both generals were opposed to any warlike entanglement provoked from our side."

Blomberg was a notoriously elastic personality, however, and once again he wavered, incapable of confronting the Führer with more objections. But not so Fritsch. Four days later Fritsch had an audience with Hitler at his mountain retreat in the Obersalzberg and tried to reason him away from what he was certain was the path to destruction for Germany. Constantin von Nuerath was supposed to follow Fritsch up the mountain, but Hitler was so vexed with Fritsch's obstinacy that he cancelled Nuerath's visit, telling the foreign minister to make another appointment some time next year. When Neurath began to suffer from heart seizures, and Fritsch left for a sixty-day leave in Egypt to ameliorate his bronchitis, the opposition grew weaker. Fritsch was never aware that Gestapo agents followed him to the Nile to watch his every move.

While Fritsch was making the tourist rounds under the healing Egyptian sun, Blomberg remained in Berlin, which was now closed in by winter snows and freezing temperatures. Blomberg was weighted down with problems at the war ministry and tortured by an acute personal crisis. Now sixty, and a widower for eight years, he frequently sought companionship in some of Berlin's seedier bars. It was at the White Deer that he met Eva Gruhn, twenty-five, who granted the field marshal her favors. The casual relationship quickly ripened into an affair that Blomberg could not control, but that he was at first desperate to conceal. Eva was common, to say the least, and her mother operated a massage parlor in an unfashionable part of town. When Eva told him she was pregnant, Blomberg knew that the only honorable course of action was marriage. But what would his fellow officers think? What would the Führer think? Despite their frequent head-on collisions, Blomberg decided to ask Göring, who was known for his ebullient camaraderie, and who moreover had the Führer's ear. *Der Dicke* (the Fat One) would provide the right counsel.

Blomberg was greeted warmly by Göring, who assured him that a marriage between a German field marshal and a "child of the people," as Eva Gruhn was described, was in the order of things under National Socialism. Göring would back Blomberg to the hilt. Elated, Blomberg now broached another problem. There was another, much younger, rival for Eva's hand, a persistent fellow who refused to bow out of the picture. Göring said that was no problem, and he was true to his word: he picked up a telephone, and shortly afterward Blomberg's rival was on a liner bound for a new job in Argentina. Before leaving, however, the suitor let Göring know that Eva Gruhn's past was much more lurid than Blomberg realized. Göring did not pass on this information to Blomberg or to Hitler, but saw to it that it was funneled to Heinrich Himmler instead. Blomberg had walked straight into Göring's trap.

At forty-five, Göring had yet to reach his penultimate goal of becoming war minister of the Third Reich. To achieve this ambition he would have to eliminate Blomberg, and after him, Fritsch. Göring still rankled over the biting criticisms leveled at him during the meeting a month earlier, nor could he forgive Blomberg for representing Germany at the coronation of George VI in London in the spring of 1937, an honor Göring felt was rightly his.

Blomberg secured Hitler's permission to marry Eva Gruhn on December 22; the wedding ceremony was conducted in the War Ministry on January 12, 1938. None of Blomberg's grown children would attend, but the lovesick field marshal was gratified when Göring and the Führer himself agreed to act as witnesses. When the brief, strained ceremony was over, Hitler dutifully kissed the hands of the bride and her mother. When the fastidious Hitler looked upon Frau Gruhn's charwoman's face he visibly recoiled.

Eight days later a criminal file on Eva Gruhn von Blomberg

reached the desk of Berlin's police president, Wolf Heinrich von Helldorf. Helldorf was flabbergasted. The file contained a number of arrests records on morals charges and a set of pornographic pictures featuring the field marshal's new wife and a male partner, both nude. Helldorf did not know what to do. He loathed Himmler and the SS, so he took the file to General Wilhelm Keitel, a frontline comrade of Blomberg's and ostensibly one of the field marshal's warmest friends. Keitel refused to get involved and suggested that Göring was the man to handle the sordid business.

On Saturday, January 22, Helldorf journeyed to Karinhall, Göring's lavish country estate northeast of Berlin, and blurted out the story. Göring, whose acting ability rivaled Hitler's, pretended to be grievously shocked and said that he would somehow gird himself to break the news to the Führer when Hitler returned from Berchtesgaden on the following Monday. When Helldorf left, Göring got on the telephone to Himmler to arrange a meeting at Karinhall on Sunday. The kill was at hand.

Hitler's private train pulled into Berlin from Munich late Monday evening. Göring confronted Hitler with the Eva Gruhn file, and the Führer groaned, "Nothing is spared me!" After the two leaders had thrashed out the lamentable Blomberg affair for several hours, Göring left the Chancellery feeling that he was near his goal.

Göring cornered Blomberg in the latter's office early the next morning. Without preamble he told Blomberg why he was there, then slapped the Eva Gruhn file down in front of the astonished field marshal. Curtly informing Blomberg that he was dismissed and that there was no appeal, Göring turned on his heel and left the office. One of Blomberg's adjutants peered through the door and saw the "hale and hearty field marshal staggering, a broken man, to his private rooms."

Blomberg was summoned to the Chancellery for the final time, having been ordered to report in civilian clothes. Hitler alternately scolded and commiserated with the fallen field marshal, then told him to absent himself from the Reich for at least a year. To soften the blow, Hitler told Blomberg that 50,000 marks (about $12,000) were waiting for him at the Reichsbank. A few days later Blomberg and his bride, "the child of the people" as he called her, were on their way to Italy.

Fritsch was next.

Less than thirty-six hours after Göring sacked Blomberg, a summons was issued to General von Fritsch to appear before Hitler at the Chancellery on Wednesday evening, January 26. Against the Führer's orders, Hitler's adjutant, Colonel Hossbach, managed to reach Fritsch and warn him that damning evidence against him now lay on the Führer's desk. What kind of evidence, Fritsch wanted to know. Hossback answered that the general faced charges of violation of article 175 of the Reich criminal code, that section dealing with homosexuality. Hossbach didn't believe a word of it, but he told Fritsch to be prepared.

Fritsch was ushered into Hitler's chambers, where Göring was standing expectantly beside the Führer's desk. Hitler presented the general with a thick dossier, and Fritsch raised his monocle to his left eye and began to read. Engrossed in the outrageous charges, he failed to notice that a fourth party had entered the room. A seedy-looking character named Otto Schmidt, a black-mailer convicted many times over, pointed a finger at Fritsch and told Göring, "Yes, that's him." Finally Fritsch looked up, and Schmidt repeated his statement; it was definitely the general whom he had seen in the shadows of the Wannsee rail station committing an unnatural act with a well-known underworld figure Bayern Seppl, or Bavarian Joe. Schmidt said this had happened in 1935, and that Fritsch had been paying him blackmail ever since. The incredulous Fritsch denied having ever laid eyes on Schmidt. The blackmailer was taken back into custody by the police, and Hitler ordered Fritsch to report to the Gestapo for further interrogation on the following morning.

The dossier was correct in almost every detail except one: the blackmail victim was actually an aged, ailing ex-cavalry captain named Achim von Frisch who lived in a shabby apartment in the Lichterfelde section of Berlin. Schmidt knew very well that he was indicting the wrong man, but he also knew it was worth his life to go against Himmler and the machinery of the SS.

On Hitler's order, Fritsch reported to the Gestapo building on the Prinz Albrechtstrasse shortly after ten the next morning to undergo the humiliation of interrogation by a civilian policeman. His interrogator, Franz Huber, was embarrassed at having to deal with the Wehrmacht's commander-in-chief, especially on such a sordid matter, but his orders were clear: get the truth out of General von Fritsch. Fritsch was offered a chair, and the questioning began. Then the blackmailer Schmidt was brought in; he reminded Huber of a sewer rat, and Fritsch averted his eyes.

Huber: "You are sure that the man sitting here is the one you saw?"

Schmidt: "Yes. I can only say once again that I am as sure as I am of the fact that I am standing here now."

Huber: "Inspector Fehling, take that man outside for a moment until I am ready to call him back here again."

When Schmidt had been hustled out of the office, Huber turned to Fritsch and looked at him questioningly. Fritsch raised his voice and said, "I can only say that this is a complete outrage!"

Schmidt was retrieved, and the process continued, largely in a circle. After three hours of assurances by Schmidt and denials by Fritsch, Inspector Huber was convinced that Schmidt was a liar, but he could not understand why the swine was trying to blacken the name of a *Herr*, a gentleman, like Fritsch.

Nor would Huber have understood the weird rite being enacted in the adjoining office while the interrogations were under way. A young SS officer named Walter Schellenberg entered the office next door by accident and gazed upon "a dozen SS officers sitting in a circle, all sunk in deep and silent contemplation." Himmler, it turned out, had assembled the group in an attempt to force a confession from Fritsch using their powers of concentration.

Fritsch's ordeal ended early that afternoon, and he returned home a bitter and dispirited man. On the next day, January 28, Hitler relieved Fritsch of his command, but Fritsch fought back and, pressured by several senior Wehrmacht generals, demanded a formal trial by military courts-martial. Hitler hedged at first, then agreed providing that Fritsch first handed in his resignation. This was done on February 3, with Göring waiting in the wings.

As it turned out, Hitler had no intention of appointing Göring, whom he considered "lazy," to yet another high post. Instead, he abolished the position of war minister vacated by Blomberg and assumed that role himself. Fritsch's job was handed over to General Walther von Brauchitsch, fifty-seven, a man who referred to Hitler as "our leader of genius." The brilliant economist Hjalmar Schacht, who had repeatedly warned Hitler that his guns-before-butter policies would inevitably bring economic ruin to Germany, was replaced by Walther Funk, a former newspaper editor and notorious homosexual; Schacht was demoted to directing the Reichsbank. Neurath lost his post as foreign minister to sycophantic Joachim von Ribbentrop, a onetime champagne salesman. Hitler completed the purge by suddenly dismissing his adjutant, Hossbach, and by sacking a dozen Wehrmacht generals known to be hostile to himself and his plans.

On Monday, February 5, Hitler summoned the remaining senior generals and admirals to the war ministry and lectured them for the better part of the morning. He castigated Blomberg, then broke the news of Fritsch's resignation, spelling out in sordid detail the charges leveled at the former Wehrmacht commander-in-chief. The news stunned everyone; not one of them had had an inkling of Fritsch's trouble prior to the Führer's revelations that morning. Hitler assured them that Fritsch would receive an open hearing and a proper trial by military court-martial. The meeting broke up and Hitler left Berlin for his snowy mountain retreat above Berchtesgaden.

The telephone rang in Walther Schellenberg's office, and the voice at the other end told him he would be having dinner that evening with his superior, Reinhard Heydrich. Schellenberg could only agree, but was puzzled when his caller told him to bring his service pistol and "plenty of ammunition." Schellenberg checked his Luger, secured two boxes of 9-mm shells, and, attired in an immaculate black uniform with silver piping, reported to Heydrich's office at 7 P.M., wondering what it was all about.

Heydrich greeted Schellenberg at the door, and they walked together toward the SD leader's office, where dinner was being laid out. Heydrich turned to Schellenberg and said, "I've heard that you are an excellent shot with a pistol." Schellenberg admitted that he was. Schellenberg faced Heydrich across the dining table, the unnatural silence broken only by the scrape of silverware against china plates. Schellenberg was fascinated and repelled by his superior's manner and appearance, the white skin, the long, predatory nose, the "small, restless eyes as crafty as an animal's," the pale, long, violinist's hands that reminded Schellenberg of spider legs. Gazing at Heydrich's face was like staring at a glacier. His voice was high-pitched, nervous, staccato.

Heydrich was a man at odds with himself. He was still bitter about being thrown out of the navy for refusing to marry a shipbuilder's daughter he was sleeping with, and his rage over false rumors that his grandmother had been married to a Jew was unquenchable. It was easy for Schellenberg to believe, as many in the SS did, that two men lived inside Heydrich's tall frame. A story making the rounds of the SS described how a drunken Heydrich lurched into his spacious bathroom and how he caught sight of his reflection in a wall mirror. He pulled a pistol from his holster and fired two shots at the mirror, crying out, "I've got you at last, you scum!"

When the last plate had been cleared away, Heydrich rose from the table and began pacing the room. He gulped down several aspirin and said to Schellenberg, "If they don't start marching from Potsdam during the next hour and a half, the greatest danger will have passed." Noting the younger SS officer's perplexity, Heydrich explained that his undercover agents working within the Wehrmacht had tipped him to rumors sweeping army barracks of an impending putsch against the SS and even Hitler himself over the outrageous treatment handed Fritsch, the pillar of the German army.

Heydrich's information was correct: there was angry talk at the Potsdam garrison, especially among the aristocratic officers of the elite 9th Infantry Regiment, of executing a sudden coup. The rebellion had no clear leader of authority, however, and words failed to be converted into action.

When, finally, Schellenberg was dismissed from Heydrich's presence shortly after one the next morning, he realized why he had been invited to the strange dinner and why he had been ordered to arm himself: Heydrich wanted a reliable marksman at hand in case the renegades of the 9th Regiment fought their way past his guards to smash down Heydrich's doors.

The court-martial of General von Fritsch began on the morning of March 10, 1938 and was adjourned *sine die* a few hours later without explanation. Fritsch and his lawyer left the courtroom wondering if Hitler was reneging at the last minute on his promise.

At four that afternoon, General Heinz Guderian, Germany's leading tank expert, was told that Hitler, up in Berchtesgaden, had decided that the time was at hand for the *Anschluss*, the annexation of Austria. Guderian had less than forty-eight hours to prepare the Second Panzer Division for movement, and Vienna was 598 miles from Berlin. Guderian was told that the SS Life Guards Division was to be alerted as well. Guderian asked General Beck if combat was in the offing, and Beck said that the Führer had assured him that fighting was quite out of the question. "In that case," said Guderian, "let our tanks move in beflagged and decked with greenery."

The two mechanized divisions moved across the Austrian frontier at 9:00 A.M. on March 12 and started down the highway for Vienna. At Linz, not far from Hitler's birthplace, they paused for an enthusiastic celebration staged by 60,000 cheering civilians and elements of the Austrian army. So unready were the two German divisions for operations that Guderian had to borrow civilian trucks for logistic help, and his tanks and armored cars depended upon Austrian gas stations along the way for fuel to get them to Vienna, which was reached an hour after midnight on March 13. Not a shot had been fired. The conquest of Austria was complete.

Fritsch's trial reconvened on the morning of March 17. So contemptuous was Fritsch of the proceedings that he alone refused to stand when the acting president of the court, Hermann Göring, lumbered into the room to take his place on the dais. Fritsch sat upright in his chair before the dark wooden table, his monocle glinting dully in the pale winter light that shone through the courtroom windows. His face was expressionless, as though he were a spectator at someone else's tribunal. His attorney, Count Rudiger von der Goltz, leaned forward, eager for the proceedings to begin; he had an open loathing for the Gestapo, and he and his investigators had gumshoed all over Berlin to lay bare the clumsy framework of lies that constituted the spurious case against Fritsch.

Fritsch was first charged with luring two unfortunate Hitler Youth to his Berlin apartment and molesting them. Goltz put Fritz Wermelskirchen and Gerhard Zeidler on the stand, and they told the court that they had, indeed, been to the general's flat—but only because they were quite poor and had been given hot lunches and tactical lessons in topography. Goltz asked if the general had ever touched them. Yes, they replied, the general pinched their ears or whacked them with a ruler when they gave stupid answers to his questions about map reading. The boys' mothers had only praise for Fritsch.

Heydrich's men had earlier grilled a great number of stable-hands where Fritsch did his afternoon riding, but the agents were angrily rebuffed and, on one occasion, threatened with physical violence if questions about their commander-in-chief's sexual preferences were raised again. Goltz put all fourteen noncoms on the stand; they defended Fritsch belligerently.

Schmidt, the blackmailer, was next on the stand, pale, nervous and sweating. Goltz asked if he had been threatened by any member of the Gestapo before the beginning of the trial. Schmidt cleared his throat and answered, "Yes, SS Oberführer Meisenger told me that if I did not stand by my former statements I would find myself on my way to heaven." Josef Meisenger who, even to his own colleagues, resembled a toad, admitted to Goltz that what Schmidt said was true, but his remark about going to heaven was meant as a "drastic warning to tell the truth."

The trial picked up again on the following morning, and Goltz incisively tore Schmidt's testimony to ribbons. Terrified of Meisenger, Schmidt at first stubbornly stuck to his story that he had blackmailed both Frisch *and* Fritsch, but when Goltz proved to the court that it was the pitiful old Frisch—and only Frisch—who was involved, Schmidt started to collapse. Since Hitler had already given Brauchitsch the job Göring coveted, and since the case against Fritsch now lay in wreckage, Göring switched his line of attack and made it appear he was on the side of Fritsch and justice itself. Alternately threatening and cajoling, Göring let fall the full weight of his histrionics and his high office on the fearful and bewildered Schmidt, who finally blurted out that he had never seen General von Fritsch prior to their confrontation in Hitler's chambers at the beginning of the year.

With Schmidt's testimony destroyed, Goltz now tried to expose the prosecution's role in the frameup. He asked that Himmler and Heydrich be summoned to court and put on the stand. Göring flared up and told Goltz it was out of the question; both men were in Austria on important state business. He reminded Goltz that the Reichsführer and his deputy were not on trial, only Fritsch.

The trial ended at noon with Fritsch found innocent on all charges. Schmidt was hurried out of the courtroom and sent to the concentration camp at Sachsenhausen north of Berlin, where he rotted in solitary confinement for four years and then was executed on orders from Himmler with Göring's hearty approval. "He should have been shot long ago," Göring commented.

Hitler formally approved of Fritsch's exoneration, but he refused his reinstatement. Instead, Hitler offered Fritsch the honorary colonelcy of the 12th Artillery Regiment, a drastic comedown that Fritsch glumly accepted. Colonel Hossbach, furious at his own dismissal and at the decapitation of the army, spent hours convincing Fritsch that the only honorable course of action left was to challenge Himmler to a duel. They worked over a draft of the letter of challenge, and Fritsch spent part of every afternoon in target practice, his pistol cracking at a bull's-eye ten paces away.

The stinging indictment of Himmler was handed over to General Gerd von Rundstedt for personal delivery to the Reichsführer. Rundstedt, however, had second thoughts; he realized that Hitler would never stand for Himmler's being shot down on the field of honor. Rundstedt went back to Fritsch on March 30 and talked him out of the idea. Fritsch resigned himself to limbo, telling his friends that if it came to war, he would accompany the regiment into combat "not as a commander, but as a target."

The unbelievably shabby treatment dealt to the leading commanders of the Wehrmacht shocked the professional German officer corps, as did the subsequent forced retirement of a number of senior general-officers known by Hitler to be antagonistic to the Nazis and their policies. Many of those who remained now realized that a bitter struggle was in the offing to maintain their cherished traditions and the army's aloofness from political infestation. The time was not yet ripe for any overt moves against the new régime, especially since Hitler was then at the height of his popularity, but some generals realized that a showdown must eventually come. Meanwhile, opposition was forming in other quarters.

Part 2

The Hunters

3

The Oster Plan

IN THE SPRING of 1936, Carl Friedrich Goerdler, the lord mayor of Leipzig, received a message from Berlin via the Nazis on his city council. The statue of Felix Mendelssohn visible from Goerdler's office must be removed, the delegation said; this monument to a Jew in Leipzig's main square offended National Socialist sensibilities. Goerdler ordered the petitioners out of his office. "When that statue goes," he said, "then so will I."

Goerdler's defiance was not surprising: he was known throughout high municipal circles in Germany as a volatile, temperamental, outspoken pragmatist who wished for the return of the monarchy as it was under Kaiser Wilhelm II before the First World War. Goerdler loathed the street-gang aspects of the Nazi party as exemplified by the SA, and the pagan demonstrations featuring torchlight parades, mass rallies with banners and bugles, and Caesar-style salutes. He refused point-blank Hitler's personal invitation to join the Party, and when local Nazis appeared to present him with a brilliantly colored swastika flag to fly atop the City Hall he ordered them off the premises. Then he locked the doors, surrounding himself with Leipzig municipal police with whom he swore to fight to keep the storm troopers out of the building.

Hitler let these incidents pass because he admired Goerdler's hard-nosed economic skills; he even persuaded the feisty lord mayor to accept the post of price commissioner and controller of foreign exchange. To facilitate Goerdler's travels, Hitler put his private Ju.52 transport plane at the lord mayor's disposal.

Goerdler would admit that National Socialism was right on two points. "We must help each other," he said, "and capital must not be allowed to yield excessive profits. Life is a struggle in which work and achievement are necessary." Hitler had drastically cut unemployment and had achieved progress in other areas.

Before long, however, Goerdler soured on Nazi methods, publicly declaring, "The Party will be shattered on the rock of moral law that makes human society possible." And as time went on, his disgust deepened: excesses like the Röhm bloodbath and the murder of the generals, coupled with Hitler's increasingly ruinous economic policies, turned Goerdler into a diehard opponent.

It didn't take the Nazis long to put Goerdler's ultimatum to the test. The lord mayor was invited to Helsinki in November 1936 to lecture before the Finnish chamber of commerce. Afterward in Stockholm he accepted a telephone call from a colleague in Leipzig, who told him, "Carl, they've taken down the statue." Goerdler caught the next plane for Germany, and the next day he faced his councillors and demanded that Mendelssohn's effigy be replaced on its pedestal. When his demand was refused, Goerdler straightaway handed in his resignation, ending twenty-seven years of municipal service.

But Geordler's protest did not end there. When Hitler vetoed an appointment offered Goerdler by the munitions magnate Gustav Krupp von Bohlen, Goerdler approached the democratic-minded manufacturer Robert Bosch in Stuttgart. Bosch, who loathed Hitler and his concepts, had given generous sums to aid victims of Nazi persecution, especially Jews and theological students of the banned Confessional church. Like Goerdler, he believed that Hitler must be somehow stopped before Europe was engulfed. He hoped Goerdler was the man to warn the rest of the world of the impending moral catastrophe.

Bosch provided Goerdler with funds with which to begin a

one-man crusade. Goerdler's tall, raw-boned figure, draped in a long, black coat, his hand gripping a heavy walking stick, became a familiar sight in Germany and in the capitals of Britain, Belgium, France, Yugoslavia, Rumania, and Bulgaria. He swept through the Mideast and touched down in North Africa. He huddled with the Swiss, even crossed the Atlantic to voice fears of Armageddon in Canada and the United States.*

When in Germany, Goerdler was a frequent visitor to 78 Tirpitzufer, the headquarters building in Berlin of the Abwehr, the German counterintelligence organization, whose master was an enigmatic little admiral named Wilhelm Canaris who stood less than five feet four with his shoes on. His size and reticent manner belied his determination and personal courage. In Canaris Goerdler found a kindred spirit.

In 1914, Canaris had been aboard the cruiser *Dresden* prowling the South Atlantic in search of British merchantmen to send to the bottom of the sea. The *Dresden* sank many such ships and survived two major engagements with British men o' war before she was destroyed. Damaged and penned against the coast of Chile, the *Dresden* was scuttled and the crew interned. With bribery, false papers, and a disguise, Canaris made his way out of South America and returned to Germany. He was then sent to Spain to spy on British activities in the Mediterranean. Arrested while on an excursion to Italy, he once again managed to escape. Canaris ended the war as a U-boat captain, having sunk eighteen Allied ships.

As peace came to Germany in 1919, Canaris settled comfortably into naval administration and command and lived sedately in a fashionable part of Berlin with his wife, his daughter, and his

---

*Ironically, Goerdler's excursions abroad were made possible by Hermann Göring. Goerdler told Göring that he feared a European war loomed on the horizon, a fear Göring then shared. Göring agreed that Berlin did not have its finger on the pulse of the world; Goerdler would find out "confidentially and unofficially to what extent Germany was endangered." Göring retrieved Goerdler's confiscated passport and enthusiastically wished him *bon voyage*.

dachshund, an inseparable companion that accompanied him even to his office on the fourth floor of the Tirpitzufer. On January 1, 1934 (his forty-seventh birthday) Canaris became head of the Abwehr, a position roughly comparable to today's head of the American CIA. Despite his powerful position, Canaris, who had no taste for the Gothic opulence of décor cherished by Hitler, Göring, Himmler, and other Party bigwigs, worked in shabby surroundings. His heavy desk was scarred and stained, resting on part of a worn Oriental carpet of uncertain vintage. Books and journals were stacked haphazardly on shelves. The dog's bed was in one corner. A signed portrait of Francisco Franco, who had befriended young Lieutenant Canaris during the First World War, hung on the wall. But it was from this unlikely interior that Canaris and his deputies directed the clandestine activities of more than 3,000 men and women at home and abroad.

Hitler and Canaris may have seen the Abwehr in the same light—Hitler wanted it to be "something like the British Secret Service—a [holy] Order doing its work with passion"—but their views of each other were vastly different. To Hitler, Canaris seemed benign, a diminutive, white-haired, blue-eyed, rosy-complexioned headmaster of some small, private English school. To Canaris, Hitler and the rest of the Nazi hierarchy were, as he confided to his predecessor, "all a gang of criminals." The wanton murders during the Röhm purge made him physically ill, and the sordid way Fritsch was humiliated and cast out of office disgusted Canaris to the depths of his soul. The same year the little admiral took office he quietly began planning ways to use the Abwehr as a tool to bring down Hitler's house.

Canaris was filled with anxiety and tortured by self-doubts in the dual role he chose for himself and his organization. He consumed tranquilizers and sought therapy in makework trips all across Germany in the back seat of his supercharged staff car. A contemporary recalled that Canaris "rushed, like King Ahasuerus, from city to city and land to land, but finding peace nowhere." With Canaris absent much of the time, the Abwehr offices on the Tirpitzufer were left in calmer and even more radical hands.

Colonel Hans Oster, at fifty, still retained his elegant cavalry-man's figure; his refined taste and insistence upon the best military tailoring in Berlin maintained his reputation as the fashion plate of the Abwehr. A Saxon, Oster had wit to match his intelligence and, as another Abwehr officer put it, took a "quick, almost light-headed delight in making decisions." He had a matinée idol's profile and the easy movements of a natural athlete. By turns arrogant and captivating, this master equestrian, around whom the handsome women of Berlin fluttered, remained unflappable in the face of emergency and exhibited a cheerful countenance when confronted by depressing events. Oster was also a confirmed monarchist who vaguely longed for the return of the Hohenzollerns, and he was unable to conceal his contempt for the entire body of National Socialism. An Austrian intelligence officer who reported for duty with the Abwehr entered Oster's presence and raised his right arm toward the ceiling. "Oh, no," Oster said, waving his hand deprecatingly, "no Hitler salute here, please."

Oster was a serving Abwehr officer under General von Bredow before Hitler's ascension to power, and Bredow's brutal execution by Himmler's henchmen gave Oster a furious hatred for everything Nazi. He battled tenaciously to keep Heydrich's Security Service, the *Sicherheitsdienst* (SD), from encroaching upon Abwehr territory, keeping his undercover agents busy ferreting out state secrets and dislodging damaging bits of evidence to be used against the Party.

Oster realized that the Abwehr alone was not capable of toppling the régime: that goal required political and military orchestration. He believed that the peripatetic Goerdler was perfectly cast in the role of civilian usurper, and he was convinced that General Ludwig Beck, chief of the German General Staff, was fully capable of galvanizing the Wehrmacht against the Führer. Oster dreamed of the day when they could place Adolf Hitler where he belonged—behind bars, or locked away in an asylum.

At fifty-eight, Beck was a graying, thin, red-eyed man with forty years of soldiering behind him. He had married once, when he was thirty-six, but his wife died a year later, and from that time forward Beck divided his time between the army and his intellectual pursuits. He was fluent in French and in English, and could quote lengthily from Nietzsche, Schopenhauer, and Clausewitz. He was also a member of the select Wednesday Club in Berlin, a collection of savants who gathered weekly to discuss philosophical and historical topics.

Beck's dislike of the leaders and goals of National Socialism began early in the régime. As with Canaris, the bloody Röhm purge left him sick to the core and when, on the afternoon of Hindenburg's death, Beck had to join the entire Wehrmacht in swearing a new oath of allegiance, he ruefully remarked that it was the blackest day of his life. The oath was indeed forceful in strange ways. It required that the swearer "render to Adolf Hitler, Leader of the German People, Supreme Commander of the Armed Forces, unconditional obedience" and be "ready as a brave soldier to risk my life at any time for this oath." No mention of constitution or Fatherland—just a promise before God of fealty to one man, a man with the ambitions of a Caesar and the morality of Attila. When, in 1935, Beck was told to work up a detailed operational plan for a "theoretical" attack on Czechoslovakia, he was appalled, calling it an act of desperation.* He stated that if the operation were ever carried out the High Command "must expect the severest condemnation, not only of its own age, but also of history." Beck threatened to leave his post rather than begin plan-

---

*At issue in Czechoslovakia, with its population of 12 million, was the fate of 3 million Germans living in self-contained communities in areas adjoining Germany and Austria. These Sudeten Germans complained, with some justification, that the Czechs treated them as second-class citizens. The unemployment rate in the Sudetenland was twice that of the other Czech provinces, Czech schools were superior, and Sudeten Germans serving in the Czech army or in civil service could not advance above certain grades unless they adopted Czech names. As the summer wore on, Hitler's public outbursts whipped up the ill-feeling, the tension heightened by frequent bloody clashes between Sudetens and Czechs. Göring referred to the Czechs as "a vile race of dwarfs," and Hitler promised the Sudetens he would soon put an end to their persecution.

ning an offensive war. The matter was dropped, but only for a while. When it came up again, it provided the impetus for the first Abwehr-Wehrmacht plot against the Nazi régime.

On April 21, 1938, Hitler once again ordered the General Staff to create a plan for a preemptive attack on its neighbor, an operation codenamed *Case Green*. This time Beck calmly put his staff to work on the tactical and logistical problems involved—then spent two weeks working on a comprehensive memorandum pointing out why the plans would be a disaster for Germany.

On May 7 the document was delivered to General Brauchitsch, Fritsch's replacement, who read it and had it retyped in letters a quarter of an inch high so that Hitler could read it without using his glasses. As the Führer impatiently skimmed the paragraphs, he rejected one by one the cogent arguments. *Russia must be regarded as an increasingly more outspoken enemy of Germany . . . Germany's military situation is not as strong as in 1914 . . . Germany's defense economy is poor, poorer than in 1917–1918 . . . France and Russia are already on the side of Britain, and America will attach herself to them . . . Britain is preparing to throw her sword into the balance should Germany march on Czechoslovakia . . . lying centrally within the continent, Germany cannot withstand a major war on land, sea, and in the air.*

Beck's pointed memorandum was based on fresh intelligence gathered by Goerdler, on staff studies carried out earlier, and on economic data supplied by Hjalmar Schacht, the disgruntled director of the Reichsbank. The paper proved to be the work of a prophet, except for the crucial assumption that Britain would risk war over the Czechs.

Hitler did not deign to even reply to Beck's arguments. Instead, he summoned the Reich's ranking military and political leaders to the Chancellery and announced, "It is my unalterable decision to smash Czechoslovakia in the near future by military action!" His audience stood in stunned silence. Then Hitler turned toward Beck and other Wehrmacht generals were standing and added, "We shall have to use methods which perhaps will not find the immediate approval of you old officers." The room remained silent. Hitler strode over to where Beck and Brauchitsch stood and continued. "So, we will tackle the Czech situation, then I will give you three or four years' time, then we will tackle the situation in the west."

Beck only stared at the Führer. He knew very well what Hitler meant: he was planning a war of conquest against France, probably using Belgium and Holland as gateways, and he wanted Czechoslovakia neutralized, ground under, first.

After the ultimatum from Hitler, Beck called Goerdler, who had just returned from a long swing through France, and arranged a clandestine meeting. Beck passed on to Goerdler the contents of Hitler's remarks, and Goerdler was so agitated that he rushed over to the Chancellery to talk to Hitler's secretary, Captain Fritz Wiedemann. Goerdler pulled from his pocket a lengthy paper protesting Hitler's plans for war, suggesting that Germany could have what she wanted—including the Sudeten part of Czechoslovakia—by negotiating with the British. Wiedemann skimmed through the report, then pushed it aside, explaining that it would be his neck as well as Goerdler's if he dared submit it to the Führer. Besides, he added, both his and Beck's information was already out of date.

Wiedemann told Goerdler that Hitler had already resolved to use whatever force was necessary to create a "German Empire which would include Poland, the Ukraine, the Baltic states, Scandinavia, Holland, Flemish Belgium, Luxembourg, Burgundy, Alsace-Lorraine, and Switzerland." Goerdler was flabbergasted and incredulous. "But that means world war!" he cried out. "Yes, it means world war," Wiedemann replied calmly. "But that is catastrophe!" Goerdler said, almost shouting.

"Yes, it is catastrophe," agreed Wiedemann, "but nothing can be changed now—Ribbentrop has convinced the Führer that the British won't fight."

Now Beck and Oster began meeting almost every day. The Abwehr offices on the Tirpitzufer became the headquarters for planning of a coup d'état, a tactic tried only twice before in modern Germany history, once by Hitler in his failed putsch of 1923.

Hitler reiterated that he "intended to smash Czechoslovakia by military means" and told his generals that the day would come no later than October 1 of that year. More plotters drew themselves into the conspiracy. State Secretary Baron Ernst von Weizsäcker joined, as did the aristocratic ambassador to Rome, Ulrich von Hassell. Generals Karl Heinrich von Stülpnagel and Georg Thomas, Chief of the War Economy Department, added their military weight to the chorus of dissent. A strapping young ex-Gestapo official, Hans Bernd Gisevius, attached himself to the Abwehr group and acted frenetically as liaison officer. There was hardly a branch of political or military activity that was not somehow represented in the circle of conspirators—except Göring's Luftwaffe, which was National Socialist almost to the core.

Beck told Oster that he would keep thrusting at Hitler through Brauchitsch. "After all," he said, "the General Staff is the conscience of the army." Oster said that he would get to work on detailed plans for Hitler's overthrow. Both men agreed that time was running out.

Beck's assignment was by far the more difficult of the two. Brauchitsch admired Beck, but he was more in awe of Hitler; worse, he was heavily indebted to the Führer. At fifty-seven, Brauchitsch, like Blomberg before him, became lovestruck and wanted a divorce. Hitler gave the general 80,000 Reichsmarks (about $20,000) in order to buy off his wife. The new bride, a hefty woman named Schmidt, pleased Hitler because, as the German ambassador to Rome pointed out, "she was 200 percent rabid Nazi."

Brauchitsch, according to one observer, "seemed almost paralyzed in the presence of Hitler," and Beck's continued badgering about morality and unpreparedness added to Brauchitsch's perpetual crisis of nerves. To Brauchitsch, Beck was a Cassandra who probed his conscience with uncomfortable results.

All that summer of 1938 Beck fought with Brauchitsch. He continued to leave trenchant arguments against Hitler's plans, in the form of short, telling paragraphs, on the desk of the Wehrmacht commander. He argued heatedly that "extraordinary times call for extraordinary measures." We must, he said, convoke a meeting of all of the army generals and put it to them that Germany should not, and could not, wage war, that they "could not accept responsibility for such adventures." To Brauchitsch, this sounded dangerously like a call for mutiny or, at the very least, a general strike.

Beck explained, "History will burden these leaders with blood-guilt if they do not act in accord with their specialized political knowledge and conscience. . . . If their warning and counsel receive no hearing, then they have the right and the duty to resign from their offices."

Brauchitsch finally gave in and convened all the army's senior commanders. He, not Beck, stood to address the generals with the red stripes down their trousers—but it was from Beck's numerous memoranda that Brauchitsch drew his inspiration. He outlined Hitler's plans, then asked each area commander how his own troops and the neighboring populace stood on the question of war. The consensus was that nobody wanted it. They debated how to convince the Führer of this truth. By no means, said General von Reichenau, should we confront Hitler *en masse;* one man alone should act as the army spokesman. Brauchitsch, then, approached the Führer on his own, only to be dressed down like some bumbling orderly.

A few days later, on August 10, Hitler summoned the members of the General Staff to dinner at Bertchesgaden, where they were forced to listen to a three-hour monologue on the Führer's political theories. The atmosphere was strained, and the generals left for Berlin late that night still, as one of them put it, "unconvinced of the Führer's genius."

On the afternoon of August 17 a wealthy Pomeranian land-owner named Ewald von Kleist-Schmenzin boarded a Lufthansa passenger plane at Berlin's Tempelhof airdrome and took off for London. Kleist's mission, like Goerdler's before him, was to warn British politicians of Hitler's intentions and to urge them to action to prevent another world war. The visit had been arranged by a distinguished British foreign correspondent working in Berlin, Ian Colvin, a friend and confidant of Admiral Canaris. Canaris arranged for Kleist's passport and briefed him on Hitler's latest plans for conquest.

Kleist had been working against the Nazis even before they came to power. In 1932 he wrote and published a broadside that called National Socialism the "dangerous sickness of our time." Hitler, he wrote, was responsible for poisoning the minds of the people; his political theories were rubbish. A year later Kleist told the SA that he would be arrested and thrown into jail before he allowed them to fly the swastika over his castle. Kleist, in fact, had been marked for extermination during the Röhm killing spree of 1934, but hid with a friend in Berlin until the frenzy had passed.

The morning after his arrival in London, Kleist was in conference with Sir Robert Vansittart, undersecretary of the British Foreign Office. He opened the conversation with a message from Beck: "Bring me certain proof that England will fight if Czechoslovakia is attacked and I will make an end of this régime." He emphasized that war was a certainty unless Britain took a strong line.

"Do you mean an extreme danger?" Vansittart asked.

"No," said Kleist, "I mean a complete certainty."

"When are the operations supposed to commence?" asked the undersecretary.

Now Kleist laughed. "Of course, you already know the date."

Vansittart said that he did not, nor did the prime minister. Kleist then said, "After September 27, anything you do will be too late." He suggested that the Foreign Office state publicly in no uncertain terms that the British would act in case of a German intrusion into Czech territory, backing up words with a massive demonstration of British seapower in the North Sea. Vansittart said he would take Kleist's suggestions and warnings under advisement when consulting with the foreign minister and the prime minister.

Meanwhile, on that same afternoon, Beck was having his last fiery meeting with Brauchitsch, who had become so exasperated with Beck that he took leave out of Berlin to avoid seeing him. He returned to Berlin on the eighteenth only to find Beck waiting on his doorstep. Beck shouted that the time had come for him to resign. Brauchitsch answered that he found Beck's suggestion unacceptable. Beck retorted that whether Brauchitsch accepted his resignation or not, this was nevertheless the last day he would serve the Third Reich as chief of the General Staff. Then he picked up his cap and marched out of the office. Hitler willingly accepted Beck's resignation three days later, remarking intuitively, "That man is capable of undertaking something."

Beck's own deputy, General Franz Halder, was handpicked by Brauchitsch to take Beck's place. Halder, fifty-four, was a stern-looking soldier, by turns crusty and emotional. His clipped dark hair stood up *en brosse*, and he wore old-fashioned pince-nez glasses high on the bridge of a substantial nose. Halder and his forebears had steadfastly served Bavarian rulers for many generations, and Brauchitsch thought him the ideal replacement for the troublesome Beck; he did not know that in private Halder referred to the Führer as a "criminal," "sexual psychopath," and "bloodsucker."

On September 1, 1938, the day Halder assumed office, events began rushing toward a climax. Staff officers in Berlin and at divisional level wrestled on paper with the thorny problems of logistics; there must be no repetition of the frantic scramble after fuel that threatened the march into Austria. Gunnery officers of the Sixteenth Army Corps, which included the 1st Panzer Division and the 13th and 20th Motorized Infantry Divisions, practiced firing at replicas of concrete-and-steel bunkers that formed part of the stout Czech defensive positions. The results were not encouraging; heavy German tanks were still on drawing boards, and the existing light tanks mounted only 37-mm guns. Göring visited a Pomeranian regiment and sought clumsily to inspire a gathering of young officers by telling them, "I know you are afraid of the Czech bunkers, but just throw your hearts over and you will come through!" Stung by what seemed to be an insult to their courage, the officers lodged a formal protest with Brauchitsch.

Along Germany's southern flank work was stepped up on the West Wall, later known as the Siegfried line. Miles of concrete tetrahedron "dragon's teeth" were being poured and deep tank traps were being dug; concrete machine-gun emplacements began sprouting in the grass. When General Wilhelm Adam complained that these raw defenses could not be held even for three weeks, Hitler exploded. He shouted back, "The man who can't hold these fortifications for three months or three years is a scoundrel!"

On September 2, and again on Spetember 5, German emissaries approached the British government—one of them, Theodor Kordt, entered through the back door of 10 Downing Street—with new warnings and with renewed pleas for British action. But they had no more success than did Kleist earlier.*

---

*The British military attaché in Berlin, Colonel Noel Mason-MacFarlane, had his own plan for averting a second world war while at the same time erasing the entire structure of National Socialism. He figured that a single rifle bullet fired from his apartment window would do it.

Mason-Mac, as his friends called him, was forty-nine, and had been taking long chances all of his life. He had broken his neck while still a schoolboy, and in France and Mesopotamia during the First World War his battlefield courage earned him the Military Cross with two bars, two mentions in dispatches, and the croix de guerre. During the Afghan war of 1919, Mason-Mac took up the local sport of pigsticking, and while chasing a wild boar he was thrown from his charger and permanently injured his back. A car crash a little later put him in hospital with ribs smashed close to the spine. As a result of these injuries Mason-MacFarlane walked with a stiff-legged gait, his body hunched forward as though leaning into a gale. He had watched the growth of the Nazi party and the rise of Hitler since his days as an attaché in Vienna in 1931 and saw the danger to world peace for what it was. He believed that direct action, not diplomacy, was the solution to the crisis over Czechoslovakia.

Mason-MacFarlane's apartment overlooked a broad avenue down which "Führer parades" passed in front of a reviewing stand; he had viewed several of these military processions from his window, gazing directly down at Adolf Hitler standing on the elevated platform to watch the troops and mechanized vehicles pass in review. With his marksman's eye, Mason-MacFarlane estimated the range at just under 100 yards. He would not, of course, fire from the living room window, which would be under observation by security police scattered

47

In Berlin, Oster and Beck feverishly put the finishing touches to the detailed plans for the coup d'état. The first move had to be a lightning strike against key government installations—radio stations, the public telephone system, ministerial teletypes, Party offices, and, above all, the various SS, SD, and Gestapo headquarters. It was not a simple matter of rushing the Gestapo headquarters at 8 Albrechtstrasse; Gestapo substations proliferated, and nobody within the Abwehr knew where they all were.

The disillusioned Gestapo officer Hans Gisevius, who flew from one level of the conspiracy to another, applied himself to the problem. He secured the help of a veteran cop named Arthur Nebe who had access to Gestapo secret files and reports, and he managed to recruit Berlin's chief of police, Wolf von Helldorf, under whom Gisevius ostensibly served. Nebe and Helldorf supplied Gisevius with the addresses of various secret police stations scattered around Berlin, some of them camouflaged as innocuous-looking private homes. These places would have to be invested by troops; but first a tactical military reconnaissance had to be carried out.

---

throughout the parade route. The shot would be made through the bathroom window instead, with the rifleman standing nine yards back inside the room, invisible from the outside. A telescopic sight would make the figure of the Führer leap forward in the narrow angle of fire permitted the shootist, and a silencer would muffle the crack when the firing pin struck home.

Sure that the plan would work, Mason-Mac flew to London and laid the scheme before his superiors, who said the plan would be taken under advisement. Then Mason-MacFarlane returned to Berlin where he confided in the *Times* correspondent, Ewen Butler, showing him the spot from where the shot could be fired. The colonel admitted that "he hadn't the slightest hope London would accept his plan, but if by any wild chance it were approved he, himself, would be the rifleman if necessary."

Butler protested that "the murder of the German Chancellor by the British Military Attaché would create a really formidable diplomatic incident."

Mason-Mac agreed with Butler, but added, "Nobody in Germany would go to war on that account, whereas while Hitler lived war is certain."

Gisevius got in touch with General Erich von Brockdorff-Ahlefeld, commander of the nearby Potsdam garrison, who agreed to execute the recon in person. Brockdorff told Gisevius that they would have to be discreet; the Gestapo had eyes and ears everywhere. Gisevius got on the telephone and called Frau Elisabeth Strünck, whose husband, Theodor, the director of a large insurance firm, had no use for Hitler. That same afternoon Brackdorff and Gisevius journeyed to a suburban railway station and were met by Frau Strünck in a gleaming cabriolet. The two "tourists" climbed in and sat on the warm leather seats to begin an afternoon of sightseeing in Berlin.

The big car cruised the streets of the capital city while General von Brockdorff furiously sketched and made notes. He ordered the various buildings circled so that he could observe possible escape routes through back gardens and over walls. They drove past the SS barracks at Lichterfelde; they wheeled around the huge radio broadcasting center at Königswusterhausen. Then they headed northeast out of town to drive past the concentration camp at Sachsenhusen, where nearly 5,000 German citizens were

---

The two men believed that the Führer's death at that time would have brought about the collapse of the National Socilaist regime, with Mason-MacFarlane well aware of the forces inside the German High Command which would "seize the opportunity to overthrow a system they had every reason to hate and fear."

Mason-MacFarlane waited impatiently for word from London, but no word ever came. A few weeks after he and Butler discussed the daring scheme, Butler told Mason-Mac that he managed to get within twenty feet of Hitler at the Anhalter railway station in Berlin, where the correspondent had no right to be. "The Gestapo security arrangement had collapsed," he said, "and I might have had several Mills bombs in my pockets. I could have disposed not only of the Führer, but most of his accomplices." Mason-Mac bitterly reproached Butler for "having missed such an excellent opportunity."

Mason-MacFarlane later learned that Whitehall and the war ministry had vetoed his plan because, among other things, the act would have been "unsportsmanlike." Both Mason-Mac and Ewen Butler held their tongues, and word of the attaché's assassination plans did not surface until thirty-one years after the Czechoslovakian crisis had passed.

behind barbed wire, most of them charged with slandering the Party or the Führer. The release of these political prisoners would prove to the rest of the world that the coup was being staged to bring back to Germany what Goerdler called "ordinary human decency."

The military commander of the risky undertaking was General Erwin von Witzleben, then commanding Wehrkreis III, the military district of Berlin. Witzleben was immensely popular with the troops, and he counted on support of the Twenty-third Infantry Division to help in the overthrow attempt. At fifty-seven, Witzleben was still lean and hard, his jaw square under an eagle's beak of a nose. Gisevius found him "refreshingly uncomplicated . . . a typical frontline general firmly rooted in the chivalric traditions of the old Prussian officers' corps . . . certainly not inclined toward the fine arts, but devoted to country life and a passionate hunter." Witzleben provided the burly Gisevius with a private office adjoining his own, an office free of Gestapo wiretaps and SD spies. Nobody could get to Gisevius without first passing Witzleben's desk. Gisevius carried false ID papers supplied by the general, who told his adjutant with a wink that Gisevius was "a close relative arranging the Witzleben family papers."

Borrowing a leaf from the Hitler-Himmler-Göring book of treachery and deceit, the conspirators decided to cloak their coup under the guise of an announced SS uprising against the Führer and the Wehrmacht, broadcasting to the people that Himmler planned to usurp Hitler's authority and replace the Wehrmacht with the SS as the nation's armsbearers. Hitler and Göring, then, were to be taken into custody by Witzleben and company for their own protection. Himmler and Heydrich were to be arrested as ringleaders of a dastardly plot against Führer and Fatherland. With this cover story in force, it was reasoned that the Wehrmacht units outside of Berlin would fall in line willingly to contain what Witzleben called the "black rabble of the SS." With the coup an accomplished fact, the real reasons for the takeover would be explained to the public and the army.

Besides the 23rd Infantry, one other division and an independent regiment were committed to provide armed backup for the takeover. General von Brockdorff's 9th Infantry Regiment would spearhead the military action inside Berlin. The 9th was a showcase outfit based at Potsdam, its officers and men handpicked. Once Brockdorff loosed this regiment inside the capital, Witzleben's greatest worry was the crack SS Adolf Hitler Life Guards Division stationed near Munich. The division was filled with Nazi fanatics from top to bottom and fully mobilized. It would have to be contained on the first day, probably by combat. Witzleben called in General Erich Hoepner, commanding the Wuppertal Panzer Division, and explained the problem. Hoepner, fifty-two, a pugnacious combat veteran and holder of the Iron Cross, First Class, from the first World War, was eager to unleash his armored division against Himmler's finest. His Panzers, then camped in a Thuringian forest north of Munich, were alerted and put in a state of combat readiness. If the Leibstandarte started to move on Berlin, Hoepner's tanks and armored vehicles would debouch from the trees with guns blazing.

Halder, whose specialty was operational planning, approved every detail of the plans drawn by Witzleben, Oster, and the others, although he found Oster dangerously irrepressible. He, like Canaris, drew the line at any talk of assassination of any of the Nazi leaders, although his hatred of Hitler grew with each personal contact.* When it was suggested that events might force Hitler's liquidation, Halder said no, certainly not while Germany was still at peace. Only if Hitler plunged the nation into war was assassination to be considered, and even then the killing must appear to be accidental so as not to turn Hitler into a martyr and a legend. If fighting started, Halder suggested, then Hitler's private train could be blown to bits with demolition charges; the blame could be placed on strafing enemy aircraft.

Halder later explained the dilemma facing him as the only surviving male member of a family who had been soldiers for 300

---

*On his first day as chief of the General Staff, he faced Hitler in the Chancellery and suggested that, as soldiers, they should form their ideas together. Hitler waved his hand and replied, "You will never learn what I am thinking. And those who boast most loudly that they know my thought, to such people I lie even more."

years. "In the dictionary of the German soldier the terms *treason* and *plot against the state* do not exist. Thus I was in the position of one who has a soldier's duty—but also a duty that I consider higher, the duty to the flag. This is the worst dilemma a soldier can be faced with."

The plans boiled down to the seizure of Hitler and the others, with Hitler to be placed on trial before the people. He was to be proved insane, incompetent to lead a resurgent nation of nearly 80 million. Oster dug from the files a twenty-year-old medical report written up after Corporal Hitler was carried to a base hospital following a mustard gas attack in Flanders during the last month of the war. Hitler, wrought up over defeat at the front and by revolution at home, went temporarily blind. A Berlin psychiatrist examined the patient, who had been in combat for almost four years continuously, and found Hitler a "psychopath with hysterical symptoms." The yellowing report, although of dubious value in certifying the Führer insane, nonetheless went into the dossier of infamy maintained by Canaris and Oster.

At Oster's home tactical details for Hitler's seizure were worked out. The task was entrusted by Witzleben to Lieutenant Friedrich Wilhelm Heinz, attached to Oster's staff. Heinz, who had fought with the Free Corps against communist armed gangs during the postwar uprisings, was a man who favored direct action. Witzleben told Heinz to recruit a company of commandos with which to storm the Chancellery, take Hitler into custody, and spirit him away to a castle in Bavaria pending a trial. Witzleben suggested that Heinz's commandos should comprise students and workers as well as Wehrmacht officers so that the world would realize that this was not a South American-style army coup, but a revolt against tyranny by a cross-section of the German people.

Heinz got busy and soon had sixty men together. He and Oster now hatched a plan of their own behind Witzleben's back. They agreed that the putsch could only be a guaranteed success if the Führer were to be killed on the spot; in their eyes, Hitler dead was unquestionably better than Hitler alive and imprisoned. At H-hour, Heinz would lead his commandos against the Chancellery, blow in the doors, and rush upstairs and arrest the

Führer. Heinz said he would see to it that an incident was provoked, providing an excuse to shoot Hitler down then and there.
"Shot while trying to escape" was the standard Gestapo and SS
explanation for executions of political prisoners, and Heinz said
the same phrase could be applied in the case of the Führer. As for
Brauchitsch, the putsch would be revealed to him only minutes
before Witzleben ordered the regular troops and Heinz's commandos to move into action.

By mid-September, the conspirators believed they had a pistol
cocked and ready, aimed at the head of the state; all that was
needed was the order to pull the trigger. The trigger-pull would
be initiated by Hitler himself when he announced publicly his intention to seize Czechoslovakia by force, and the hammer would
fly forward when the British and the French handed down their
decision to go to war over the principle of safeguarding the integrity of small nations—as Beck was convinced they would.

All of Europe tensed for the coming of the evening of Monday,
September 12, 1938, when Hitler was to speak at the annual
Party rally held at the gigantic outdoor stadium in the medieval
city of Nuremberg. Nobody knew what Hitler would say. Beck,
Canaris, Oster, and the others deeply involved in the conspiracy
thought that Hitler would use the opportunity to hand down an
ultimatum to the Czechs to cede the Sudetenland or face war—in
which case Witzleben's various armed groups would be placed on
full alert. Others felt sure that the Führer would demand only a
plebiscite, thus pulling the Sudeten Germans under the Reich's
wing in that peaceful way.

The Führer's arrival at Nuremburg stadium at two minutes
before seven that evening was heralded by the simultaneous
switching on of massed batteries of searchlights that sent brilliant
blue-white shafts racing vertically into the threatening skies. The
stadium exploded with hoarse, passionate cries of *Sieg Heil! Sieg
Heil! Sieg Heil! Sieg Heil!* that followed Hitler for a full ten minutes while he marched purposefully through the hysteria toward
the rostrum. He stared straight ahead, left thumb hooked in his
belt, his right arm raised in the Party salute.

It was 9:00 P.M. in Moscow, 6:00 P.M. in London, midnight in

53

New York, and 9:00 P.M. Sunday in Los Angeles. When the uproar died down, Hitler placed both hands on the lectern and began to speak. The world listened to learn if the Führer of Germany had decided for peace or war, and none listened more carefully than the plotters in Berlin.

What followed was a puzzling anticlimax. Hitler opened with a lengthy, droning account of the early struggles of the Party, then finally raised his voice and launched an attack on Czechoslovakia. He abused the nation, its history, and its president, Eduard Beneš. But there was no talk of war, no demand for a plebiscite. The tirade was vaguely threatening, but that was all. Following another enthusiastic chorus of Sieg Heils, Hitler marched out of the stadium and, instead of returning to Berlin, continued south to Berchtesgaden. This change in plans added to the frustration felt by the conspirators in the capital.

Despite the lack of specific provocation, Sudetens left their radios and rushed out into the streets and milled around excitedly, some of them carrying pistols and hunting rifles. Inevitably, firing broke out, and martial law was declared. Czech troops moved in to quell a disturbance in the town square of Tachau on the following morning, and before it was over eleven Sudeten Germans lay dead on the cobblestones. Beck and Oster looked for reaction from Berchtesgaden; the reaction came instead from elsewhere, and was totally unexpected.

At midmorning on Wednesday, September 14, the British prime minister, Neville Chamberlain, announced to the press gathered at 10 Downing Street that he was going to fly to Germany to meet with Adolf Hitler. The news was quickly flashed to world capitals, creating joy in London, exultation in the streets of Berlin, and deep gloom in Prague. Admiral Canaris became so depressed that he lost his appetite and could not finish his dinner that evening.

Chamberlain, sixty-nine, boarded an airplane for the first time in his life early the next morning, flew through bad weather to reach Munich, and from there traveled by car to Berchtesgaden. He and Hitler and an interpreter sat in the Führer's cavernous salon, and while a wind-whipped rain beat against the windows they discussed the Czech crisis. When Hitler was first informed of the intended visit he believed that Chamberlain would arrive bearing an ultimatum; he quickly learned that the elder statesman was there to find out what Hitler wanted and to find ways of making accommodations. The British were not against a plebiscite, but were against the Germans using force of arms to acquire the disputed territory. Chamberlain left Berchtesgaden after a three-hour discussion, promising to return after he had consulted with the French and with his own government.

Chamberlain was back a week later, this time for a meeting at the Rhinish resort town of Bad Godesberg. He brought with him news that Britain and France agreed upon the dismemberment of Czechoslovakia on a peaceful, step-by-step basis that would cause the Czechs a minimum amount of economic loss. Hitler began to rant over continued incidents of "persecution" of the Sudetens; he would move against the frontier with his Wehrmacht despite what the British and French had guaranteed the Czechs. The arguments seesawed for three days and ended with Hitler's agreement to extend the deadline for occupying the Sudetenland until October 1, with a promise of no precipitate military action until final concessions were wrung from the Czechs.

Hitler returned to Berlin only to work himself up to a new rage against the Czechs and President Beneš. He addressed 20,000 Germans in the Berlin Sportpalast and screamed that Beneš was a Bolshevik bent on eradicating the German minority. If Beneš failed to give the Sudeten Germans their freedom, then Hitler would seize their freedom by force. He was still enraged the next day and told a British diplomat that he didn't care a fig if the British and the French struck in the west. "I am prepared for any eventuality!" he shouted. "It's Tuesday today, and by next Monday we shall all be at war."

Early the following morning in London, hundreds of sweaty workers carrying picks and shovels descended upon Saint James's Park and began tearing into the soft, grass-covered earth. Similar scenes were enacted in parks all over England, where air raid trenches were being dug for a bewildered public already being issued cheap gas masks.

On that same day, Hitler ordered a Panzer division with supporting infantry to parade through Berlin. The crowd stood sullenly and watched them pass. The Führer had hoped for enthusiasm; watching the apathetic reaction from a Chancellery window, he was disgusted. He turned away and said to his adjutant, "I can't wage a war yet with people like that."

Inside the Abwehr offices on the Tirpitzufer, frantic activity swirled around the still-despondent Canaris. Oster had agents planted in all of the major government offices bringing him current reports, especially from the Foreign Office. Göring was tapping telephone conversations between Jan Masaryk, the Czech ambassador, and the British Foreign Office. These scrambled conversations were unscrambled by Göring's technicians and translated into clear German. Oster's agents secured carbons of these transcriptions and delivered them to the Abwehr.

Gisevius believed the "time was right for the final spurt." War was obviously only days, if not hours, away. But Oster for once was pessimistic and told Gisevius that the Western powers were bound to yield. Irritated, Gisevius shot back, "You deserve a post with the Propaganda Ministry."

Gisevius's estimate of the situation was given added credence when Oster was handed a copy of the latest letter from Hitler to Chamberlain, filched from the foreign ministry. The Führer had changed his mind again; the Czechs, he told Chamberlain, had until 2:00 P.M., Wednesday, September 28, to meet his demands. Oster convened an emergency meeting early Wednesday morning with Beck, Witzleben, and Halder who, Oster observed, uncontrollably broke into a brief fit of weeping after reading the note. Beck suggested that Halder go immediately to Brauchitsch and urge him to confront Hitler to try to talk him out of moving militarily against the Czech defenses without one more effort at negotiation. Halder got control of himself and departed for the war ministry, where he found Brauchitsch willing to try.

Witzleben hurried back to his headquarters to await developments, ready to spring into action. Heinz's commandos, secreted in safe houses in the area of the Chancellery, were told to stand by. Witzleben found Gisevius waiting for him in his office, and said excitedly, "Gisevius, the time has come!"

But the time had not come. Brauchitsch again stumbled badly in the presence of his Führer and was subjected to such a vitriolic tongue-lashing that he left Hitler's study drained of color, thankful that he still had his job.

With Hitler's deadline less than three hours away, the Italian ambassador arrived with an offer from Benito Mussolini to mediate the differences. Hitler accepted. Mussolini's offer was relayed to London, and early the next afternoon the third and final conference was held, this time in Munich, to decide for peace or war. An agreement acceptable to everybody except the Czechs—who were not even invited to the conference table—was finally wrenched into shape at one-thirty the following morning.

Hitler got everything he wanted except a blitzkrieg through Czechoslovakia to the Carpathians, and complained immediately afterward that "Chamberlain has spoiled my entrance into Prague." Chamberlain returned to London a savior, and Hitler to Berlin a conquering hero. The Führer had worked another bloodless miracle, confounding his critics. Beck's premise upon which the coup d'état was based had been wrong: France and England would not yet fight for a smaller nation's integrity.

Even the most diehard of the plotters realized that the opportunity to eliminate Hitler was a flower that had bloomed spectacularly, then withered suddenly with the decision at Munich. The moment had flown. Halder would later explain: "With a stroke of the pen a victory was secured. I do not know if a non-military man can understand what it meant to have the Czech Army eliminated with a pen stroke, and Czechoslovakia stripped of her fortifications and standing naked like a new-born babe. I stayed the order of execution because the whole basis for the action was taken away."

While the chosen elements of the Wehrmacht moved peacefully across the Czech frontier to occupy the Sudentenland, the conspirators gloomily dismantled their machinery for a takeover.

"Our revolt was done for," said Gisevius. "Schacht, Oster and I sat around Witzleben's fireplace and tossed our plans and projects into the fire. We spent the rest of the evening meditating, not on Hitler's triumph, but on the calamity that had befallen Europe."

Oster, however, retained his original three-page handwritten draft of the operational plans in his office safe. He knew it would be needed, probably sooner than the others sitting before Witzleben's autumn fire might think.

4

Alone against
the Führer

THE APATHY OF the German public toward Hitler's cherished torchlight parades and displays of the Wehrmacht's growing might was brought on by fears that their newly found stability and relatively improved living conditions would vanish with the coming of another war. Fewer than 1 million Germans were out of work in 1938, compared with 6 million five years earlier, and the number of jobless was shrinking all the time.

Although there was bread on the table, it was put there at heavy personal cost to the worker. Hitler had abolished trade unions and the right to strike, and he forbade industry to increase wages from the 1936 average of the equivalent of $6.29 per week; if a worker wanted more income he had to spend longer hours at his lathe producing more. He was, in fact, an industrial serf doing piece work. Workers were forced to stay with the job they had, but on the other hand they could not be fired at the whim of employers without permission from the Labor Front, the Nazi-controlled organization that had replaced all of Germany's unions. Hitler had created no worker's paradise, but compared with the freedom to starve the worker had enjoyed during the chaotic Weimar Republic, he was grateful for his current spartan stability.

Germans had to accept the virtual confiscation of their children by the state. Hitler warned in 1937, "This new Reich will give its youth to no one, but will *itself* take youth, and give to youth, its own education and its own upbringing." From the age of six until being drafted into the Wehrmacht at eighteen, German boys were indoctrinated with Nationalist Socialist philosophy in either special Party schools or in public schools, where teachers were forced into joining the Nationalist Socialist Teachers' League and required to swear an oath of fealty to the Führer similar to that forced on members of the Wehrmacht. Children were encouraged to observe their parents' reactions to the Nazi régime and to report unfavorable remarks made in the home about the Führer. Parents learned to watch what they said in front of their uniformed children, whose costly tattling could send them to Dachau or Sachsenhausen.

Perhaps at no time in history had a people's lives been so thoroughly dominated by a state as during the years of the Third Reich. The government tightly controlled the newspapers, radio broadcasting, films, and even symphony concerts. The eyes and the ears of the Gestapo and the Security Service of the SS were everywhere, alert to the slightest criticism of the Führer and his works. A revolt of the people against Hitler was never remotely possible; indeed, those German citizens who wanted to take a shot at the Führer would have been hard-pressed to find the weapon handy enough for their desires—one of the first moves the Nazis made when Hitler gained power in 1933 was to confiscate every private handgun in Germany, leaving only registered fowling pieces, which are poor tools for assassination.

However, a handgun was used in the next attempt to stalk Hitler, a gun smuggled into Germany by a foreigner engaged in a one-man crusade.

In the early summer of 1938 a twenty-two-year-old Swiss theological student named Maurice Bavaud walked out of the gates of a French seminary in Brittany, ostensibly bound for his summer holiday. But when Bavaud boarded the train for his native town of Neuchâtel in western Switzerland, he knew he would not be coming back. After almost three years of dedicated religious study, Bavaud had become obsessed with a higher calling: the destruction of Adolf Hitler.

The idea of doing away with the German leader was planted in Bavaud's mind by a fellow seminarian, Marcel Gerbohay, twenty-four, who exerted a mystical influence over the younger Bavaud. Hitler, Gerbohay said, was the devil incarnate. He was bent on destroying the Mother Church. His speeches rang with talks of peace, which disturbed Gerbohay because it proved that Hitler had no intention of waging war to rid Russia of communism, the archenemy of Catholics everywhere. Gerbohay confided to the credulous Bavaud that he was a direct descendant of the Romanovs; he could take his rightful place as one of the rulers of Russia only when the communists were ousted. Since Hitler apparently was not going to do the job, he had to be gotten rid of. Bavaud said he would take on this responsibility himself even though he was a devout Catholic and murder was anathema. Surely God would pardon him for doing away with the antichrist.

Bavaud moved back in with his parents and five brothers and sisters. He helped his mother at the small greengrocer's shop she ran that provided additional income to her husband's salary as a postal worker. To prepare himself for the great undertaking that lay ahead, Bavaud began studying German and familiarized himself with the Hitlerian prose in a French edition of *Mein Kampf*. When the British and the French surrendered at Munich and the Wehrmacht moved into the Sudetenland, Bavaud decided it was time to act. He left Neuchâtel on October 9, 1938, telling his family that he was going to Germany to find work as a draftsman, having worked at that trade before entering the seminary.

Bavaud spent ten days with relatives in the German resort town of Baden-Baden, then told them he was going on to Mannheim in the north to look for work. Instead, he caught a train for the Swiss frontier town of Basel, 100 miles to the south, where he spent part of his meager funds for a small automatic pistol and some 6.35-mm ammunition. Assuming that Hitler was in Berlin, Bavaud bought a ticket for the capital and traveled 400 miles northward. He reached Berlin on October 21 and learned the next day that the long train journey was wasted; the Führer was not in Berlin but at his mountain retreat above Berchtesgaden, 300 miles to the south. Bavaud got on another train and headed

61

for Bavaria, the pistol nestled in an overcoat pocket. He checked into an inexpensive hotel in Berchtesgaden on the twenty-fifth, wondering how he could get up the mountain and within range of his intended victim.

Hitler had been coming to the mountain, the Obersalzberg, that overlooked Berchtesgaden since 1925. His first residence had been a small, rustic house on the Obersalzberg, rented for the equivalent of twenty-five dollars a month. He bought the house and a small plot of ground outright in 1928, and in 1935 embarked on a massive expansion scheme, borrowing drafting instruments from Albert Speer, his personal architect, and hunching over a drawing table to execute ground plan, elevations, and final rendering. The result was derivative of typical two- and three-story Bavarian guest houses seen in the area. Speer later commented, "The ground plan would have been graded D by any professor at any institute of technology."

Hitler designed a huge picture window that overlooked the village of Berchtesgaden, 1,650 feet below, the city of Salzburg off to the right, and the mountain named Untersberg across the valley, where the Emperor Charlemagne was buried. Hitler loved his house, the Berghof, more than any other place in Germany. "By night at the Berghof," he once said, "I often remain for hours with my eyes open, contemplating from my bed the mountains lit up by the moon."

Through purchase of surrounding land and acquisition of nearby state forest preserves, Hitler's domain in 1938 spread across 1,728 acres. Maurice Bavaud, sitting at an outdoor café, could see a parade of trucks moving slowly up and down the winding, hairpin road that led to the Berghof. Construction was going on all over the Obersalzberg. Martin Bormann was building a house there; Hermann Göring was laying foundations for a place of his own; new SS barracks and a garage to house the motor pool were rising in brick and concrete behind the Berghof, hidden by tall trees. The security on the Obersalzberg during that early autumn of 1938 was far from formidable. The outer perimeter was surrounded by a nine-foot-high barbed-wire fence circuiting nine uninterrupted miles. Closer to the Berghof itself, there was an inner fence two miles in circuit. But there was never more than forty of the black-uniformed SS guards patrolling the vast area at any one time; a determined man could have cut his way through the wires dressed as one of the workmen and conceivably could have gotten within firing range of the Führer as he stood on his terrace gazing across the valley.

Bavaud was more persistent than imaginative, and in any case he once again lost his quarry. On the day that his train pulled into Berchtesgaden, the Führer's special train, the *Amerika*, left the valley to carry Hitler to Austria and then to the occupied areas of Czechoslovakia. Bavaud decided to wait out Hitler's return. He bought some extra cartridges for the Schmeisser pistol and took long walks in the hills surrounding Berchtesgaden. A lifetime spent largely indoors poring over books and in front of a drafting table was poor preparation for assassination. Bavaud knew little about firearms and nothing at all about the fine art of pistol marksmanship. From what distance could he trust his aim with the unfamiliar pistol? Bavaud decided that the maximum range at which he would risk a shot at Hitler would be twenty-five feet. He chose a tree with a girth about the same as a man's and paced off the distance. He raised the pistol, squinted through the sights, and made the clear forest air ring with the cracking of the Schmeisser as he fired round after round, sending bark flying and birds rushing into the sky.

In town, Bavaud discovered that his sporadic German studies enabled him to order meals, inquire about the time, and exchange the usual tourist greetings—but was hopelessly inadequate for carrying on conversations or learning anything about how he could penetrate the Berghof's defenses when Hitler returned. He was relieved to meet two local French teachers at an inn; now he could converse freely in his native language. Bavaud left the impression that he was an ardent admirer of National Socialism and the wonders Hitler was working for his people. Could they help him meet the Führer? The teachers said they would like to help, but there was nothing they could do.

Just then Captain Karl Deckert, a police official sitting at the next table, intervened with a fateful suggestion. Deckert said that he could not help overhearing the conversation between the earnest young Swiss and the two schoolteachers, and that since his job involved security he was in a position to help. He was sure Bavaud would never be able to secure an audience with the Führer at the Berghof; he should try instead to go through channels in Munich, preferably with a letter of introduction, and failing that he could at least see the Führer and other Party officials during the annual ceremonies commemorating the putsch of 1923. Deckert explained that Hitler and the others would march through the streets of Munich as they had done fifteen years earlier on November 9. Bavaud thanked Captain Deckert and said he would follow his advice.

Bavaud took the train for Munich on October 31, just one day ahead of the peripatetic Hitler, who stayed in the Bavarian capital only overnight before climbing into a car for a whirlwind tour of southern and central Germany. He was gone for a week, during which time Bavaud tried to prepare himself for the ultimate confrontation.

He decided to familiarize himself with the parade route through Munich's streets that Hitler and the other "Old Fighters" would follow on the day of the march. The 1923 route was a matter of public record, but Bavaud's job was made easier with the publication in a Munich newspaper of the particular streets with their twists and turnings into this square and that. Armed with a copy of the newspaper and a tourist map, Bavaud set off on his own solitary march.

He began at the eastern edge of the city in front of the Bürgerbräukeller, the cavernous old beer hall, and walked westward across the great stone Lugwig's Bridge that spans the green, swift-flowing Isar River. He left the bridge, paced up Zweibruckenstrasse, the street leading to the frescoed stone gateway known as the Isartor. He passed under the archway and continued westward along a broad avenue known as the Tal leading into the Marienplatz, roughly halfway to his destination. Bavaud now turned north and kept going until he reached the spacious Odeonsplatz where, all those years before, Hitler's putsch had been stopped by gunfire that left sixteen of his followers sprawled dead on the pavement. Bavaud hoped he would leave Hitler in the same state long before the Führer could reach the Odeons-platz this time.

There remained the problem of securing a prime vantage point from where Bavaud could loose off several rounds of automatic fire that were sure to hit the mark without, he hoped, striking any innocent bystanders come to cheer their Führer. The Swiss learned that even foul weather had not deterred the citizens of Munich from thronging the parade route during the previous three years' marches. Wooden grandstands were erected at stra-tegic spots along the line of march, and Bavaud decided to try to bluff his way onto one of these. After several fruitless attempts to secure a pass, he finally was given a ticket for a place on one of the grandstands near the Marienplatz. Bavaud's story that he was a correspondent for a chain of Swiss newspapers went un-challenged, so the precious ticket was his.

As the day of the commemorative march approached, Bavaud fretted over the quality of his marksmanship. There was no se-cluded place near the city where he could practice, so he jour-neyed twenty miles west of Munich to a large, pretty lake, the Ammersee, and rented a rowboat. He oared himself some dis-tance away from shore and stopped. He fashioned several small, boatlike targets out of newspaper and set them adrift. When they bobbed away to a distance Bavaud estimated to be twenty or twenty-five feet, he raised the pistol and fired, the automatic bucking in his hand. The firing seemed to pass unnoticed; he rowed back to shore unmolested and returned to Munich.

The morning of November 9 broke cold with overcast skies. Adolf Hitler rose long after sunrise and entered the bathroom and shaved himself. Then he started dressing for the day's events. He pulled on a pair of khaki, military-style riding breeches, then a pair of brown leather boots that reached the knee. He buttoned up his khaki shirt, put on a black tie, and checked the Iron Cross, Second Class, pinned just underneath the golden Party badge. The wardrobe was completed with the addition of a Sam Browne belt. He picked up the khaki military cap, but it would not be worn during the long walk through Munich's crowded streets; the

65

marchers would go uncovered in deference to the dead of 1923.

Maurice Bavaud was up much earlier. He dressed, then checked the Schmeisser pistol. The seven-round clip was firmly seated in place. Bavaud pulled the action back, then let it slam forward to inject a shell in the chamber. He flicked on the safety, then put the weapon in his overcoat pocket. He hurried out into the streets and made his way rapidly through the crowds to reach the bleacher near the Marienplatz. He found an empty space down front and sat down to wait in the chilly outdoor air. The bleacher filled quickly, and crowds gathered to stand shoulder to shoulder up and down the street as far as Bavaud could see. Ranks of brown-shirted SA members stood solidly two-deep with backs to the crowds. Small children held red, white, and black paper flags, ready to wave them upon parental command when the Führer came into view. When Bavaud put his hand into his right overcoat pocket for warmth, he could feel the cold, heavy metal of the automatic postol, loaded and waiting.

Suddenly off to the right, the crowd noises grew in intensity. *The Führer is coming!* Bavaud gripped the pistol in his overcoat pocket, rising from his seat with the others to catch the first glimpse of Hitler, who would be leading the solemn procession. Bavaud craned his neck, straining for his first glimpse of the man he hoped to kill. Then Hitler came, marching up the street flanked by Göring, Himmler, and some others Bavaud did not recognize. Bavaud's heart fell—Hitler was going to pass on the opposite side of the street, a full fifty feet away, twice the distance Bavaud was willing to risk a shot. Hitler led the others steadily on, and Bavaud thought wildly of trying to shove his way past the packed bodies of the storm troopers, dash into the center of the street, and open fire. But Bavaud realized he could never fight his way past those burly guards. Hitler strode past the bleacher; a forest of arms were raised in his honor. The pistol was never taken from Bavaud's pocket.

Bavaud went back to his hotel to think out a new plan. Time was now critical for the would-be assassin; he had now been away from home for four weeks, and he was running low on cash with no means of getting more. His parents believed him to be still in Mannheim looking for a job. Bavaud fell asleep, only to be wakened later by what appeared to be rioting in the streets of Munich. There were hundreds of thousands wakened that night all over Germany by screams and the sounds of shattering glass. The orgy of destruction, directed against Germany's Jews, had been sparked by shots from a pistol wielded more efficiently than Bavaud's.

The pistol had belonged to Herschel Grynspan, a distraught Polish-Jewish émigré who had shoved his way into the German embassy in Paris, bent on assassinating the ambassador. He encountered instead Third Secretary Ernst vom Rath and opened fire. Rath died of his wounds in a Paris hospital on the afternoon of the ninth, while Hitler was still celebrating the events of the day. It was the moment some of Hitler's henchmen had been waiting for. Heydrich, with Goebbels's help, organized a nightlong pogrom that resulted in the murder of thirty-six German Jews and the destruction of 815 Jewish-owned shops and nearly 200 private residences. At dawn, more than 100 synagogues lay gutted and smoldering from flames set in the darkness. Hitler approved the order that local police, the SS, and the SA were not to interfere with the rioters. Because of the number of plate-glass windows that were smashed, more than $1.2 million worth, the night went down in history as Crystal Night.

The event was important to Bavaud because of the implications for his own plan. No German Party official had been assassinated since February 1936, when a Swiss-Jewish medical student named David Frankfurter had gunned down Wilhelm Gustloff, deputy leader of the Nazi party in Switzerland, in a shooting spree in Bern. Now Grynspan's action might cause a tightening of security around Hitler, making Bavaud's task more difficult than ever.

Remembering the suggestion made by Police Captain Deckert, Bavaud bought some stationery and envelopes, sat down in his Munich hotel room, and composed a forged letter to the Führer. This letter of introduction was signed "Pierre Flandin," the name of the current foreign minister of France; it explained that Bavaud had yet another, and more personal, letter for Hitler's eyes only. To cover this, Bavaud slipped a blank sheet of paper inside a second envelope, sealed it, and wrote Hitler's name on the front. Bavaud stuffed the phony documents inside his pockets along with the pistol and, on the same day, Thursday, November 10, caught a tram for Munich's Hauptbahnhof, where he boarded a train for Berchtesgaden to seek an audience with the Führer.

Bavaud had guessed wrong again; Hitler was still in Munich lecturing representatives of Germany's controlled press. Bavaud's train pulled into Berchtesgaden late in the afternoon, and the Swiss hired a taxi to take him up the winding road to the Berghof. He was of course stopped long before he reached the house, and after the usual problems with translation and after telephone calls on the part of the guards, the driver was told to take his passenger back down the hill; the Führer was not on the mountain. The frustrated Bavaud caught the next train back to Munich. Hitler, unbeknownst to Bavaud, the following day boarded the *Amerika* and left Munich to spend the weekend on the Obersalzberg.

While Hitler was relaxing at the Berghof eighty miles away, Bavaud traipsed the streets of Munich vainly trying to track down his quarry in one government building after another. He was turned away from them all, not unkindly, and it was suggested that if he still wished to deliver his letters in person he might try to reach the Führer through the Chancellery. Bavaud knew that it was out of the question to go all the way to Berlin, but he learned that there was a Chancellery representative in the small town of Bischofshofen, eighteen miles south of Berchtesgaden.

Bavaud was in a quandry; it was already late Saturday afternoon, and a search of his pockets turned up only sixteen Reichsmarks and a few pfennig, just under four dollars. He decided to make a final effort. He bought another train ticket and journeyed past Berchtesgaden, past the Obersalzberg where the lights were being turned on in Hitler's house, and reached Bischofshofen as the sun disappeared behind the forested mountains. There was no money left for a taxi, so Bavaud wearily started trudging up the streets for the Chancellery office, the pistol in his overcoat pocket bumping against his leg with every other step. He stopped and turned around before reaching the Chancellery office, realizing that his quest was hopeless; nobody would be on duty to receive him that late on Saturday night to help him bluff his way into the Führer's presence. There now remained the problem of getting out of Germany.

He only had five marks left, but that was enough for a train ticket to Salzburg, where he could seek help from the Swiss consulate for funds to return to his home at Neuchâtel. He could contact his parents and ask for money for the same purpose. He could sell the Schmeisser automatic pistol for enough cash to get him to the Swiss frontier, about 150 miles to the west of Berchtesgaden. Bavaud was not a criminal, not a wanted man, yet he now acted like one. Instead of getting rid of the incriminating evidence, the gun and the phony letters addressed to Hitler, he kept them and bought a train ticket for the small town of Freilassing, thirty miles to the north, above Berchtesgaden. He now had one mark, fifty-two pfennig in his pocket, and an uncertain future.

Bavaud's ticket was no good beyond Freilassing, but he managed to sneak himself aboard one of the coaches bound for Paris that were hooked up to the train that he had picked up in Bischofshofen. Once the train chuffed its way out of the station and headed west for Munich and Augsburg, the failed assassin was liable for arrest. He still had time to shred the letters and flush them down the toilet, to toss the gun out into the darkness, but he did neither.

Bavaud's luck held until shortly after the train pulled away from Munich, when the conductor caught him without the right ticket and with no money to buy one. Bavaud was escorted from the train at Augsburg by civilian police who automatically turned him over to the Gestapo because he was a foreigner. Incredibly, the Gestapo swallowed Bavaud's story that target practice was a favorite form of recreation and that he carried the Schmeisser wherever he went. The forged letters, he explained, were only to be used in an attempt to see the Führer and discuss the future relations between their two countries. The Gestapo made no immediate connection between the gun and the letters, and Bavaud was turned over to civilian authorities to face charges of trying to ride free on Reich railways.

Three weeks later, on December 6, Bavaud was sentenced to sixty days in the Augsburg jail for fraud. Despite the damning evidence in the hands of the Gestapo, it seemed that Bavaud had gotten away with his abortive attempts to shoot Hitler dead. But the Gestapo had not been idle; they traced his movements from one town to the other, and they tracked down the place and date of the purchase of the handgun. In late January 1939, the Gestapo descended upon Bavaud in his cell and after lengthy interrogation wrung a confession from him that he had, after all, come to Germany to assassinate Adolf Hitler.

German justice in Bavaud's case was sure but not swift. Bavaud was held for eleven months in Berlin's Moabit Prison before being brought to trial before the People's Court. He was found guilty as charged and sentenced to death. Again, his captors were in no hurry. Bavaud languished another seventeen months in prison before being taken out of his cell early one morning and beheaded. In one of his last letters to his parents, Bavaud wistfully commented, "Ah, if only I had remained at the seminary in God's service . . . if I had not forsaken the light for the shade, I would not be here now."

The Bavaud affair prompted Hitler to speak to his dinner guests about the probabilities of assassination. "The confessions of this Swiss," he said, "interested me in so far as they confirmed my conviction that not a soul can cope with an assassin who, for idealistic reasons, is prepared quite ruthlessly to hazard his own life in the execution of his own object. I quite understand why ninety percent of the historic assassinations have been successful . . . the really dangerous elements are those fanatics who have been goaded to action by dastardly priests, or nationalistically minded patriots from one of the countries we have occupied. . . . In the midst of crowds it is easy for some fanatic armed with a telescopic-sighted firearm to take a shot at me from some corner or other."

Hitler was not impressed with his bodyguards or local police when it came to his personal safety, commenting, "I owe my life not to the police, but to pure chance." He referred back to the time when he entered Vienna during the Anschluss when "the Gestapo plainclothesmen dressed themselves in such an astonishing collection of clothes—rough woollen mackintosh coats, ostler's capes and so forth—that I, and indeed any moron, could recognize them for what they were at a glance.

"The only preventive measure one can take," he concluded, "is to live irregularly—to walk, to drive and to travel at irregular times and unexpectedly." This philosophy, which had helped balk Bavaud's plans, would frustrate other aspiring assassins as well.

5

Clandestine
Missions

ALTHOUGH THE BRITISH-French capitulation at Munich dealt the conspirators a severe psychological blow, the loose confederation committed to Hitler's liquidation did not collapse. Instead, as time rushed on, more and more Germans from various strata of political, military, and religious spheres threw themselves into the anti-Hitler movement. But for months after the decisive confrontation at Munich the conspirators floundered, wondering how next to strike at a Führer who seemed infallible, a leader capable of pulling miracles of conquest out of the nearest hat.

Throughout that fall and winter the momentum was all Hitler's. He boasted to a convocation of generals at the Berghof, "There will probably never again be a man with more authority than I now possess. My existence is therefore a factor of great value—but I can be eliminated at any time by some criminal or lunatic. There is no time to lose! War must come in my lifetime."

At 6:00 A.M. on the snow-blown morning of March 15, 1939, German motorized infantry, motorcycles, and light tanks boomed out of the Sudetenland and rolled unopposed into Bohemia and Moravia, all that remained of Czechoslovakia. Hitler arrived to occupy Hradschin Palace that same night; his troops filled the square below, and swastika flags flew from the battlements overhead. Poland was now flanked to the south, and Hitler turned his attention northward where the Polish corridor cut through pre-1918 frontiers to the Baltic Sea, cutting off East Prussia from the main body of the Third Reich. Within the corridor lay the free city of Danzig, populated almost entirely by Germans, a Prussian enclave awash in a sea of largely hostile Poles.

Hitler demanded the return of Danzig and a German corridor through Poland to reach that city. The Poles refused and looked to Soviet Russia as an ally. Then Chamberlain handed Hitler a shock on the morning of March 31 when he faced the House of Commons and announced that if Polish independence were threatened, "His Majesty's Government would feel bound at once to lend to the Polish Government all the support in its power." France, he added, would back Britain in the military action required. Hitler reacted three days later by ordering the General Staff to begin strategic and tactical planning for the invasion of Poland. Hitler's war directive put the Wehrmacht on notice that it had until September 1, only five months away, to gear itself for the opening round of what would undoubtedly become a second world war.

Chamberlain's pronouncement and Hitler's reaction provided the catalyst needed to stir the civilian conspirators into action again. Hans Gisevius and Hjalmar Schacht, who had again been fired by Hitler, this time from his post as president of the Reichsbank, agreed to meet secretly in Switzerland with Goerdler to try to keep the lines of communication open with England and France. Switzerland was chosen for the rendezvous because they felt it was no longer safe to be seen with foreign emissaries in Berlin.

Gisevius and Schacht went on ahead by train, and as they approached the frontier Gisevius "felt his heart thump." He wondered if they were being followed by spies, and what interpretation the German border police would put upon their trip. While waiting for Goerdler they walked restlessly through the countryside near Lake Maggiore. It seemed to Gisevius that Schacht's perpetual equanimity was only a façade, that the older man "had adopted the habit of wearing high stiff collars in order more easily

to present an inscrutable appearance to the outside world." Gisevius noted that Schacht's habit of scratching at his skin when his
nerves were on edge produced small, ulcerating sores, a sure sign
that the ex-finance minister was fighting some secret inner battle.

Goerdler rang through under an assumed name and summoned
the others to the resort town of Ouchy. Goerdler and Schacht were
like terriers at a first meeting: wary, circling, and circumspect.
"Goerdler did not like Schacht's iridescent brilliance and vivac-
ity," noted Gisevius, "while Schacht could not endure Goerdler's
insistency, loquacity and obdurateness." Schacht and Goerdler
could not agree on which tack to follow in their approach to the
French and the British. Goerdler wanted only to convince the
Western powers that if they acted strongly and in concert against
Hitler, he would back down over Poland; Schacht, looking into
the future, insisted that the French and the English be fully informed of Germany's breakneck armaments program and be
made to understand that Hitler saw Danzig merely as a way station to Warsaw, to the oil fields of Rumania, and to the rich
grainlands of the Ukraine.

The distillate of the Ouchy conference was delivered to the
French prime minister, Edouard Daladier, by Dr. Reinhold
Schairer, a well-known German educator and political philoso-
pher. Daladier thanked Schairer and put the memorandum away
in a wooden file cabinet. Schacht journeyed to Basel and conferred with an old friend, Norman Montagu, governor of the
Bank of England, emphasizing his conviction that "the longer
responsible statesmen give ground before this satanic trouble-
maker, the bloodier the final accounting will be." Montagu duly
delivered the message to Chamberlain in London; but the prime
minister replied that since Schacht and the others were without
political influence, he would continue to deal directly with Hitler.

Of course Chamberlain was right, but he could not grasp the
point that Schacht and the others were making every effort to
regain their political influence through the overthrow of Hitler
and then, as they saw it, to restore sanity inside Germany. With
each polite rebuff the conspirators wondered why the British

seemed uninterested in building up contacts with the German underground, why London could not realize "the political and strategic importance of having informants in the enemy camp in case of war."

Despite the unpromising reactions, emissaries continued to shuttle back and forth across the Channel. Goerdler went to see Winston Churchill, then leader of the opposition, in May and found the old statesman keen to learn about the resistance to Hitler within the higher echelons of the Wehrmacht; but Churchill promised nothing. He was followed by the studious-looking Berlin attorney, Fabian von Schlabrendorff, who allied himself with the Abwehr in 1938. Canaris chose Schlabrendorff primarily because the jurist's great-grandfather had been personal physician to Queen Victoria; this tie, Canaris felt, would provide Schlabrendorff the entrée needed to the highest circles in Britain.

The little admiral's hunch was correct. Schlabrendorff was first invited to Windsor Castle, then to a conference with a member of the House of Lords, George Ambrose Lloyd. He found Lord Lloyd "sympathetic . . . but pessimistic as far as his country was concerned." Schlabrendorff astounded his host by telling him that the Abwehr was on to Hitler's secret plans to conclude a nonagression treaty with Soviet Russia—a country Britain was then courting. Lord Lloyd reached Lord Halifax, the foreign secretary, with this startling piece of intelligence, but what were termed "competent experts" within the Foreign Office assured Halifax that any such treaty between Hitler and Josef Stalin was quite out of the question.

Schlabrendorff next paid a visit to Churchill at his country estate, Chartwell, in the Kentish hills. Facing Churchill, who sat "compact and solid on the sofa beneath the portrait of his famous ancestor, the Duke of Marlborough," the German felt that Churchill was "the personification of England at the very height of her greatness."

Schlabrendorff opened by stating, "I am not a Nazi, but I am a good patriot."

"So am I!" Churchill shot back.

Churchill wanted to know if Schlabrendorff could guarantee a successful outcome of any attempt to overthrow Hitler. The German hesitated, then said he could not. Schlabrendorff went back home, but other emissaries followed in his wake—so many, in fact, that Sir Robert Vansittart was moved to comment, "We have no need of a Secret Service in Germany, for these fellows are bringing us all we want to know."

In June, the German General Staff sent one of its key field-grade officers to London to ingratiate himself with the British; they wished to persuade Whitehall and the war ministry to stand up to Hitler in the face of the plans to invade Poland. The officer chosen was Lieutenant Colonel Count Gerhard von Schwerin, an urbane, aristocratic career officer considered by the upper echelons of British naval intelligence as a "very acceptable type of German with charming manners who spoke perfect English, was unobtrusive, receptive and a good mixer." Schwerin was taken under the wing of Admiral J. H. Godfrey, Britain's director of naval intelligence, and soon was mixing with the best of British military and political society.

Unlike Goerdler, Schlabrendorff, and the others, Schwerin offered concrete suggestions concerning how best to intimidate Hitler. He drove home the point that Hitler "took no account of words—only deeds." Schwerin suggested that the Royal Air Force stage mass bomber and fighter exercises over French air space, using airfields belonging to the Armée de l'Air for refueling and maintenance, to demonstrate Allied military solidarity. He said that maneuvers by the British fleet in the North Sea would impress Hitler, whose own navy was short-budgeted in Wehrmacht expansion plans.

Then Schwerin suggested to Admiral Godfrey: "Take Churchill into the cabinet. Churchill is the only Englishman Hitler is afraid of. He does not take the Prime Minister [Chamberlain] or Lord Halifax seriously—but he places Churchill in the same category as Roosevelt."

Schwerin's proposals bore fruit. The RAF staged flights to France, and fleet maneuvers were readied. But after a strenuous press campaign and an acrimonious debate in Whitehall, Chamberlain stubbornly refused to have Winston Churchill in the cabinet. Schwerin returned to Germany and reported to General Halder what he had seen; the British were growing stronger, especially in the air, and he was certain they would fight over the question of Polish integrity. The word was passed on to Hitler, who refused to believe any of it. "I saw my enemies at Munich," he said, "and they are little worms."

In Berlin, General Georg Thomas of the Army High Command (OKH) joined in with the Abwehr conspirators in a final effort to avert war. Thomas knew better than any one else in OKH that Germany was bound to lose a long war of attrition. He drafted a concise memorandum that spelled out the harsh realities of Germany's economic and raw materials position and took it to Hitler's chief of staff at the Wehrmacht High Command (OKW), General Wilhelm Keitel, on August 17. Because in personality and military capability Keitel was little more than an elevated office boy, he suited Hitler perfectly. Keitel was known as "General *Ja-Ja*" by his subordinate officers; not once had he ever contradicted the Führer on the slightest point.

Thomas had barely begun reading the memo when he was interrupted by Keitel, who protested that Hitler would never lead Germany into a world war. "The Führer," continued Keitel, "knows that the French are a degenerate and pacifist race. The British are much too decadent to come forth with real aid to Poland. And America will never again send a single man to Europe to pull the chestnuts out of the fire for England—much less those of Poland." When Thomas pointed out that those who really knew the foreign situation held altogether different views, Keitel sharply replied that Thomas was "apparently infected by the pacifistic crew who refused to see Hitler's greatness." Keitel dismissed Thomas and pigeonholed his report.

Five days later, on August 22, Hitler gathered the senior commanders of the Wehrmacht at the Berghof and announced his intention to destroy Poland with a blitzkrieg, a lightning war. Canaris, seated unobtrusively at the rear, took notes on the two-hour harangue that followed. According to Hitler's scenario, neither the British nor the French would react. A naval blockade would not be effective as in 1918 because Germany was now much more self-sufficient. And as for the Russians, he would be able to announce momentarily the signing of a nonaggression pact with the Soviets. He had the confidence of the whole of the German people. Although Poland was nearly as large as Germany, victory would come in a surprisingly short time—it had to if the tanks and infantry were not to get bogged down with the coming of autumn rains on Poland's notoriously poor roads. "A quick decision," he said, "in view of the season."

The Polish campaign would require nearly all of Germany's first-line divisions, fifty-two in all. Forty-four of these would be hurled against Polish defenses, leaving only eight combat-ready divisions, plus seventeen reserve, training, and second-echelon divisions to defend Germany's western borders. General Siegfried Westphal and the other western-front commanders were aghast at the proposal of having to stave off 2 million French troops, complete with armor and artillery, with the motley of divisions at their disposal. "We felt our hair stand on end," Westphal has recalled, "when we considered the possibility of an immediate French attack."

General Thomas huddled with Abwehr official Oster and economist Schacht, and they decided to try reasoning once again with the Führer. On Sunday, August 27, Thomas appeared before Keitel with sheafs of neatly rendered statistical charts which, Thomas told Keitel, "demonstrate clearly the tremendous military-economic superiority of the Western Powers and the tribulation we face." Hitler rejected the evidence the next day; there was no need for anxiety over the danger of another world war.

No amount of economic or military logic could sway the Führer, and events ran their course. At 4:45 A.M., September 1, 1939, the Wehrmacht rolled through low-lying ground fog and struck all along the Polish frontier. An hour later, when visibility improved, Luftwaffe bombers and fighters took to the air and wreaked carnage upon horse-drawn columns of Polish reinforcements moving up to face the blitzkrieg. German Ju.87 Stuka divebombers were especially effective; an entire cavalry brigade,

The SA helped Hitler to power, then he smashed it
during the Night of Long Knives.

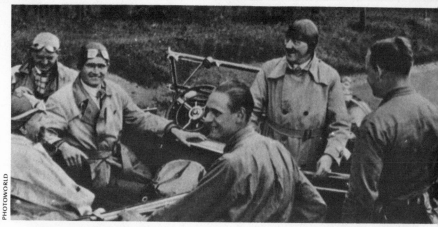

Hitler's open roadster sped him to
Bad Wiessee, where he personally
arrested Ernst Röhm (*right*).
General von Bredow (*left*) was
shot down at home, as were the
unsuspecting General von
Schleicher and his wife (*lower
right*).

General von Fritsch (*left*) and General Blomberg (*center*)
were victims of sordid Nazi plots.

Hans Oster, dedicated patriot-traitor

Wilhelm Canaris, enigmatic head of the Abwehr

Lord Mayor Carl Goerdler

Finance Minister Hjalmar Schacht

Colonel Henning von Treskow

General Ludwig Beck

Hitler's armored Mercedes-Benz 770-K weighed 10,000
pounds and secreted enough small arms and ammunition
to thwart any assassination attempts while the Führer
was on the road. He is shown here with supporters,
including Goebbels, during a 1936 parade in Berlin.

Georg Elser, the master craftsman whose bomb came close to ending Hitler's career

November 9, 1938: Hitler has passed the point where Maurice Bavaud waited on a Munich street with a pistol, loaded and ready.

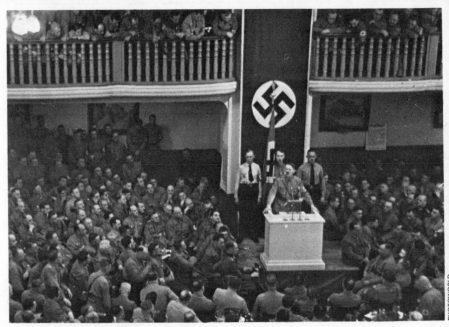

Hitler speaks inside the Bürgerbräukeller. Just above the swastika, Elser's clockwork mechanism wound down to zero.

Elser's bomb destroyed the interior of the beer hall where the birth of National Socialism was celebrated. The Führer escaped death by minutes.

3,000 men and horses, was annihilated from the air with bombs and machine guns. The Wehrmacht's tank regiments rolled across Polish fields and down narrow roads, raising clouds of dust, virtually unopposed.

In Cologne, the commander-in-chief of Army Group A decided that soldier's oath or not, the time had come for personal intervention; Hitler must be seized, and executed if necessary. General Kurt von Hammerstein-Equord, sixty-one, had been pulled out of retirement only that year to command one of the army groups responsible for the defense of the lower Rhine. Hammerstein had been commander-in-chief of the Reichswehr during its formative years, serving from 1930 until 1934 when he was retired and replaced by Fritsch. Tall and powerfully built, Hammerstein was still physically active, continuing to indulge himself in his lifetime passion for stalking game animals in Germany's deep woods. Now, Hammerstein, to whom Nazis had always been "brown scum," was determined to snare his biggest trophy, the Führer himself.

Hammerstein sent one of his staff officers to Berlin to confer in secret with the Abwehr's Fabian von Schlabrendorff. What the general wanted, the aide explained, was to lure Hitler to group headquarters on a morale-boosting inspection trip, arrest him on the spot, and "render him harmless once and for all, even without judicial proceedings." Hammerstein wanted the British informed of this plan so that, if it were successful, they would delay their own offensive movements in the west. Hitler's liquidation was bound to create chaos inside Germany, for however short a time, and Hammerstein envisioned that the Wehrmacht would have to deal with the SS before stability could be achieved. He realized as well that once locked in combat with Anglo-French forces, the Wehrmacht would have terrible difficulty extricating itself.

The British-French ultimatum on Poland ran out at 11:15 A.M. on September 3, the very hour that Schlabrendorff was seated with Sir George Ogilvy Forbes, counselor of the already vacated British embassy, at the Adlon Hotel. Germany was now officially at war with Britain and France, and Schlabrendorff was uneasy at being seen in the open with one of the "enemy." While he was spilling out Hammerstein's plans in discreet tones, Schlabrendorff looked over his shoulder and saw two SS officers talking to the head waiter and looking in his direction. Schlabrendorff's pulse raced. *They're after me,* he thought.

The black uniforms strolled over to the table where the German and the Englishman were seated, and Forbes was called aside. Schlabrendorff could not hear what they were saying. After a few minutes the SS officers strolled out of the lobby, and Forbes returned to the table to explain that the SS only wanted to inquire about details of the imminent departure of the embassy staff.

At about the same time that Schlabrendorff and Forbes were having their discussion, State Secretary Weizsäcker was having his own anguished talk with Erich Kordt, the energetic chief of the Ministerial Bureau. Outside, along the broad Wilhelmstrasse, apathetic crowds watched troops passing by in trucks, headed eastward. There was no cheering, no flag-waving. Kordt asked, "Is there no way to prevent this war?"

Weizsäcker, who believed that "the enemy will never conclude a peace with Adolf Hitler or Herr von Ribbentrop," thought it over. Then he said to Kordt, "Do you have a man with a pistol? I regret that there has been nothing in my upbringing that would fit me to kill a man."

That same morning, Canaris was taking his usual stroll in the Tiergarten, the sprawling wooded park in the heart of Berlin. He noted the approach of the Spanish military attaché's car and waved him to a stop. Canaris and the attaché were on intimate terms and spoke freely. The Spaniard smiled broadly and said to Canaris, "Naturally, Germany has calculated out this war to the last detail of ultimate victory."

Canaris looked up sadly and replied, "Calculated nothing at all."

In Cologne, Hammerstein awaited impatiently for an answer from Hitler regarding his visit to Army Group A. So far, with

German tanks chewing their way towards Warsaw, not one shot had been fired along the western front, no German cities bombed by the RAF. It was as though the rest of Europe was asleep under the blazing summer sun, unaware of the cauldron that was now Poland. Now, Hammerstein knew, was the time to end it before the war had fairly begun. At first Hitler agreed to a quick visit, but then from faraway Poland where the Führer was inspecting the fresh battlefields came word that the visit was cancelled indefinitely. Hitler's fabled sixth-sense was evidently at work. A short time afterward Hitler ordered Hammerstein's relief and permanent retirement.

On August 17 the Red Army inundated Polish defenses and rolled westward to occupy its promised half of the ruined nation, and on August 22 the Wehrmacht was at the gates of Warsaw. The 12th Cavalry Regiment was engaged in heavy fighting in front of the Warsaw suburb of Praga, and among those crawling through the fields was the regiment's honorary colonel, the former commander-in-chief of the Wehrmacht, Werner von Fritsch, who had never fully recovered from his disgraceful court-martial. At the forefront of the fighting ever since the campaign opened, Fritsch acted as though he were a fledgling lieutenant eager to prove himself in front of his fellows.

Fritsch insisted upon leading a patrol to scout Praga's defenses pending an all-out assault. While making his way back to HQ, the red lapels of his general's greatcoat caught the eyes of Polish snipers holed up in a wrecked farmhouse. Bullets began to crack overhead and spat against the ground, driving Fritsch and his adjutant into a nearby ditch running beside a stone wall that marked the boundary of the field. A machine gun opened up from a house 100 yards to the east, forcing Fritsch to get his head right down in the dirt. Bullets whined and richochetted off the stone wall, then Fritsch felt a hammer blow in his right thigh. Blood spurted up through the torn fabric; the general's femoral artery had been severed by the spent slug. An adjutant moved to apply a makeshift tourniquet—and would never forget how Fritsch waved him away with one hand while removing his monocle with the other. "Just leave me be!" he ordered. Fritsch died ninety seconds later, at 9:40 A.M., while the adjutant watched helplessly, the bullets still singing over his head.

Fritsch died as he wished, in the field with his men, just five days before the campaign ended. Warsaw was a smoking ruin, reduced to rubble by Göring's bombers in the first saturation raid of the Second World War; unopposed by fighters, Ju.52 transports wheeled over the stricken city while crewmen literally shoveled incendiary bombs out of open doors. At home in Berlin, General Ludwig Beck, retired as chief of staff, tuned in to BBC radio to listen to a eulogy delivered by a retired British brigadier who had served briefly with the Imperial Guards Regiment in Berlin before the First World War. He lauded the gentlemanly behavior of the German officers he had known, then asked "where those men could be today after Poland had been so brutally dismembered." The broadcast ended with the BBC orchestra playing a soulful rendition of the sentimental soldier's ballad, "Ich hatt' einen Kamaraden." Beck's guests remembered how the sad-eyed general uncontrollably burst into tears.

Even as the Polish campaign was under way Hitler's policies of "resettlement" and liquidation intensified the loathing of the SS by the officers and men of the Wehrmacht. Reinhard Heydrich's special extermination squads, *the Einsatzgruppen*, were busy rounding up Poland's elite—clergymen, professional men, intellectuals—and killing them out of hand. Canaris's agents in the field fed details of atrocities to the Tirpitzufer, prompting Canaris to report to army headquarters that "SS commanders are boasting of killing two hundred Poles a day." Jews of all classes were being dragged from their homes and herded together like cattle for eventual extermination *en masse*. Still outraged, Canaris went to Poland and confronted General Keitel aboard the Führer's special train on a siding near Illnau. Canaris laid a sheaf of atrocity reports on Keitel's desk and said, "The world will one day hold the Wehrmacht responsible for these methods since these things are taking place under its nose!"

Keitel lamely replied that if the Wehrmacht did not want to take part in "these things," then it had no right to complain when the SD and the SS carried out the work of liquidation. The killings were carried out in the open; few members of the Wehrmacht were unaware of what was happening. Wehrmacht officers refused to shake hands with SS officers, even in the presence of Hitler at Führer headquarters.

General Gerd von Rundstedt, the commander-in-chief of the East, ordered the most notorious of Himmler's killers, SS Obergruppenführer Udo von Woyrsch, out of Poland when he got wind of the particular horrors inflicted upon Silesian Jews by von Woyrsch's men: Jews were flogged out of synagogues with leather whips; they were forced to smear their own fear-induced excrement in the faces of their fellow Jews; they were hung upside down and torn to shreds by savage dogs, and they were stood before open pits and shot down in droves. Woyrsch complained that he was only following Hitler's policy to "ensure that the Polish intelligensia cannot throw up a new leader class . . . Jews, Poles and similar trash to be cleared from the old and new Reich territories."

By the end of the campaign Heydrich could report: "Of the Polish upper classes in the occupied territories, only a maximum of three percent is still present."*

---

*Heydrich later changed his methods. Following a reign of terror as protector of Bohemia and Moravia, Heydrich suddenly switched policies and successfully began to woo Czech workers and housewives by increasing food rations and clothing. He requisitioned expensive hotels and turned them into workers' spas; he overhauled the Czech social security system for the benefit of the common man. Initial Czech resistance to Heydrich began to fade among the workers and peasants as a result of this change in tactics. A British member of parliament, R. T. Paget, has explained what happened next: "Partisans often deliberately provoke reprisals in order that hatred of the occupier may be intensified and more people can be induced to resist—this was our general idea when we flew in a party to murder Heydrich."

On the morning of May 27 Heydrich's green Mercedes cabriolet slowed for a hairpin turn on the outskirts of Prague. Two Czech assassins, parachuted in by the British, leaped from cover, one brandishing a Sten gun and the other armed with grenades. The car slowed to a stop. The Sten failed to fire. The other Czech tossed a grenade that exploded underneath the car. Heydrich, who probably wished the

The flagrant barbarism added fresh fuel to the flames of opposition, reignited in any case by Hitler's declaration in October that he intended to prosecute the war to the fullest: the Wehrmacht was ordered to prepare itself for an assault on the West sometime in November. The shortest line to victory, he said, lay through the neutral nations of Belgium and Holland.

Senior Wehrmacht officers were aghast. There were serious shortages of artillery shells, aerial bombs, and even rifle ammunition. They remembered the Flanders quagmires of the last war during November, and many of them were shocked at the idea of smashing through small countries still at peace with Germany. Gisevius commented: "In time we became accustomed to such violations of neutrality, but in 1939 our concept of international law had not yet been blunted, so that even the generals were tormented by scruples."

The Oster study on how to stage the coup, hidden in a safe at army HQ since the Czechoslovakian takeover, was now removed and reread. General Halder, chief of the General Staff, ordered the original 1938 plan updated for the seizure of Adolf Hitler and his cohorts and the occupation of Berlin by designated infantry and armored divisions. Captain Friedrich Heinz got back in touch with his sixty commandos and told them to see to their rifles and ammunition. A list was at hand of those to be arrested and done away with. Hitler's name was at the top, followed by Ribben-

---

marksman Schellenberg were with him now, jumped out of the door with drawn pistol, firing and shouting at his befuddled attackers, who fled down the street, one shooting wildly over his shoulder. A startled bystander later recalled that the scene was reminiscent of the wild west. Heydrich fired up the whole clip, then staggered and sat down on the cobblestones. The bomb had driven bits of steel springs and leather from the seat into his spleen and stomach. Heydrich died eight days later, and the SS went berserk, arresting more than 10,000 Czechs, wiping out an entire village, and slaughtering at least 1,300 people.

Heydrich's death caused no mourning in Czechoslovakia; his successor continued to carry out his policies after the bloodbath. Only his wife, Lina, Himmler, and Hitler considered Heydrich a martyr to the cause.

trop, Himmler, Heydrich, Göring, Goebbels, and Sepp Dietrich, commander of the SS Life Guards.

To the German generals who feared that the British and the French would take advantage of the postoverthrow chaos inside Germany and launch their own attack in the west, it was explained that with Hitler and the others safely out the way, General Beck would come out of retirement; he would not only head the Wehrmacht but a provisional government until fresh elections would be called.

At the Foreign Office, Erich Kordt and others drew up a long memorandum designed primarily to convince General von Brauchitsch to lend active support to the planning for the new coup. Kordt anticipated the objection that an attempt to overthrow Hitler on the heels of a brilliant military campaign would find no support by stating: "The debacle will only be recognized once it is there. The coup d'état would then, of course, be popular—but it would come too late and would no longer ward off the catastrophe into which we would all be plunged, with or without Hitler, and even with our fine Polish laurels. For once the fury of war is let loose, it cannot be coaxed back by reason. The relative unpopularity of the undertaking must, therefore, be accepted with the necessary amount of civic courage." Regarding the soldier's oath, Kordt said that the oath was no longer valid because Hitler "is planning to sacrifice Germany to his own diabolic aims."

The most that could be wrung from Brauchitsch was the guarded comment, "I won't do anything, but I won't oppose it if someone else does."

Hitler now set the date of the attack in the west—November 12. Oster, using his privileged lines of communication, warned the Dutch and Belgians of the imminent violation of their territory. Halder irresolutely slipped a small automatic pistol in his pocket with the vague intention of using it on Hitler when summoned before his Führer. The motivation and the means were at hand, but Halder could not bring himself to draw the weapon and kill Hitler in cold blood. He nonetheless kept the pistol with him against the remote chance that his aversion to assassination might somehow be overcome.

Halder and Brauchitsch mustered their courage and faced Hitler on November 5 to present their objections to launching the new offensive. Hitler's violent outburst drove them out of the office, whereupon Halder panicked in the belief that Hitler was onto the plans for the coup. He got on the telephone and ordered all of the incriminating documents destroyed. He now wanted nothing to do with the putsch.

Exasperated, Kordt went to see Oster and said that he was willing to take care of Hitler himself. Kordt had free access to the Chancellery and was, as far as he knew, above suspicion. If the Abwehr could provide him with the necessary explosives, he would enter Hitler's office and blow him to bits, regardless of the danger to his own life. Oster told Kordt that he would procure the needed materials to fabricate the kind of bomb Kordt had in mind. How soon? asked Kordt. Oster said he would have what was needed by November 11.

Then there occurred a totally unexpected event that made Kordt's brazen scheme impossible to execute.

6

The Craftsman

HITLER'S ERRATIC SCHEDULES, sudden changes in plans, and unannounced visits to far-flung parts of the Reich continued to make him a difficult target to pin down for would-be assassins outside his own immediate circles. He had a complement of thirty SS and SD bodyguards, all fiercely loyal and sworn in personally by the Führer himself. In 1938 the Mercedes-Benz factory in Stuttgart had manufactured to Hitler's order a Mercedes 770-K open touring sedan, armor-plated in front, back, on the sides, and underneath in case of a mine or a rolling grenade attack. Daimler perfected quarter-inch bulletproof glass for the windshield and the roll-up side windows.

When Hitler set off on long journeys in the new Mercedes, there were seldom fewer than twenty bodyguards in trail. The guards and their cars were mobile arsenals. Each SD officer carried two 9-mm pistols and fifty rounds of ammunition. Stashed in various places inside the escort sedans were another six pistols in reserve, a half-dozen submachine guns, and a light machine gun, standard infantry issue, with 4,500 rounds—enough handguns and automatic weaponry to stave off a platoon-sized attack. When out in public, Hitler usually wore a special officer's cap reinforced inside with an oval steel band weighing 3½ pounds. He carried a small automatic pistol in his pocket, but he never expected to use it; he relied instead on human intuition and animal instinct for continued survival.

It was a thirty-six-year-old cabinetmaker from Württemberg, acting completely on his own, who came closest to solving the problem of how to get at the Führer, obviating the hedgehog defense and the frustrations of trying to track an eccentrically moving target. Johann Georg Elser planned to assassinate a victim rooted firmly to one spot, in full view of hundreds of admirers. The precise time of the killing would be chosen by Elser, but the place of execution would be predetermined by Hitler himself.

Elser was raised in the small mountain village of Königsbronn in the Swabian Alps, where his father and mother eked out a living from a small hillside farm to feed two sons and three daughters. The father got drunk at the village *bierstube* every Saturday night and did not neglect the other nights in the week. He rolled home late at night, waking up the household, and when Georg was old enough he alternated with the others in helping pull his father's boots off. Georg also shared beatings with his brothers and sisters at the hands of their father, who boasted that, on the other hand, he never struck his wife "with his hands, with a chair, or with a lantern."

In 1910, when Georg was seven, he was happy enough to be sent to school, where he excelled in drawing, mathematics, and penmanship. His teachers remembered young Elser as obedient, peaceful, and meditative. Georg and the other children shared the farm labor with their parents in the hours left to them after school, and while helping his father at the grindstone sharpening the wood-cutting ax, Georg caught his right hand in the gears, shearing off his little finger. This minor deformity failed to upset his perpetual tranquillity, nor did it keep him from getting a job in a local steel mill when he finished school in 1917.

Although only fourteen and a poorly paid apprentice, Elser was content with laboring in the mill, watching white-hot metal form into bolts, angle braces, and wheel hubs for use by horse-drawn transport wagons along the western front. Two years of this work wore down his inherently fragile health, forcing him into another trade. He was taken on as an engraver's apprentice and excelled. He bought cabinetmaker's tools and built himself a complete suite of furniture to put in the farmhouse cellar where his father allowed him to live.

Elser next learned the rudiments of watchmaking, and when his German employer burned down the small factory for the insurance in 1928, Elser went to the small Swiss town of Bottighofen and got a job where he could apply his new skills. He lived in a small pension in Constance on the German side of the lake and bicycled to work and back, a total of twelve miles each day. There he became friendly with, and in time impregnated, a waitress named Mathilde. Thus Elser became the father of a boy named Manfred, and although he provided for mother and child as best he could, the pittance he earned argued against marriage. Elser was offered a slightly better-paying job in a small town near Constance overseeing the handcrafting of exquisite little wooden boxes into which watches were placed for sale. In the spring of 1932, when the Depression was at its worst, Elser and everybody else in the shop were dismissed.

Now twenty-nine, Elser returned to the dour little mountain village of Königsbronn, where the chances of finding work were remote. Anticipating this difficulty, he had planned to earn a living temporarily as a musician; the harder the times the more people crave entertainment, and in the hours left to himself while at Constance, Elser had learned to play the zither. He was accepted by the local folk-music group, a dozen members in all, which played the local hotel and festival halls.

Zither playing was far from lucrative, so Elser rented the cellar of a Königsbronn couple's home and set up a workshop where he executed small furniture commissions, including the making of wooden marionettes at five marks apiece. He moved back into his old cellar room at the falling-down farmhouse and tried to help his mother and father, but by now the place was so debt-ridden that all hope for its survival had vanished. Elser, whose alcoholic intake never exceeded one or two beers at a sitting, could not understand why the worse things became the more his father drank.

In the winter of 1935 the entire place was put on the block for 6,500 Reichsmarks, about $1,650. Elser's mother took the youngest daughter and moved to another town, and his father gave it all up and disappeared in an alcoholic haze.

Georg Elser had never been considered handsome, but he had bright, shining eyes, a shock of unruly black hair, and a shy, somehow engaging personality. Else, the lady of the house in Königsbronn where he had his workshop, was more than happy to rent him a spare room after the family farm was sold. In the months that followed, Else's husband discovered the devastating effect the self-effacing artisan had upon his wife, and he left town in a rage, divorcing Else a year later.

Thanks to a chance acquaintance made at a local inn, Elser obtained a job as a common laborer in a munitions factory at Heidenheim, north of Königsbronn. Elser reported for work on December 29, 1936. By then, Adolf Hitler had held supreme power over Germany's destiny for two years and four months. That fact, and Elser's feelings about the consequences, combined with his proximity to explosives being turned out by the rapidly expanding Wehrmacht, set in train the most meticulously thought-out plan to liquidate a tyrant by an individual so far recorded in the twentieth century.

As Elser would later confess, he decided to do away with Germany's leader in the fall of 1938, not long after German troops marched into Czechoslovakia; he was formulating his plot at the time that the Abwehr conspirators were shelving theirs for later use. Elser proved immune to the hypnotic effect exercised by Hitler on so many of his countrymen. Nazi pageantry—torchlit parades, drums and bugles, broad avenues festooned with Hakenkreuz flags—moved him not at all. Nor could he be swayed by the barrage of Goebbels-inspired propaganda. Georg Elser never listened to Hitler's hysterical speeches on the radio; he only occasionally read a newspaper. He was completely uninterested in organized politics, never joining any party; the only card he carried was one identifying him as a member of the Woodworkers' Union.

Elser's reasons for plotting Hitler's death were political, how-ever. He knew that Hitler was determined to plunge the nation into war, and he was incensed over the ruthless putting down of any opposition to the régime. He was especially bitter over what he felt was the worsening of the lot of the German workers under National Socialism. "The workers find themselves under con-straint. Under the new laws, for example, they cannot change the place where they work; they cannot move to another town to look for a better job. No, that is forbidden." He brooded over the fact that although the German economy had improved under Nazism, the German worker was worse off financially than he was before the Nazis seized power: the minimum hourly rate in 1929 was one mark, but had dropped to sixty-eight pfennig in 1938; worse, withholding taxes had jumped from 10 to 20 percent, too much of it, Elser felt, going into the coffers of the SS. To Elser, the ques-tion nagged: *How can one eliminate these oppressive social conditions?* Elser finally decided that the only logical solution was to blow Hitler to eternity.

Where, Elser asked himself, could he be sure Hitler would ap-pear without fail and on a date as fixed as the stars? Of course—at the famous old Bürgerbräukeller in Munich on the evening of November 8 of any year. In Elser's memory the Führer had never failed to appear to address the Old Fighters of the Party. Elser planned to turn the beer hall into an abbatoir, striking down not only the devil himself, but many others of the Nazi hierarchy.

It was now too late in 1938 to plan and carry out his scheme—Elser scheduled it in his mind for 1939—but the timing was per-fect for a first reconnaissance in Munich. After that, the patient killer would have an entire year at his disposal to perfect each de-tail of the assassination, which would be crafted with the same painstaking care one would observe in assembling a fine watch or dovetailing the joints of an expensive armoire.

Late on the afternoon of November 8 Elser boarded a train for the eighty-mile trip westward to Munich, a city he had seen only once nearly twenty years earlier. The train pulled into the station at 7:00 P.M., and Elser went over to an information kiosk provided by the Nazi party as a service to tourists. An hour later he was installed in a modest hotel in Munich's eastern sector. He stayed long enough only to register and see his room, then struck out on foot for Rosenheimerstrasse and the Bürgerbräukeller.

The area of the beer hall was packed with people hoping to catch a glimpse of the Führer, and Elser milled around in the cold with the others until 10:30. Hitler concluded his speech and marched out of the hall with his cohorts, but Elser was so far away he could not get a look at the man he intended to kill. Elser entered the beer hall and had a late supper of beer and sausages. Now largely emptied of people, the place seemed much larger than he had imagined it to be.

At eleven the following morning Elser was standing on the sidewalk across the street from the Bürgerbräukeller with several thousand others awaiting the arrival of the Führer, who showed up in boots, khaki uniform, and Sam Browne belt. With Hitler, Göring, and Himmler in the lead, the Old Fighters started off on the long march through the streets of Munich, followed at a discreet distance by the crowd that included Elser. He could hear up ahead the *Sieg Heils*! that marked Hitler's passage. Elser walked past the grandstand opposite the Church of the Holy Spirit, where Maurice Bavaud was sitting, futilely clutching the pistol in his overcoat pocket.

The procession broke up in the Odeonsplatz, and Elser kept walking toward the railway station. He was back home that same evening.

Elser's superficial inspection of the beer hall convinced him he had chosen the logical place to carry out his plans for assassination; there was no checking of who came and went, no guards posted inside to hinder free movement in the great hall. Elser decided that he would manufacture a time bomb and secrete it inside one of the great square pillars at the back of the hall, only a few feet behind the table where the Party leaders sat flanking the Führer's rostrum.

By March 1939, Elser reached the conclusion that he would never be able to steal explosives from the munitions plant where he worked; security was too tight. He picked a fight with his supervisor and managed to quit his job. On April 4 Elser took the train to Munich and headed straight for the Bürgerbräaukeller. He walked through the main entrance, past the small dining rooms and approached the swinging doors that led into the great festival hall where the Nazi gatherings were held. He noted that these doors were not fitted with locks. He walked over to the center column and took its dimensions with a pocket tape rule. He noted the figures in a small notebook, made a few quick sketches of the base of the column, and was back outside on the street within five minutes.

Elser spent a week in Munich trying to land a job in the Bürgerbräukeller as a waiter, even offering to buy a job away from a beer-loving waiter he became friendly with, but his efforts came to nothing. He did, however, manage to ingratiate himself with three plump serving girls and persuaded them to pose for his camera in front of the pillars at the rear of the main hall. The resulting negatives were much too thin to print, and Elser abandoned photography as a research tool, relying instead on his facile hand with pencil and paper.

His job searching in Munich having borne no fruit, Elser went back to Königsbronn, where he received permission from the Nazi labor office to apply for a job as hod carrier with the local stone quarry. He was taken on by the quarry's director, Georg Vollmer, who later would bitterly regret his decision to hire the inoffensive-looking Elser. The hard work taxed Elser's strength, but it was exactly what he wanted; the quarry stored large amounts of explosives and detonators, and security was lax.

The entrance to the explosives storage bunker was sealed by a steel door, to which Vollmer held the key. Elser secured three different keys of the approximate size and returned to the quarry late one night to try them all. Two would not penetrate the keyhole; the third went in easily enough, but would not turn. Elser patiently filed down the key until it turned and the tumblers in the lock slipped out of place. The door swung open to reveal a treasure trove of explosives. It was as easy as that.

Throughout the summer of 1939 Elser slipped into the bunker four or five times a night between the hours of ten and one to steal small quantities of Donarit and Gelatine. The Gelatine came in small paper cartridges, the Donarit in compressed tablets a quarter-inch thick and three-quarters of an inch in diameter. The thefts were unnoticed. At first Elser hid the explosives under the dirty laundry in his room, but as the pile grew he knew he had to find a more secure hiding place. He fashioned a kind of footlocker with a double bottom, the lid secured with a heavy padlock, which was kept under his bed. When his landlady asked Elser what was in the large box, he told her it contained his money and plans for a secret invention that would one day make him famous. Nestled at the bottom of the box were 110 pounds of high explosive, 125 high-capacity detonators, and coils of quick-burning fuse.

In the middle of May a heavy stone fell on Elser's foot, putting him out of action and out of work for two months. He used the time to attack the problem of how best to set off the charge once it was planted. Realizing that a hissing fuse was out of the question, he experimented with using a pistol shot to trigger the explosion, but this would mean Elser's presence at the beer hall; if he weren't killed by the blast, then arrest was certain. He settled on electricity supplied by storage batteries to provide energy to spark the detonation, using a clock set to close the electrical circuit at a precise time. When the package blew, Elser planned to be far from Munich, inside Swiss sanctuary.

On August 5 Elser left Königsbronn aboard a train headed for Munich. He took with him the heavy, double-bottomed box which he wrestled into a rented room at 94 Türkenstrasse. Then Elser had a friend forward his tool kit and a box stuffed with odds and ends. To execute the complicated work that lay before him Elser had at hand an assortment of wood planes, three hammers, two set squares, two tin shears, two graving tools, a padsaw, a precision ruler, scissors, pliers, wood clamps, and several rasps and fine wood files. Aside from the fifty kilograms of high explosive, Elser also possessed six clock movements, insulated wire, and a six-volt battery. He brought along an empty, 180-mm brass artillery casing that he planned to use to encase part of the explosive.

Now Elser began the work he had dedicated himself to ten months earlier. He took supper each night in the Bürgerbräukeller, quietly making friends with the waitresses and with the beer hall mascot, a large German shepherd named Ajax to whom Elser fed tidbits of sausage. Elser's leisurely meal was usually over by ten. After paying the bill Elser would pick up the small rucksack filled with tools and walk unhurriedly through the doors leading into the darkened and empty hall. He would climb the staircase leading to the gallery and peer over the balustrade. Directly below was Hitler's table upon which Elser hoped to drop several tons of rubble and timber.

Elser's life assumed a clockwork pattern. He hid himself in the gallery, not moving, until the place closed at 11:30 each night. The final ritual of the evening occurred when the old lady who sold cigarettes padded into the deserted hall to feed the cats that were permanent residents there.

Working by the weak beam of a flashlight shrouded with a blue handkerchief, Elser carefully prised away the molding that surrounded a rectangular section of the column. Then he carefully drilled a small hole in one upper corner of the veneer panel and inserted the tip of a special cabinetmaker's saw. With exquisite care Elser began cutting away the panel. He worked three or four hours, then cleaned up evidence of his work before falling asleep in a chair. The painstaking sawing a few millimeters at a time, the replacing of the molding, the picking up of each grain of sawdust after each stint of work—none of this tried the craftsman's patience. He spent three nights just removing the panel. No trace of his tampering could be detected.

Elser left the beer hall at eight each morning, just after opening. He walked out of the front door, seen but unnoticed, to return to his lodgings on Türkenstrasse. To explain his upside-down schedule to his landlord, he said he was working on a secret invention in a shop open to him only after midnight and was never questioned further.

Elser next attacked the column itself, a massive structure of tightly compacted brick, stone, and cement. He chipped out a cavity bits and pieces at a time using one of the hammers and steel

TO KILL THE DEVIL

hand drills of various diameters. Each tap reverberated throughout the empty hall, sounding to Elser like pistol shots. When
some obstruction required heavier blows than usual, he waited
for noises from the street to cover the sounds. Since he worked
during the predawn hours, he often had to wait a long time between hammer blows. To facilitate the work Elser swung the re-
movable panel on small brass hinges fastened to the wood on the
inside. The heavier pieces of brick and rock debris were placed in
his rucksack and thrown into the Isar when nobody was around.

Elser was discovered only once while in the gallery. He had
working through the night and was on the point of leaving when
the main doors flew open and a waiter hurried up the staircase to
fetch an empty carton. Elser saw him coming and tried to hide
behind the jumble of empty boxes stored behind the pillars. But
the waiter was followed by the big dog, Ajax, who sniffed out
Elser and began wagging his tail in the joy of discovery. The
waiter looked Elser in the eye, then hurried back down the stairs
to fetch the owner. Elser calmly descended the stairs and seated
himself at a table, took out his pencil and notebook, and began
scribbling. The waiter and the irate owner approached Elser; the
owner demanded what Elser thought he was doing there at that
early hour of the morning. Elser replied that he had come to write
a letter. "Go outside in the garden to write your letter," shouted
the owner. "You have no business here." Elser shrugged, picked
up his sack, and went into the garden where he ordered coffee,
taking his time about drinking it. He was careful to pay and to
leave a tip before strolling unconcernedly away. The owner was
the same man Elser had applied to for a job nine months earlier,
but Elser went unrecognized.

The war that began on September 3, nearly a month after Elser
began his work in the Bürgerbräukeller, had not the slightest effect on him. The streets were blacked out and the inside of the
beer hall became even darker, but Elser was used to working with
the small flashlight by then, so the lighting made absolutely no
difference to him. In any case, he was oblivious to everything except the task at hand.

The slow excavation inside the pillar to create a cavity large

96

enough to hold the explosives and timing device was well along when, at the beginning of October, Elser began to suffer excruciating pains in his right knee. The knee mysteriously began to suppurate, making the act of kneeling before the pillar physically impossible. Elser packed away his tools, sealed the hidden edges of the door with a fine iron wire, and hobbled off to see a doctor. He was partially immobilized for two weeks, but when he returned to the pillar he found his work undisturbed.

Work on the column continued by night; work on the machine to trigger the explosive charge was carried out by day inside Elser's room. The primary mechanical action was based upon two fifteen-day alarm clocks, one of which provided a parallel back-up system should one of the movements fail. Elser fabricated a series of cog wheels and levers which, when soldered to the backs of the movements, would work together to actuate the timing. The mechanical functions were complicated but were flawlessly designed and engineered. Elser's innovations gave him the option of timing the explosion up to 144 hours, six days, after starting the mechanism.

The clockworks were fitted inside a box that was completely sealed except for two small holes through which the ignition wires were fed. But Elser worried about the residual ticking noise through the box and through the pillar. He chanced to read a short item in a technical journal that described a new material created for insulating clocks against the extremes of heat and cold. For one Reichsmark Elser bought enough of this material to shroud his clocks.

Only one item of construction remained. He bolted a thin sheet of steel to the rear of the hinged panel against the possibility that some security guard might make the rounds of the beer hall and start tapping the columns in a search for suspicious hollow sounds. Now Elser was ready to install the explosives and the timing mechanism.

On Thursday night, November 2, Elser let himself inside the Bürgerbräukeller through the service entrance on Kellerstrasse and mounted to the gallery. He swung open the hinged door and began placing the explosives and detonators in the hollowed-out

97

interior. He installed fifty pounds during the first night, and the remaining charges on Saturday. He left at 6:30 Saturday morning through the service entrance without being seen. Back in his room he tested the clockwork mechanism for the last time. It worked perfectly.

A ball was scheduled for that same Saturday night, a rare but Party-connected affair at the Bürgerbräukeller. Elser saw no reason why the festivities should interfere with his plans. He packed up the box containing the clockworks, entered the hall through the front door after buying a ticket, and went straight up to the gallery. He put the sack containing the box in an inconspicuous place and leaned over the railing to observe the dancers and drinkers below. When the party ended and the hall was once again in darkness, Elser withdrew the box from the sack and opened the door in the column. He had great difficulty in trying to fit the box inside. It wouldn't go quite all the way in no matter how he shifted it around. He closed the port and slept until daylight, then let himself out the service entrance once again to return to his room, where he planed down the box until he was sure it would fit inside the pillar. Shortly before 1:00 A.M., Monday, November 6, Elser opened the door in the pillar and carefully pushed the box inside; it slipped in smoothly, a perfect fit. Elser braced the box in position with angle irons, hooked up the wires to the two detonators, and then, finally, set the mechanism going. It was now 6:00 A.M. The heavy charge would detonate precisely sixty-three hours and twenty minutes afterward. Elser carefully closed the panel, left the Bürgerbräukeller by the fire exit, and walked outside into the cold, foggy air.

He drank two cups of coffee at a café on the Isartorplatz, then returned to his room to check out. The landlord asked him if he had succeeded in perfecting his invention. "Yes," Elser answered, "yes, I have." Elser caught the 10 A.M. train for Ulm, where he changed for an express that would carry him to Stuttgart. The double-bottomed box, now empty of its deadly contents, followed Elser in the baggage car. Elser had spent thirty-five nights working alone at his task in the gallery. The job demanded every skill he possessed; the result was a masterpiece of craftsmanship. He was content.

In Stuttgart Elser's sister and brother-in-law were surprised to see him. Elser spent Monday night with his relatives, offering no explanation for his long silence or for the twelve weeks spent mysteriously in Munich. He told them he was going to try to cross the Swiss frontier within the next two days, and when they asked why, he replied, "Because I must!" He presented his brother-in-law with the double-bottomed box after removing an assortment of laundry from inside, and on the afternoon of Tuesday, November 7, he left Stuttgart to return to Munich for one final inspection of his handiwork; he wanted to be sure that the clockwork mechanism was still winding down toward the climactic instant he had planned and worked for for more than a year. When he left Stuttgart all Elser had to sustain him was thirty marks ($7.50) borrowed from his sister, a pair of pliers, a pocket knife, and a half-pound of sausage.

Elser reached Munich at 9:00 P.M. and headed directly for the Bürgerbräukeller. He walked through the front door and continued straight through the main hall, then dark and deserted. Gently he pried open the panel with a knife blade, then opened the inner box. He struck a match and saw that the primary clock was running smoothly and on time. He closed the box, closed the door, then pressed his ear to the flat surface of the panel. In the silence of the hall he could hear the faint and regular *tick-tick-tick* of his engine of destruction. He slept that night in his usual place, and at 6:30 on Wednesday morning he let himself out of the fire exit and started for Switzerland.

At 7:30 P.M., while Elser's train was nearing Constance, Adolf Hitler stepped out of the door of his Munich apartment and climbed into the back seat of his Mercedes for the drive to the Bürgerbräukeller and the sixteenth reunion of the Old Fighters. The hall was already packed, the chairs and benches filled with the Party faithful, lights blazing down from baroque chandeliers. Waitresses hurried back and forth with their fingers locked around the handles of steins foaming over with beer and thumped them down on wooden tables already laden with empties. The place was clouded with cigar and cigarette smoke, redolent of comradeship, victory, anticipation of the Führer's arrival.

At eight sharp Hitler entered the hall to a sudden, respectful silence. Chairs scraped back; everyone stood while Hitler strode past a forest of arms raised in salute. The band struck up the refrains of the Horst Wessel song, and when it was over they all sat down again to listen to a worshipful introduction by one of Bavaria's leading Party officials, a onetime horsetrader named Christian Weber. Hitler took his place at the lectern at 8:10 P.M. His back was directly behind a column draped with a long swastika banner—Elser's pillar.

"Comrades of the Party! Comrades of the Party!" he began. "My comrades of the German people! I have come to you in order to relive with you the memory of the day which was for us, for the movement and for the German peoples, a day of the greatest importance." After a few minutes of reminiscence, Hitler launched into a tirade against England. He reproached the British for speaking of liberty while dominating the lives of 480 million people scattered across 40 million square kilometers of conquered territory. He castigated the British government for speaking of civilization while allowing millions of their own to live in such notorious slums as Whitechapel. He pointed to the plight of the Palestinians and the Egyptians under British control. He sarcastically remarked, "How this new British crusade would appear noble if only it had been prefaced by the proclamation of liberty of 350 million Hindus and the granting of independence and the right to vote to all the other British colonies!"

Hitler's words were interrupted frequently with sharp bursts of applause and cries of approval, cut short with a dramatic wave of the Führer's hand. Behind him, Elser's clocks continued to tick.

Elser stepped off the train at Constance and started walking south for the Swiss frontier, 1,500 yards away. He moved easily through the darkness down familiar streets to reach a small park, the Wesserberggarten. Moving along the iron fence until he came across an unlocked gate, he stepped inside and began walking across the grass, intending to pass by the main lodge and slip across the frontier only 100 yards away.

Elser did not see the two frontier police standing with slung carbines outside the lodge window, their ears cocked to a radio blaring inside with Hitler's speech. Noticing Elser approaching, they unslung their carbines, trotted across the lawn, and placed him under arrest. At the guardhouse, he was told to empty his pockets. Elser produced a handkerchief, a pocket knife, some bills and coins, a clock spring, some small cogs, a tiny aluminum tube, and a picture postcard of the interior of the Bürgerbräukeller. Not knowing what to make of Elser or of his strange possessions, the guards decided to take him to Gestapo HQ there in Constance.

Elser, dressed in a worn dark-blue suit, a brown pullover, and black shoes, stood befor Criminal Inspector Otto Grethe, who inspected the array of personal effects laid on his desk. He studied Elser, who appeared "harmless and inoffensive." Grethe switched off the radio carrying Hitler's speech, and the interrogation began. It was shortly after 9:00 P.M.

Hitler was winding up his talk. "Comrades of our National Socialist movement, our German people and, above all, our victorious Wehrmacht—*Sieg Heil!*" Hitler flashed his arm in the air, marched down the steps of the podium, and made his way through the crowd and into his car waiting to rush him to the railroad station. It was 9:12 P.M. Hitler's speech, at fifty-seven minutes, was much shorter than usual, and it had begun twenty minutes earlier than scheduled. Most of the Nazi hierarchy followed in Hitler's wake, but hundreds of diehard beer drinkers stayed on to order another round and to sing the old songs.

Waitress Maria Strobel was busy clearing away the Hitler table, still littered with empty steins and full ashtrays. She was upset because the Nazi bigwigs had rushed out of the hall without paying their bill. At 9:20, eight minutes after Hitler had left the hall, the ceiling exploded as though it had been struck with an artillery shell. Inexplicably, Maria Strobel did not hear the cataclysmic explosion. She felt the blast of superheated gases at her back, picking her up and flinging her through space, down the length of the hall and through the doors. She lost consciousness momentarily, waking to the screaming and cries for help. She lay sprawled amid broken glass and crockery and torn garlands ripped from the walls. The air was filled with brick dust and stank of cordite. Bruised and bleeding, she was picked up and carried outside.

Hitler's table lay smashed and buried under six feet of broken timber and rubble. When Elser's pillar shattered into fragments of wood and brick, the rearmost parts of the ceiling collapsed, the fallen beams lying at random angles. Dazed rescuers heaved these beams aside to get to the dead, the dying, and the injured. Ambulances were called from every part of Munich to carry away the remains of six killed outright and sixty-five others who were pulled from the wreckage too badly hurt to walk on their own. Of these, two later died, raising the final death toll to eight.

Elser's clockwork mechanism triggered the explosion fifteen minutes earlier than he had intended, but this minor malfunction would have worked in his favor *if* Hitler had begun his speech twenty minutes later, as he first planned, or *if* the speech had lasted the usual ninety minutes. Unquestionably Hitler would have been crushed under the several tons of wreckage that cascaded upon the speakers' table were it not for the *ifs*.

At first, Inspector Grethe could get little from Elser except polite protestations that he was not attempting to illegally jump the Swiss frontier; he was, he said, on his way to see an old friend and had somehow become lost. The interrogation was interrupted by the appearance of a messenger who handed the police official a telegram. The message was identical to hundreds of others wired to customs and border police throughout southern Germany: it gave the bare details of the assassination attempt on Hitler and warned all frontier posts to be alert for suspicious characters. Grethe now could make the connection between Elser's flight, the clock spring, the aluminum detonator part, and the postcard of the Bürgerbräukeller's interior. Else finally gave in and admitted that he, and he alone, was responsible for the explosion in the beer hall. Inspector Grethe picked up the telephone receiver and called the secret state police. Elser was on his way to Gestapo headquarters in Munich early the next morning.

The news of the attempt on his life reached Hitler aboard his train at the first stop out of Munich. The news stunned him into a long silence, then he said it was a "miracle" that his life had been spared. The train continued its journey to Berlin where Hitler had scheduled a meeting early the next morning with senior Wehrmacht commanders to discuss the impending invasion of France and the Low Countries, set for November 12. It was because Hitler had to catch the early train out of Munich that he had left the beer hall so suddenly. Knowing nothing of Elser's arrest at this point, Hitler jumped to the conclusion that the bomb was the work of the British Secret Service.

Since mid-October Colonel Walter Schellenberg of the SD, Heydrich's right-hand man, had been working an intelligence operation against two of Britain's top Secret Service agents, Major S. Payne Stevens and Captain R. H. Best. Schellenberg, using an assumed name, believed he had convinced the British agents that he represented a lique of dissatisfied German generals bent on Hitler's removal; he hoped by this ruse to pump genuine information from Stevens and Best about the real underground movement inside Germany. Now Himmler, who was beside himself over the beer-hall incident and wished to prove the efficiency of the SS to his Führer, got on the phone when Hitler's train reached Berlin and called Schellenberg in Düsseldorf, waking him from a sound sleep.

Schellenberg listened to Himmler's excited description of the events in Munich, then jerked fully awake when the Reichsführer SS said: "There's no doubt that the British Secret Service is behind it all. The Führer says—and this is an order!—when you meet the British agents for your conference tomorrow you are to arrest them immediately and bring them to Germany. This may mean a violation of the Dutch frontier, but the Führer says that is of no consequence."

Schellenberg started to protest, but Himmler shouted back, "There's only the Führer's order, which you will carry out!"

Shortly after three the next afternoon Schellenberg was sitting at a café in the Dutch border town of Venlo, waiting for Stevens and Best. Just over the border, also waiting, was a heavily armed SS detachment. As the British agents and a Dutch intelligence officer drove up to the café in a black Buick, the SS car roared across the border, and a lively exchange of gunfire began when the Dutch officer opened up with a pistol. Several SS men dashed over to the Buick and wrenched open the doors to drag Stevens and Best from the interior. They and the mortally wounded Dutchman were hauled over the border into Germany. The kidnapping had taken less than five minutes to execute.

Elser stubbornly stuck to his story of acting as a lone wolf, despite intensive grilling that included injections of truth serum and sessions involving experienced hypnotists. Elser said he had never heard of Stevens and Best, knew no one in the British Secret Service, and was not connected in any way with any communist organization. The interrogation report was forwarded to Himmler, who read it with mounting anger and scrawled across the opening page in his angular script, "What idiot conducted this interrogation?"

Himmler flew to Munich to confront Elser in person. The chief of the Gestapo Criminal Investigation Department in Munich, Dr. Böhme, described what happened next: "With wild curses Himmler drove his boots hard into Elser's body. He then had him removed by a Gestopo official and taken to the lavatory where he was beaten with a whip until he howled with pain. Elser, still handcuffed, was dragged back at the double to Himmler, who once more kicked him and cursed him."

The dreaded Heinrich "Gestapo" Müller was called in to try his hand against Elser, but of course he had no better luck than the others, because Elser was telling the truth despite the cost to himself in pain and bruises. They all gave up and concentrated instead on getting details of Elser's plans, including the engineering of the infernal machine itself. Elser told them everything. His memory of dates, places, and movements was phenomenal. Müller provided Elser with tools and a place to work. Elser, now in his element, painstakingly reconstructed a model of his timing device down to the smallest detail while Müller looked on in amazement. Since the Gestapo had not smashed his hands during the interrogations, Elser was able to complete the job in record time. His meticulous engineering drawings later found their way into a Gestapo handbook used for advanced criminology classes.

Hitler had wanted a public trial with Stevens, Best, and Elser in the dock together, but there was no evidence to link them. Elser's confession was complete, but Hitler could not bring himself to accept that Elser was a lone agent, and he continued to blame Himmler and the SS for failing to find the "real culprits." Georg Vollmer, the quarry owner, was imprisoned for two years for his negligence in guarding the explosives bunker from which Elser helped himself.

Elser was not tried. Instead Himmler ordered him confined to solitary at Sachsenhausen under twenty-four-hour guard in case Elser should try to kill himself. But suicide was not on the cabinetmaker's mind. His craftsman's hands grew restless, and he began scrounging matchsticks and small scraps of wood with which to make a zither.

7

The Traitor-Patriots

THE NEWS OF Elser's epic assassination attempt stunned the conspirators within the Abwehr. Some speculated wildly that Göring had engineered the plot with the help of the Gestapo; others suggested that Hitler could have staged the event in order to generate fresh waves of sympathy for himself among the Wehrmacht and the German people. Calmer minds pointed out that despite the Führer's admitted personal courage, he was not likely to stake his life on the workings of an alarm clock with fifty kilograms of high explosive set to detonate a few feet behind his back. They all worried about what effect the unexpected development would have on their own plans.

Erich Kordt told Hans Oster that he still intended to get Hitler with a bomb of his own, and Oster assured him he would try to secure the needed explosive from the Abwehr's own stores so that Kordt could "throw the bomb which will liberate the generals from their scruples." Oster sought out Major Erwin Lahousen, chief of Abwehr Section II, Sabotage, and told him what he wanted and why. Lahousen, recruited from Austrian counterintelligence by Canaris in 1937, had no use for the Nazis and willingly agreed to help.

Kordt's plan was to secure an appointment with the Führer on the evening of November 11, ostensibly to talk over some urgent Foreign Office business. Once inside Hitler's office in the Chancellery, he would set the fuse and somehow get the explosive package close enough the Hitler to assure success, even if it meant sacrificing his own life. On the afternoon of the eleventh Kordt appeared at Oster's home in Berlin to pick up the explosive; but Lahousen had failed to secure it. Elser's outrage caused a tightening of security measures regarding explosives throughout the Reich; not even an ounce of black powder could be issued without written justification for its intended use and by whom.

"Then I will just have to try it with a pistol," Kordt said. "We've got to stop the attack in the west."

"Kordt," Oster replied, "there's not a chance in a hundred. Don't try an act of insanity. You can't get Hitler alone, and in the anteroom there are all those adjutants, orderlies, and visitors. You wouldn't have an opportunity to fire." Oster went on to explain that Hitler had postponed the assault on the Low Countries due to begin on the following morning until November 28; the conspirators now had nearly two more weeks to figure something out.

As it turned out, they had a great deal more time than that. Hitler repeatedly postponed the attack, and almost six months would go by before his Panzers would leap forward into France and the Low Countries. In the meantime opposing troops idled behind the Seigfried and the Maginot lines, suffering only from the boredom and the cold. The Germans called it *Sitzkrieg;* the French, *drôle de guerre;* the British, the Phoney War.

The Abwehr group and two active-duty general officers— Georg Thomas and Wilhelm Ritter von Leeb—were convinced that the edgy winter of 1939–40 provided the right climate for Hitler's overthrow by the army, then held in great esteem by the German people. Hitler and his entourage were in Berlin and could be gotten to. The fanatics of the SS were still relatively few in number and could easily be dealt with by the army's superior forces. But everything hinged on full and active cooperation from Chief of Staff Halder and Brauchitsch, commander-in-chief of the army, without whose firm orders the army entire would not march.

Halder was approached and responded with two strange ideas.

Believing, erroneously, that Hitler listened to a favored Berlin astrologer and used the readings as a basis of determining political and military strategy, Halder offered to help raise a million marks to bribe the astrologer to convince Hitler that the juxtaposition of stars and planets spelled disaster for the offensive in the west.

Halder additionally proposed a meeting between Brauchitsch and a leading German industrialist, Hugo Stinnes, hoping to add corporate weight to military arguments against stepping up the war. At the meeting, Brauchitsch gloomily predicted that Hitler's offensive was doomed to failure but said that he was powerless to intervene. "What can I do?" he asked. Stinnes had no reply. Brauchitsch confided that "the situation is such that he might arrest me, or I him." He complained, "None of my generals will talk to me." He wondered aloud to Stinnes if any of the generals would follow him. "I don't know what to do," he said. Brauchitsch ended the self-pitying monologue with melodrama, hinting to Stinnes, a virtual stranger, "Perhaps we shall never again see each other in this life." Baffled at the commander-in-chief's plaintive attitude, Stinnes felt he was playing priest to a troubled parishioner.

Brauchitsch's apparent moral collapse removed much of the stiffening in Halder's own spine. Toward the end of November Canaris met with Halder and urged him onward; after all, Halder had been active for more than a year in seeking ways to get rid of the Führer and indeed was more tolerant of the idea of assassination than the admiral himself. How many times, for example, had Oster or Gisevius heard Halder mutter darkly, "Is there no way to get rid of the dog?" Now Halder, who had found himself unable to shoot the Führer in cold blood, primly said to Canaris that it was unthinkable that he should take a personal part in plans to overthrow Hitler because he "could not go down in history as the first German General Staff officer to participate in treasonable actions."

Halder sought more pragmatic reasons for disassociating himself from the Abwehr and Carl Goerdler circles. He made a ten-day tour of the western front and returned to Berlin impressed with what he had seen. The armies used in Poland were now refitted and expanded. Fifty-two divisions would become a hundred and fifty by early spring. Constant training exercises had put a knife edge to the troops, and morale was high. Moreover, the factories in the Ruhr were beginning to create adequate reserves of tanks, guns, and aircraft, untroubled as they were by any Allied bomber. It seemed to Halder that the British and the French were doing their best to cooperate with Hitler by giving him all the time he needed to build the Wehrmacht into an irresistible force.

General Ludwig Beck persuaded Halder to walk the cold streets of Berlin with him on the morning of January 16, 1940, in a final effort to persuade the chief of staff to take action, Brauchitsch willing or no. But Halder refused to budge, saying that chances of military success now looked good and that only a severe reverse of arms could again provide the incentive for Wehrmacht and public acceptance of Hitler's overthrow. With that, plans for a coup seemed as far away as ever: the last hope rested with their man in Rome, Josef Müller.

Müller, assigned to the Abwehr for just this purpose, had been in Italy since September of the previous year. He had gone to persuade Pope Pius XII, the former Cardinal Pacelli, to act as a peace intermediary between German oppositionists and the British. Müller scored a success almost at once, working through the Pope's private secretary, Father Leiber. Father Leiber reached the British minister, Sir Francis d'Arcy Osborne, and the dialogues had begun. The Canaris group was once again in solid contact with London, thanks to the unimpeachable relay point established by Müller within the Vatican. Once the Pope was informed that General Beck was behind much of the planning, he had no hesitation in vouching for the entire opposition group.

Events moved slowly, and it wasn't until mid-January 1940 that Osborne was able to transmit to London the gist of the German proposals. Müller warned of Hitler's forthcoming "violent, bitter, and unscrupulous" offensive, which might be launched at any time. But the dogs of war need not be loosed if the British could only guarantee the plotters a fair peace once Hitler was overthrown and his Nazi régime toppled. The new German gov-

ernment would work out agreements to restore Poland and Czechoslovakia, but Austria would remain part of Germany. The reaction at Whitehall was disappointing; the consensus within the
cabinet was that the proposal was ethereal and that the plotters
should first wipe out the Nazi régime before any useful discussions could take place.

Müller kept trying. Three weeks later the Pope had in hand
written assurances that revolutionists—for that is what they
were—would replace the dictatorship with a decentralized, conservative, and federalized government. This aspect interested
both Prime Minister Chamberlain and Foreign Secretary Lord
Halifax, who sent word back to the Vatican that should the Nazis
be replaced by a democratic form of government "within a rea-
sonable time," the British and the French would not launch a
western offensive of their own during the chaos that would surely
come on the heels of the proposed coup d'état. As for Austria,
that question could best be settled by plebiscite.

The essence of the British stance was drafted by the Abwehr in
Berlin into what was called the X-Report, and efforts were made
to present this encouraging document to Halder. Meanwhile
Hitler had made another of his lightning decisions that astonished
Army High Command (OKH) and Wehrmacht High Command
(OKW) alike. On March 27 Hitler announced that the planned to
invade Norway and Denmark by sea and air during the first week
in April. The move, he said, would secure Germany's iron-ore
shipments from Sweden via Norway, and he planned to invest
Norway before the British did.

Halder was immersed in the frantic logistic and tactical planning for the unexpected military adventure, and it wasn't until
April 4, five days before the invasion was to begin, that General
Georg Thomas was able to get inside Halder's office to present
him with a copy of the X-Report. Halder studied the contents
and took the report to Brauchitsch the same night.

Brauchitsch was aghast. "You should not have shown me this!"
he shouted. "What is happening here is sheer treason. We are at
war! It is all very well to talk about foreign contacts in peacetime,
but in wartime we soldiers can do no such thing. Besides, this is

not a struggle between governments but a contest of ideologies. To eliminate Hitler now would serve no purpose." Brauchitsch paused, then added, "Who brought you this paper in the first place? I'll have him arrested!"

Halder replied, "If anyone is to be arrested, you had better start with me." He picked up the paper and left.

When the Abwehr was alerted to the invasion of Norway and Denmark, Hans Oster knew what he had to do. The agents Canaris had planted in Scandinavia flooded the offices on the Tirpitzufer with coded messages containing information needed by the army and the Luftwaffe. The offices hummed with activity around the clock. An observer recalled Oster at work. "He had four secret telephone lines, and it was a terrifying experience to watch him speaking to four unseen agents, giving different instructions without batting an eyelid. His right hand never dared know what his left was up to. All this took place in an atmosphere where treason and high treason were no longer distinguishable."

Oster did not consider his next move an act of treason. Since, despite their best efforts, they could not halt any of Hitler's invasion plans, Oster decided to try to wreck the invasions themselves. Oster reasoned that if the Führer's increasingly risky military adventures were brought up short, if the Wehrmacht were to suffer an overwhelming defeat, then Hitler's aura of infallibility would vanish, his popularity would plummet, and the climate for a coup d'état would once again be established.

Oster reached his friend, Colonel Gisjbertus Sas, the Dutch military attaché, and gave him full details of the impending assault on the two Scandinavian countries. Warn the Danes and the Norwegians, he said, and above all get the information to the British, whose navy could shoot the invasion armada out of the water. Sas fired off an encoded telegram to Ansterdam, then tracked down Ulrich Stang, a member of the Norwegian legation, in the bar of the Adlon Hotel, and informed Stang of Hitler's intention to invade Norway on the following Tuesday. Stang thought the idea "nonsense"—the real danger, he said, was from the British. (In this, the Norwegian guessed, in part, correctly: the British were already at work on plans to land troops at Bergen, Trondheim, and at Narvik, above the Arctic Circle.)

What Sas did not know was that Stang was an ardent admirer of Hitlerian politics and wanted Norway molded after the Nazi state; he had no intention of warning Oslo of what lay ahead. Worse, for some unfathomable reason the Dutch Intelligence Service failed to alert the British to the coming invasion. Thus the efforts of Oster and Sas went for nothing. The assaults were successfully launched on April 9, Denmark fell the same day, and the Norwegians were doomed to fight a battle they could not win.

On May 6 Wilhelm Schmidhuber, a reserve officer attached to the Abwehr in Berlin, was in Rome with a message for the Pope from Josef Müller: Hitler's western offensive was now set for May 8, weather permitting; any changss would be communicated from Berlin over the telephone using a prearranged oral code. The Pontiff passed the information on to the French, the British, and the Belgians.

On the evening of May 9 Colonel Sas drove to Oster's home and learned that the long-dreaded offensive, after twenty-eight postponements, was slated to begin within a few hours, at daybreak on the following morning. The Luftwaffe meteorologists promised clear weather for May 10. Oster explained that if no further word came before 9:30 that evening cancellation would be impossible. They drove on OKW headquarters, and Oster went inside to check.

He came back out shortly after ten and said to Sas, "Now it's really all over, my friend. There have been no counterorders. The swine [Hitler] has gone off to the western front. I hope we will see each other again after the war." Sas hurried off to the Dutch embassy to make his telephone call, hoping to give his tiny country a few precious hours to prepare for the onslaught.

Oster twice put his life and his honor at stake in passing German military information to Hitler's victims, and twice his warnings went unheeded. Holland was prostrate within five days, Belgium in nineteen. The remnants of the British Expeditionary Force were swept into the sea at Dunkirk on June 2, and twelve days later Paris was abandoned. The French capitulated at Compiègne on June 21; all of Western Europe was now a Hitler fiefdom. Hitler had accomplished in forty-one days what the Kaiser could not achieve in more than four years. The cost to the Wehrmacht was trifling. Hitler now stood triumphant from the Arctic Circle to the Bay of Biscay, a heroic and unassailable figure. His bitterly disappointed opponents in Berlin would now have to bide their time until Germany faced inevitable ruin before they could strike again.

By the beginning of 1942 it was clear that the worst predictions of Beck, Goerdler, Canaris, Oster, and the others were coming true. The Wehrmacht was deep inside Russia struggling for its existence; Hitler had recently declared war on the United States; Britain—despite the Führer's promises—remained unconquered, and German civilians were caught between merciless bombardment rained down from above and a cruelly repressive police system at home.

War with Russia began in the summer of 1941, and six months later Germans had penetrated 600 miles inside Soviet frontiers. Three million Germans were fighting, freezing, and dying along a front measuring more than 1,600 linear miles. Army Group North was within eight miles of Moscow, but they would get no closer, and nearly 800,000 German troops were on the casualty rolls as killed, wounded, or missing. There were no winter uniforms, and a medical officer named Heinrich Haape was moved to write:

> The icy winds from Siberia—the breath of death—were blowing across the steppes, winds from where all life froze. The thermometer stood at only 12 below zero—but soon would fall to minus 48. It was beyond comprehension. These Arctic blasts had scythed through our attacking troops, and in a couple of days there were a hundred thousand casualties from frostbite alone. . . . If a soldier fell and lay where he collapsed until it was too late the wind blew over him and everything was leveled indistinguishably.

The supply system had broken down under the unexpected demands—unexpected because Hitler, Halder, and others at OKW had grossly underestimated the problems involved in supplying armies operating inside Russia during winter, the blame to be shared between the Abwehr's often inept intelligence-gathering apparatus and Hitler's boast that he would be in Moscow by August and the war ended before the year was out.

On the heels of the advancing Wehrmacht had come more of Heydrich's Einsatzgruppen, like jackals following the lions. One group was assigned to each of the four German armies, 3,000 men in all trained to hunt down and kill Russia's 5 million Jews. These special SS units made no attempt to keep secret their murderous work. Jews were rounded up in many instances even before the combat troops had cleared the town of Russian defenders.

At Zhitomir the commanding officer of the 528th Infantry Regiment, Major Ernst Rösler, was drawn out of his quarters by sudden ragged volleys of rifle and pistol fire. He dashed outside to see what all the shooting was about. Reaching the top of an embankment, he gazed down at a pit filled with fresh corpses of Jewish men, women, and children. Rösler's reaction spoke for the majority of the Wehrmacht: "It was a picture of such barbaric horror that the effect of anyone coming upon it unawares was shattering and repellent." Rösler noticed an old, white-bearded man clutching a cane who showed signs of life. He ordered one of the executioners to put the old man out of his misery, but the soldier refused, saying to Rösler, "I've already shot him seven times in the stomach. He can die on his own now." Such scenes were hourly occurrences throughout the occupied territories, and the Wehrmacht was powerless to intervene because the Einsatzgruppen were under Himmler's direct operational control. The SS were meticulous record keepers, and by the winter of 1941–42 reported that 481,887 Russian Jews had been liquidated.

The Russians were also savage. On December 24, 1941, Canaris noted in his diary: "In the retreat from Moscow we had to abandon German field hospitals. The Russians dragged out the sick and wounded, hanged them upside down, poured gasoline on them and set them on fire. Some uninjured German soldiers were forced to watch this torture; they were then kicked in the groin and sent back to German lines to describe how the Bolsheviks were reacting to news of mass executions and barbaric treatment meted out to their comrades in German captivity. On another occasion German prisoners were beheaded and their heads laid out to form the SS symbol."

Added to the abhorrence most German generals felt toward Hitler's racial policies in the East was growing anxiety about the Wehrmacht's ability to deal the Russians a knockout blow. More than 12,000 Red Army tanks were destroyed during the first six weeks of the campaign, but fresh waves of Russian T-34s kept appearing on the battlefield to overrun German positions. Because Göring had failed to provide long-range bombers for the Luftwaffe, Russian tank factories beyond the Urals roared unhindered around the clock to make good the losses at the rate of 1,000 tanks per month, nearly double the German production capacity. As early as November 1941 Hitler's munitions minister, Fritz Todt, told the Führer, "Given the arms and industrial supremacy of the Anglo-Saxon powers, we can militarily no longer win this war."

The climate for a coup was reestablished in the fateful year of 1942, when the first stirrings of civilian revolt were beginning to be felt within the German homeland.

8

Revolt
in Munich

IN THE SPRING of 1942 Professor Kurt Huber, fifty, stood beside a hectograph machine committing treason. The copy that issued from the matrix was an 800-word broadside directed at the Third Reich, and Huber knew that it was worth his life if he were caught.

The contents of Huber's broadside were drawn from inflammatory sermons delivered earlier by the Bishop of Münster, Count Clemens von Galen, long an active and outspoken critic of Hitler's policies. The bishop condemned the Führer's euthanasia program that sent 70,000 mental patients, cripples, and seniles to internment between 1939 and 1941 (when the program inside Germany ended), and he attacked the Gestapo for its seizure of Münster's monasteries and the expulsion of the priests, nuns, and brothers of the Society of Jesus.

"At this moment," said the bishop, "we are not the hammer but the anvil. Others, outsiders and apostates, are hammering on us. They have set about by force to reshape our people and our youth, to turn them away from God. What they are forging is illegal imprisonment, exile and expulsion of the innocent." The bishop was not persecuted for his remarks, but three priests in the city of Lübeck were seized and executed for distributing the text of sermons to German soldiers. Professor Huber wanted the bishop's words remembered throughout Germany.

Born in Switzerland, Huber migrated to Germany after the First World War and became a naturalized citizen of the ill-fated Weimar Republic. He rose to head the philosophy and psychology departments at the venerable University of Munich and was one of the most popular lecturers there. Students crowded his classrooms and enjoyed tea and academic discussions with him in the afternoons; but he kept his dangerous clandestine activities to himself.

Huber cranked out the final page on the hectograph machine and sat down at his desk to collate and staple together the leaflets that, if traced to him, would send him the way of the Lübeck priests. He slid the leaflets inside envelopes already addressed to a cross-section of Munich's citizens and stuffed them inside a worn leather briefcase. An hour later they were safely inside letter boxes, and Huber was at home eating a spartan wartime dinner.

One of Huber's leaflets arrived at the home of the Scholl family in Ulm and was read by Hans Scholl, then on leave from his studies at the University of Munich. Scholl, twenty-four, turned to one of his sisters, Inge, and said, "Finally a man has had the courage to speak out." His own early enthusiasm for Hitler having long since evaporated, Scholl had wanted to speak out himself for a long time.

Scholl had grown up in the village of Kochertal, where his father was mayor, during a time when Germany was prostrate. More than a million men were on the streets without jobs, and the national currency was literally not worth the paper it was printed on. Hitler's speeches promising a return of honor mesmerized Scholl, and in 1934, when he was fifteen, he joined the Hitler Youth, as would 8 million other German boys and girls between the ages of ten and eighteen. He could not at first understand why his father failed to share his dedication to the new Germany and its leaders, whom the elder Scholl called "wolves and deceivers" who were leading the nation to destruction. Hans was caught up in the Führer's challenge to German youth to become "quick as greyhounds, tough as leather, and as hard as Krupp steel."

Scholl's disillusionment began when the other German youth

organizations, many of them chartered when Hitler was still living hand-to-mouth in Vienna painting picture postcards, were one by one declared illegal and the members ordered into the Hitler Youth. Scholl and other youthful rebels in Ulm went underground and kept alive the traditions of the outlawed *Bündische Jugend*. They continued the pursuit of philosophical enlightenment untainted by political dogma, and they savored the carefree joys of roaming the outdoors unwatched and unregimented. In speaking of these suppressed youth organizations, Hitler proclaimed, "He who is not prepared to bear my name will not be regarded as a friend of National Socialism," and the arrests began.

Scholl and his friends were seized from their homes by the Gestapo and thrown into jail. Their libraries were ransacked. Adolescent song books, photo albums, and diaries were confiscated. Volumes by forbidden authors were taken and thrown into the trash along with everything else. The Gestapo missed one of Scholl's books on the flyleaf of which he had inscribed, "Tear out our hearts—and they will burn you."

Hans Scholl was released from jail a changed and bitter youth, but he was more fortunate than other, older recalcitrant Hitler Youth members. A Catholic youth leader named Adalbert Probst was "shot while trying to escape" the Gestapo, as was another named Ernst Lämmermann. Others were carted away to concentration camps and were never heard of again.

Scholl was drafted into the army in 1937 when he was nineteen, then released after two years of mandatory service. In 1939 he entered premed school at the University of Munich, but eight months later he was back in the army serving as a medical corpsman during the hectic campaign in France. The victory seemed swift and easy in the newsreels, but Scholl worked at the bloody receiving end of a field hospital in the wake of the advance and dealt only with the garbage of war.

The army allowed Scholl and other medical noncoms to resume their studies at the university, but they were formed into a student company and led schizophrenic lives. Their time was divided between barracks, military hospitals, and classrooms, where they felt out of place wearing heavy boots and stiff, woolen Wehrmacht uniforms.

The pleasure of the small freedoms allowed Scholl was soured by news from home. A trio of Gestapo agents had appeared in the middle of the night and hauled his father off without explanation. His wife and daughters never expected to see him again, but he showed up at home the next morning, pale and enraged. At work in Ulm's town council offices, Herr Scholl had referred to Hitler as "God's scourge to mankind," and was immediately turned in by one of his female assistants. The Gestapo turned him loose, but warned that he had not heard the last of them.

It was then that Hans Scholl returned to Ulm that weekend to be electrified by Professor Huber's illegal pamphlet. He went back to Munich and spent much of his sergeant's pay on a duplicating machine, ink, and paper, the tools of treason with which to forge active, intellectual resistance. He found allies in the student medical company, idealists like himself who had bumped against reality in the field with the Wehrmacht: Alexander Schmorell, twenty-four, born in Russia and the son of a well-known Munich physician; Christoph Probst, twenty-four, the son of a scholar and married with two small children; Wilhelm Graf, twenty-four, born in the coal regions of the Saar, intense, dedicated, and once thrown into jail for adhering to a Catholic youth organization.

On May 9, 1942, Hans was at the Munich train station to meet the incoming train from Ulm. Aboard was his sister, Sophia Magdalena Scholl, wearing a daisy in her hair and carrying a wicker basket inside which her mother had packed a bottle of Mosel wine and a spice cake, baked with the last of the sugar ration. It was Sophie's twenty-first birthday, and she was in Munich to matriculate at the university. Sophie's dark, heavy hair was brushed until it gleamed like a seal's coat. Her eyes, large and brown under substantial brows, gazed on a world that often seemed "infinitely strange, empty, and a God-forsaken void," as her sister, Inge, observed.

Sophie Scholl arrived in Munich following a disagreeable year of enforced duty with the Reich Labor Service for Young Women. She lived with more than a hundred other girls in one of the 2,000 hastily erected camps scattered throughout Germany under disciplinary conditions hardly less severe than those found in Wehrmacht training centers. Up at sunrise, the girls, dressed in coarse clothing, a heavy apron, kerchief, and rubber boots, spent seven hours doing a field hand's work on nearby farms. Sophie hated every minute of it, and now in Munich she looked forward to the university atmosphere where she could pursue her father's wishes for his children to "live in uprightness and freedom of spirit."

Hans Scholl began producing the first resistance leaflets a few weeks after Sophie's arrival, but she was not let in on this secret activity. Scholl's impromptu organization was called *Die Weisse Rose*, a name he chose from a novel by the mysterious B. Traven called *The White Rose*, which Scholl had read in translation. The novel is an outright adventure story set against a Mexican background, and the plot has no bearing on Scholl's ideas of resistance, but it seemed to the rebellious Scholl good cover, as well as romantic.

Scholl and Alexander Schmorell labored over the text of the first leaflet. They journeyed as far back as the ancient Greeks in their search through the classics for ideas to lend weight to their own literary outrage. They pored over volume after volume, extracting sentences, paragraphs, and entire poems. They covered dozens of sheets of paper with script, adding, crossing out, rearranging with scissors and paste. They finally melded the crosscurrents of thought into a thousand-word whole that pleased and excited them both. It began:

> Nothing is so unworthy of a civilized nation as allowing itself to be "governed" without opposition by an irresponsible clique that has yielded to base instinct. It is certain today that every honest German is ashamed of his government. Who among us has any conception of the dimensions of shame that will befall us and our children when one day the veil has fallen from our

eyes and the most horrible of crimes—crimes that infinitely outdistance every human measure—reach the light of day?

The leaflet asked if the German people were already too corrupted and crushed in spirit to raise a hand against the infamies in their own country. Were Germans already too far along the road to becoming a spiritless, cowardly mass? Scholl quoted Goethe and Schiller and called for passive resistance against fascism before all of Germany's cities were turned into rubble, before "the nation's last young man has given his blood on some battlefield for the *hubris* of a subhuman."

Passages were quoted from *The Lawgiving of Lycurgus and Solon*, which includes warnings against founding a state on the principles of Sparta, where "there was no conjugal love, no mother love, no filial devotion, no friendship, where all men were citizens only, and all virtue was civic virtue." Scholl and Schmorell extracted act 2, scene 4 from *The Awakening of Epimenides*, a dialogue that describes a creature rising from the abyss to conquer half the world, only to return to the abyss, dragging down all those who stood with him.

The text reflected the writers' academic background and addressed itself to an introspective, literate reader; but the message was clear enough, and the contents sufficiently treasonous to cost the lives of the authors. Scholl carefully typed the master, then spent hours bent over the gelatin platen transferring the purple tinted words to sheets of white foolscap. He worked in a room with the windows shut and the blackout curtains tightly drawn; the place smelled of glycerine, stale cigarette smoke, and jasmine picked wild in the country. He finished the job, stacked the leaflets, and hid the hectograph materials in the back of a closet.

Scholl gained entrance to the university before dawn and placed most of the leaflets in stacks where they could not be missed by passing students and faculty; the rest he mailed to professional men of Munich whose names he picked, as Professor Huber had, from the telephone directory. Sophie Scholl read the incriminating pamphlet and suspected that it was her brother's

121

work. She asked him if he knew where the leaflets came from. "It's better not to know," he replied.

Scholl and his comrades turned out three more of the White Rose leaflets within the next thirty days. They attacked National Socialism as a betrayal of the people. Scholl called *Mein Kampf* a book written "in the worst German I have ever read." German intellectuals, he said, had "fled to the cellars, there, like plants struggling in the dark, away from light and sun, gradually to choke to death." Jews were being slaughtered in accelerating numbers. Daughters of the Polish nobility were being shipped to Norway to serve in bordellos run by the SS. Germans who would not rise and take a stand were *guilty, guilty, guilty!* Germany had been reduced to a dictatorship of evil. The leaflets called for sabotage in war industries, in universities that lent their technical facilities to the war effort, in branches of the arts that depended upon the Nazi party for handouts, in newspapers that defended the current ideology. The leaflet pointed to the rising casualties in Russia. Hitler was the greatest liar in human history. "His mouth is the foul-smelling maw of Hell, and his might is at bottom accursed." The leaflet urged that the defeat of the Nazis must become the national priority and warned that a fascist German victory would have frightful consequences for the entire world.

The fourth and final leaflet in the series concluded with a reminder and a promise. "We will not be silent. We are your bad conscience. The White Rose will not leave you in peace."

Scholl's leaflets were in the hands of the Gestapo within hours after distribution inside the university, but they could not be traced—duplicating machines in a city the size of Munich were almost as common as the wartime paper upon which the seditious messages were printed. The Gestapo assigned a number of underground agents to the campus, hoping to catch the traitors in the act of distribution, but the leaflets disappeared as suddenly as they had surfaced.

In early July of 1942, Scholl and the rest of the student medical company were given one day's notice to muster fully uniformed at Munich's main railway station for transfer to active duty on the eastern front. Scholl hurriedly secreted his duplicating machine, gathered together his gear, and the following afternoon was aboard a crowded troop train headed for the Russian Caucasus, more than 1,000 miles away.

The train rolled across southern Germany and through unravaged Czechoslovakia to cross the Polish frontier. It halted outside of Cracow, where Scholl observed through the window a labor gang of Jewish women and girls hacking unenthusiastically at an embankment with picks and shovels. Scholl got off the train on an impulse and offered a young girl the first thing that came to hand, his iron ration. He later recalled how the girl, who was dressed like a scarecrow and wore the identifying yellow Star of David, looked at him with an expression of "infinite sadness" and let the foil-wrapped bar drop at her feet. The train started to move, and Scholl hurried back aboard, watching the girl stoop to pick up the bar and slip it into a pocket. Now Scholl would have to somehow find another ration; to lose it except under the extremities of combat meant court-martial.

Scholl's medical company arrived in Russia at the height of the new summer offensive and was attached to Army Group South, whose panzers and motorized columns of infantry were chewing their way toward the oil fields of Maïkop.* The medics worked in crushing heat inside fetid tents serving as field surgeries that leapfrogged along the wake of the advancing combat units. The workload was heavier than Scholl believed possible; German casualties in Russia totaled 1.4 million by the end of July 1942, and

---

*General Ewald von Kleist led his First Panzer Army through fanatical Russian resistance to reach the Maikop oil fields. They found a wasteland: the derricks lay toppled, and the pumps were shattered, blown with high explosive laid by Russian combat engineers. The great circular storage tanks were crumpled, split apart, smoke-blackened, empty. Abandoned vehicles, cannibalized for parts, had been turned into charred heaps of metal. No sign of life remained. Farther on, cracking plants and refineries reared against the summer sky in twisted shapes. It was all a smoking ruin. The hugely expensive battle, prodigious in its wastage of lives and generating countless human agonies, had been for nothing.

averaged 33,000 killed, wounded, and missing every ten days along the front that now stretched 1,200-miles northward to Leningrad.

Scholl discovered that his brother Werner's battalion was only a few kilometers away. He borrowed a war-weary Wehrmacht horse and plodded off across the parched and cratered countryside for a reunion. Sheltering inside a bunker, Scholl withdrew from his blouse pocket a letter recently received from Ulm. It described how the Gestapo had once again dragged their father off to court where a judge sentenced him to four months in prison on the old charge of verbally abusing the Führer. Werner Scholl was speechless with anger and could only stare fixedly into space. Hans Scholl told his brother not to take it so hard. "After all," he pointed out, "it *is* a distinction."

Scholl remained in Russia throughout the summer and into the fall, when cold winds howling across the empty steppes brought the first stinging flakes of snow—harbingers of another disastrous winter. He and the others of the university medical company were detached from Army Group South and entrained for the long ride back to Germany. Behind them the Sixth Army was clawing its way forward into the frozen tomb of Stalingrad.

Back in Munich, Scholl returned to his cramped apartment and registered for the fall classes at the university. He and his friends Schmorell and Probst were objects of curiosity to the rest of the medical students, who lacked their frontline experience in the treatment of gunshot wounds, burns, and amputations. Scholl brooded over newspaper and word-of-mouth accounts of casualties in Russia and arrests and executions of dissidents at home.

Copies of the four leaflets distributed during the spring and early summer had found their way to cities all over Germany, including shattered Hamburg 400 miles to the north. The leaflets were duplicated and passed from hand to hand inside the major universities. Planted Gestapo agents were no more successful in stopping the flow of pamphlets in Hamburg and in Berlin than they had been in Munich, but in December 1942 they wrecked the communist *Rote Kapelle* (Red Orchestra) organization and made sure the coup was widely publicized. Scholl read how fifty of the leaders charged with espionage were tried in Berlin and died at the end of a garrotte three days before Christmas. Others, many of them youthful Social Democrats only marginally allied with the Red Orchestra, were thrown into concentration camps to perish at leisure. Not a few of them ended their days at Dachau, eight miles down a poplar-lined side road, beyond the northwestern outskirts of Munich.

A painter friend of Scholl's was drafted and sent to the Russian front, but before leaving he turned over the keys to his studio apartment to Scholl. The studio was a converted garden shed located on a back lot not far from Scholl's apartment; equipped as it was for painting and graphic arts, it provided ideal cover for what Scholl had in mind. By now, Sophie Scholl had been taken into her brother's confidence, and in December she helped in moving the duplicating equipment into the studio where Scholl set to work composing another attack on the Nazi régime.

Scholl's sobering experiences in Russia had had their effect; the fifth leaflet in the series was shorn of literary allusions, the work was shorter by half, the sentences terser, the message unmistakable. The romantic-sounding title *White Rose* was scrapped in favor of the more pointed *Leaflet of the Resistance*. Scholl chided his fellow Germans for blindly following their seducers into ruin, saying that the war was already lost. He warned that retribution was at hand, that "judgment will be meted out to those who stayed in hiding, who were cowardly and hesitant." Scholl, Sophie, Probst, and Schmorell worked in the painter's studio at odd hours during the day and through consecutive nights until they had a stack of leaflets nearly two feet thick, 3,000 of them destined not only for Munich but for cities in southern Germany and in Austria.

In mid-January 1943, the youthful conspirators began their travels. Sophie Scholl boarded a train for Augsburg, forty miles to the west. Like all German wartime trains, it was packed, and she had trouble finding a place to stash the leather suitcase stuffed with leaflets. Then she moved down the aisle of the coach, away from the suitcase, for the ride to Augsburg. The city had long been noted for its Gothic churches, its Renaissance palaces, and its textile industry. With the coming of war, however, it went on the target list of the Royal Air Force, because it housed August Diesel's engine factories and the sprawling aircraft manufacturing plant run by Willi Messerschmitt, which turned out single and twin-engined fighters on an around-the-clock basis. The sky over Augsburg was hazy with industrial pollution mixed with smoke and motes of brick dust raised by the four-engined bombers of the RAF that came by night.

The train pulled into Augsburg station, and Sophie joined the shuffling line of soldiers and civilians as they moved down the aisle. She retrieved the suitcase and stepped off the train under an open sky; the great glass dome that covered the Bahnhof was now an empty metal latticework. She walked down the tracks toward the main waiting room, expecting to feel the hand of the Gestapo on her shoulder. Every train station in Germany seemed to crawl with civil police, military police wearing the silver crescent shield of their office on their chests, and with men of the Gestapo, whose long leather coats and narrow-brimmed, English-style Trilby hats had become a cliché.

Sophie Scholl walked through the crowd toward one of the station mail boxes, withdrew a handful of envelopes from the suitcase, and stuffed them through the slot. She quickly emptied the suitcase and walked away. No one noticed her, no one halted her progress. She was back in Munich that same evening.

Hans Scholl got on a train and traveled seventy-five miles southeast to Salzburg—just below Hitler's eyrie a mile in the air at the Berghof—and mailed 150 leaflets to Salzburg's elite. Schmorell journeyed to Linz, not far from the Führer's birthplace, and then on to Vienna, where he posted a thousand leaflets, and dispatched 400 more to Frankfurt-am-Main. When he returned from the 500-mile round trip, he and Scholl walked the darkened streets of Munich and scattered leaflets by the hundreds.

The Gestapo remained baffled as to the source of the antiwar, anti-Nazi, anti-Hitler campaign, but in Berlin the SD discovered that it was having an effect. Reichsführer Heinrich Himmler told the SD to take a covert sampling of public opinion, and agents eavesdropped on conversations throughout Germany. The SD chief, Ernst Kaltenbrunner, had the information collated for select distribution. One of Kaltenbrunner's reports sent to Himmler noted that "rumors concerning the activities of oppositional circles are spreading and disturb the population . . . one talks of handbills and posters of Marxist content on public buildings in Berlin and other places. Some sources of our information stress the point that the population apparently no longer meets such manifestations as before, by prompt removal of the inflammatory writings or the handing over of leaflets, but instead reads the contents and passes them on . . . a sharp rejection of this punishable action can be observed only rarely."

The expenses of the leaflet campaign outstripped the sergeant's pay of Scholl and other medics, who earned only 250 marks, about $62, per month. Scholl decided to visit a long-time friend of his father's, Eugen Grimminger, in Stuttgart to ask for money. Grimminger, fifty-one, was the economic adviser for the city of Stuttgart and known by the Scholls to be passively opposed to the Hitlerian régime. Scholl and Schmorell boarded the train for Stuttgart and five hours later were admitted to Grimminger's home. The economist donated 500 marks in cash.

By now, word of the Munich activities had spread via the university underground throughout Germany, and Scholl learned that the leaflets were being duplicated and distributed in Hamburg, Bonn, Freiburg, and Heidelberg, all centers of higher learning. To Scholl, this was heartening news; he envisioned resistance cells composed of the youthful elite of Germany who would work concertedly on the consciences of their elders until support of the war effort would collapse.

Sophie Scholl spent Sunday afternoon, February 14, alone in her brother's apartment waiting for his return from some unexplained errand. Night fell. She drew the blackout curtains and turned on a light that illuminated an array of treasures resting on the wooden table in the center of the room: strudel, a jar of marmalade, apples, 250 grams of butter, and fresh cookies. They had been mailed from home, and Sophie could only wonder what her mother had traded, quite illegally, to some farmer outside of Ulm for luxuries that had long since disappeared from any shop in Germany. An hour passed, then two. She brewed tea and sat at the table writing in her diary: "For each of us, in no matter which age we live, have to be prepared to be called to account by God. After all, do I know whether or not I will be alive tomorrow morning? Tonight a bomb could wipe us all out. . . ."

It grew late; wondering, *Where was Hans?* Sophie lay down and slept.

Outside on the streets of Munich Scholl and Schmorell were extremely busy. Dressed in workman's clothes and carrying brushes and buckets of paint—good, prewar stuff Schmorell had scrounged—they walked furtively in the darkness close to the walls of the buildings in central Munich. On the Marienplatz they stopped and flew into action. Schmorell withdrew a stencil he had cut himself and slapped it against the side of the Town Hall. Scholl dipped a brush into a bucket of paint and slid it across the stencil. They hurried away, leaving the words *Nieder mit Hitler*, Down with Hitler, to dry on the stone.

They walked north to Maximilianstrasse and applied stencils to the outside of the National Theater. *Freedom! Hitler the Mass Murderer.* They continued west on the Residenzstrasse—down whose cobbles Hitler had marched twenty years earlier in the abortive beer-hall putsch—and paused to brand the walls of baroque and rococo palaces of the complex of buildings known as the Residenz, homes of former dukes, kings, and electors of Bavaria. They reached the impressive Ludwigstrasse, running north from the Odeonsplatz, and painted slogans on the outside of the cherished Field Marshal's Hall. They kept going, alert for foot patrols of Munich's police, who stalked the streets looking for blackout violations and shaking doors against the possibility of burglars, who had become increasingly bolder as the war went on.

Stencils and brushes were applied to the façades of museums, state libraries, government buildings, and private homes. They continued up Ludwigstrasse until they reached the university, where they used the last of the paint in a flurry of brushwork that left *Freedom! Freedom! Freedom!* emblazoned on the columns fronting the university's main entrance. They hid the brushes and stencils in the studio, picked up fellow conspirator Willi Graf, walked back to the apartment, and woke up Sophie Scholl to boast of what they had done during the night.

Crews of Ukranian women, brought back to Germany to perform menial chores, were hard at work early Monday morning trying to scrub away the inflammatory signs on more than seventy of Munich's more prominent buildings and homes, but the paint was stubborn and the Gestapo ordered the still-legible smears plastered over with patriotic posters.

On Tuesday, February 16, the University of Munich student body was herded into the cavernous assembly hall to listen to an address by the district party leader of Bavaria, Paul Giesler. When the students were seated, black-uniformed SS guards stationed themselves at the entrances to the auditorium, and the speaker entered. Giesler was a long-time Nazi, and his appearance elicited no cheers.

He began his speech by calling for more sacrifices on the home front and loyalty to the Führer. Then he launched into the meat of his address: student unrest and rebellion. He threatened to have the male student body combed for slackers and the faint of heart. He warned that any German male unwilling to support the war would quickly find himself in Russia, whether medically fit or not. Many of the men there had already seen heavy campaigning, and many of them had been wounded in combat. These men began to growl and curse openly.

Giesler switched to another tack, the role of German women students during wartime. "They have healthy bodies," he cried, "let them bear children! That is an automatic process which, once begun, continues without the least attention. There is no reason why every girl student should not, for each of her years at the University, present an annual testimonial in the form of a son." The noise inside the auditorium grew louder, and Giesler was forced to raise his voice in order to be heard.

"I realize that a certain amount of cooperation is required, and if some of the girls lack sufficient charm to find a mate I will assign to each of them one of my adjutants whose antecedents I can vouch for. And I can promise her," by now he was almost screaming, "a thoroughly enjoyable experience!"

The auditorium erupted in pandemonium. The outraged students rose to their feet, shouting insults at the stage. Pushing and shoving and shouldering aside the SS guards, they flowed out of the auditorium and into the streets. It was a signal for a day-long demonstration in Munich that triggered similar outbursts among students throughout Bavaria. Giesler ordered the public telephone exchange in Munich shut down for three days and the radio station off the air for a week. The mushrooming juvenile gangs, whose members were largely orphaned by the war or blown out of their homes by British bombs, took advantage of the temporary chaos to infiltrate marshaling yards where they wrecked train signals and set fires blazing.

On Tuesday night, only hours after Giesler's truncated address, Scholl and Professor Huber, who were now working together, were at a table composing another broadside. The electric events of the day convinced them that the seeds of successful revolt had already been sown within German universities. The new message would be directed to students exclusively. The copy referred to Giesler's infamous suggestions, and begged German students to "get out of the party organizations which are used to keep our mouths sealed and hold us in political bondage! Get out of the lecture rooms of the SS corporals and sergeants and party bootlickers! We want genuine learning and real freedom of opinion. . . ."

On Thursday, February 18, the morning dawned clear and cold. Hans and Sophie Scholl left the apartment early and headed for the university. They walked in the crisp sunshine carrying satchels stuffed with leaflets. The doors to the lecture rooms were still locked, so they separated and walked along the corridors, depositing leaflets in stacks outside the doors. Sophie Scholl paused at the top of the third floor landing and gazed down the light well.

Below, unseen, building superintendent Jacob Schmidt stared

up through the diffused light at the girl silhouetted against the glass panes of the skylight. He watched her reach into a bag and fling handfuls of paper sheets into the air. They fluttered down like heavy snowflakes and landed on the stairs and on the polished floor. Schmidt hurried off to get one of the resident Gestapo plainclothesmen, and five minutes later the building exits were sealed.

Hans and Sophie Scholl were seized and hustled into the back seat of a waiting sedan. They drove in silence down Ludwig-strasse, where Scholl could see the posters pasted over his own work executed only four days before. The car turned right on Briennerstrasse and pulled up in front of the Gestapo headquarters. They were ushered up the stone steps, booked, searched, and locked in separate cells.

The Scholls were grilled separately in sessions that began that Friday afternoon and lasted until daybreak Saturday. "The Painters," as they were called, denied having anything to do with the White Rose affair eight months earlier or with the more recent outrages until they were shown the brushes, stencils, and hectograph equipment ferreted out during a search of the studio. With tentative confessions in hand, the Gestapo teams allowed the exhausted prisoners to return to their cells.

They were roused from sleep a few hours later, and the questioning began all over again. What about Probst? Schmorell? Sophie, who knew that Probst's wife was in a Munich lying-in hospital, having just given birth to their child, said that Probst and Schmorell were only comrades, that they were not involved. Hans tried to shift the blame for everything onto his own shoulders, telling the Gestapo that he was the sole instigator, and that Sophie and the others were only unwitting dupes.

Sophie's interrogator, Egon Möhr, offered her a cup of coffee and a cigarette and lectured her as a father might a child on her errant ways. His talk was ridden with clichés about the glories of National Socialism, the infallibility of the Führer, and the disservice done to the brave German boys fighting at the front. Möhr suggested that had Sophie been aware of the facts he had just explained, she would not have engaged in such reckless activity.

131

Sophie replied, "You're wrong, Herr Möhr. I would do exactly the same thing all over again. It is you, not I, who has the mistaken *Weltanschauung.*"

Events now moved swiftly. On Saturday night, February 20, Christl Probst was hauled into jail and charged with treason. On Sunday afternoon Sophie Scholl was similarly charged and told that she and the others would go on trial for their lives on Monday morning.

Sophie and the other Painters were convinced that the trial would be a routine formality. They were appointed a youthful defense counsel, but he, like all other practicing attorneys in Germany, was a member of the Nazi Lawyers' Association. The selection of the judge to preside over the case was immaterial; under a section of the Civil Service Act promulgated by Hitler, any judge who failed to "act in the interest of the National Socialist State" was permanently removed from the bench and replaced by a younger zealot who could be counted upon to place the law above justice. The traditional balance between judge, prosecutor, and defense counsel was altered so that the prosecutor was mantled with extraordinary powers—including the right of fixing sentence—and the defense counsel remained primarily a passive bystander. The number of capital offenses was increased from three to forty-three during the first ten years of Hitler's seizure of power. As one observer noted, the proponents of Nazi justice returned to Nietzsche's dictum, "Penal law consists of war measures employed to rid oneself of the enemy."

The prisoners slept in cells washed in the harsh glare of incandescent lights that burned throughout the night. Shortly before nine Monday morning they were taken outside and driven to the Palace of Justice, which flanked the botanical gardens laid bare by winter. Scholl and Probst were handcuffed and rode together; Sophie was unmanacled and rode alone.

The defendants sat at a wooden table and faced the infamous president of the special People's Court, Roland Freisler, whose mastery of terroristic judicial procedures used in the USSR during the 1930s so endeared him to Hitler. Freisler's face looked like a death mask, an effect he cultivated successfully despite a brace of oversized ears that stood out like flaps and might have looked comical on anyone else.

The evidence was presented routinely and drew no objections from the defense. When Freisler unlocked his face and launched into a vituperative assault intended to evoke shame and fear, Sophie Scholl replied, "What we said and wrote is what many people are thinking—only they don't dare to express themselves." Probst and Scholl admitted every deed they were charged with, Probst explaining that his actions were explainable by a "psychotic depression" brought on by the conditions inside Germany. For the most part, the three said little and refused to be intimidated by Freisler.

While Freisler and his cohorts were going through the motions of deliberating, there was a commotion at the door. The elder Scholls had just arrived from Ulm and grudgingly were given seats in the back of the courtroom. The red-robed Freisler rose, placed a black velvet cap on his balding head, and intoned the sentences:

"Hans Fritz Scholl . . . *Tod.*"

"Sophie Magdalena Scholl . . . *Tod.*"

"Christoph Hermann Probst . . . *Tod.*"

As the death sentence was decreed, Frau Scholl collapsed and was helped out of the room. Herr Scholl leaped to his feet and cried out, "There is a higher court before which we all must stand!" Freisler left the bench and walked out of the courtroom. Bailiffs escorted the three convicted youths through a rear door; Herr Scholl helplessly watched them go.

Shortly after 1:00 P.M. they were put back in the Gestapo sedans and driven to Stadelheim Prison on the southern outskirts of Munich, at the edge of the gloomy Perlach Forest. They were locked in separate cells and told to write their last letters. Probst, whose wife had no idea what had befallen her husband, wrote her a note and asked to be baptised into the Roman Catholic church. The Scholl parents were granted an exception and allowed to spend a few agonizing minutes with their doomed children. Sophie seemed calm; Hans remained stoic.

A half-hour after the Scholls were escorted out of the prison gates the executions began.

Sophie, in deference to her girlhood, went first into the clean chamber. So swift and practiced were the movements that the condemned barely had time to notice the guillotine, the lidded basket, and the sawdust on the floor. Still wearing her school skirt and blouse, Sophie was stretched out on the wooden rack with her hands tied behind her back. The catch was released, and the heavy blade dropped.

The chamber was sluiced out, fresh sawdust spread on the concrete floor, and Hans Scholl was brought in and killed. Guards remembered how he cried out, "Long live freedom!" in the final seconds of his life. Probst went at 5:08 P.M., and it was over. Statistics carefully kept by the Germans indicate that the average time elapsed in such executions was seven seconds from the opening of the chamber door to the fall of the blade.

Heinrich Himmler insisted that the first summary executions would serve as a mortal warning to other German malcontents, but instead the scheme backfired as Goebbels had said it would. The Munich *Neuste Nachrichten* carried the story of the trial and executions that same Monday afternoon; the accounts were set in type while the students were still alive so as to meet the deadline. The story was picked up by Swedish and Swiss newspapers, and the events in Munich created a shock wave that rippled outward.

In New York, Eleanor Roosevelt addressed a protest rally staged at Hunter College and paid tribute to the courage of the students. Exiled Thomas Mann, himself an alumnus of the University of Munich, addressed the nation on radio, calling Probst and the Scholls "good, splendid young people" who carried the torch of freedom at a time when Germany was still enveloped in the darkness of night.

The news reached Russia, where German prisoners formed the Free Germany Committee. The POWs created their own resistance leaflets and wrote speeches designed to put further cracks in

Wehrmacht morale. With Russian help, the leaflets were scattered from the air behind German lines and the scripts broadcast on Wehrmacht frequencies.

In Germany, others involved in the White Rose conspiracy were relentlessly tracked down.* Meanwhile, in Russia, a plot undreamed of by undergraduates was about to unfold.

————

*Professor Huber, Alexander Schmorell, and Wilhelm Graf were arrested on February 27, 1943, went to trial on April 19, and were beheaded on July 13.

9

Flight from
Smolensk

I NSIDE HEADQUARTERS, ARMY Group Center, near the ruined city of Smolensk, the senior operations officer worked at fitting together the final pieces of the jigsaw of assassination. Colonel Henning von Treskow had been trying to balk Hitler's plans since the summer of 1941; now, as 1943 loomed, Treskow was bent on tyrannicide as the only means of preventing the ruination facing Germany. Seven hundred miles to the southeast 330,000 German troops were about to be swallowed up in the cauldron that was Stalingrad; the Americans and the British were preparing to throw Field Marshal Erwin Rommel and his Afrika Korps out of Tunisia after their long tenure in North Africa; German cities were being churned into flames and rubble by thousand-bomber raids.

The war of attrition between Hitler and his generals continued to accelerate. He first fired Brauchitsch as the army's commander-in-chief, naming himself as replacement, then Heinz Guderian, the tank expert, then Chief of Staff Halder. None of these sackings affected plans to liquidate the Führer, for Beck and the others had long ago given up on Halder and Brauchitsch. Treskow's main task, Beck stressed, was to persuade General Günther von Kluge, commanding Army Group Center in Russia, to fall in line with an attempt on Hitler's life for the good of Germany.

Kluge, obsessed with the terrible military problems he faced (his entire army group was down to 167 tanks), still found time to listen to Treskow's arguments. But just when Treskow believed he had won Kluge over, the latter would change his mind and declare that he wanted nothing to do with a coup. Treskow would patiently have to begin all over again. Treskow's aide, Schlabrendorff, called Treskow "the watchmaker who wound Kluge up every morning and made him run all day."

Treskow's primary plan was brutally simple: to lure Hitler to Kluge's headquarters and have him gunned down by troops especially picked for the job—an Einsatzgruppe, if you will, whose target was not some hapless Jew but the German head of state. He found no lack of volunteers for this special commando unit formed by Lieutenant Colonel Georg von Boeselager, twenty-eight, a fire-eating reconnaissance officer and holder of the Knight's Cross with oak leaves and swords. Boeselager was built and moved like a whippet; a service report evaluated him as "a spirited cavalry officer who thinks boldly and surely in taking decisions, but who is modest and unassuming, the idol of his men."

Boeselager picked his men from his own command, Cavalry Regiment Center, a force of 2,200, of whom 650 were Russian Cossacks enlisted in the fight against Stalin. Treskow and Boeselager sketched out alternate plans, all depending on Kluge's acquiescence and the field marshal's ability to persuade Hitler to visit his battered troops under the pretext of pumping up their morale. Boeselager's regiment would be charged with field security on the day of the Führer's visit, his men strategically placed in and outside of the towering woods that sheltered the headquarters complex. Hitler could be shot down not long after he stepped off his aircraft while walking through the woods to Kluge's HQ. Boeselager's men, hardened combat veterans equipped mostly with Schmeisser submachine guns, would then deal with Hitler's SS bodyguards in the firefight anticipated after the Führer had been mown down. If for some reason action could not be initiated before Hitler reached HQ, then he would be shot while seated in the mess hall; a dozen officers from one of Boeselager's battalions unhesitatingly volunteered for the job to be carried out at the command of Colonel Berndt von Kleist, a one-legged officer of Hitler's own General Staff.

Back in Berlin the old 1938 plans for takeover at home were once again dredged up for overhaul. Speculating in a successful assassination in Russia, Oster and Beck coordinated their efforts with the deputy commander of the Home Army, General Friedrich Olbricht, fifty-five, known for his quick wit, affability, and lack of political ambition. Olbricht had long known Goerdler and others in the underground resistance, but his real value to the projected coup lay in his power to issue orders to troops stationed near major German cities. The moment word was flashed from Russia that Hitler was finished, Olbricht would order the seizure of Berlin, Cologne, Munich, and Vienna. "Give me eight weeks," Olbricht said to Treskow's aide, Schlabrendorff; then he set to work.

Hans Gisevius was again provided with a private office in the Bendlerstrasse where he could have instant access to Olbricht. The general assigned Gisevius the task of updating the maps that pinpointed major SS installations, which had proliferated throughout the Reich since the war began. Up to this point the Abwehr had failed to penetrate either the SS or the Gestapo, and Gisevius racked his brains for ways to find out the location of new SS units. Then somebody in the Abwehr mentioned to Gisevius that wherever the SS went, funds followed to set up private brothels for Himmler's elite. When an Abwehr agent persuaded the head of the Berlin vice squad to turn over a list of newly established joy houses in Germany, Gisevius was able to bring his map up-to-date. At the end of February 1943, Schlabrendorff flew back to Berlin at Treskow's request, and Olbricht told him: "Now we are ready. Operation Flash can begin."

Canaris, ever the worrier, decided that a final conference was needed to tie everything down. On March 7, 1943, an Abwehr passenger plane cleared the runway at Berlin-Gatow airfield, reached altitude, and bored eastward through the winter sky for Smolensk, three and a half hours away. Aboard were Canaris;

Abwehr sabotage chief Lahousen; Hans von Dohnanyi, former justice of the Leipzig Supreme Court and special friend of Oster, plus various aides. Cover for the mission was provided by Canaris, who convened Army Group Center intelligence officers down to battalion level. The plane left a Berlin clearly showing the effects of the night marauders of the RAF. Only six days earlier a hail of high explosives and firebombs had left 35,000 homeless and 700 dead. Buildings were gaping shells; smoke still drifted in the air.

The plotters reached Smolensk without incident, and that same evening, after the obligatory intelligence conference broke up, Treskow, Schlabrendorff, and Dohnanyi arranged a secret conclave to exchange details of what was to happen at both ends of the chain of conspiracy. Treskow told Dohnanyi to pass the word to Oster and Olbricht that the Führer had at last consented to pay a quick visit to Smolensk, but as usual he was vague about the date.

Hitler was on the move. In mid-February he left his East Prussian headquarters at Rastenburg and flew south 750 miles to Field Marshal Erich von Manstein's headquarters in the Ukraine at Zaporozh'ye. He stayed long enough for a war conference, then, with Russian gunfire clearly audible to the east, flew to his own HQ in Russia—Vinnitsa, 300 miles back to the west. Here he granted an audience to an ailing and harassed Field Marshal Rommel come to beg for reinforcements and supplies to shore up his collapsing front in Tunisia. The next day, March 10, Hitler was in the air headed back for Zaporozh'ye to congratulate Manstein, whose two counterattacking Panzer armies had just finished thrashing a Russian army corps north of the Dneiper River, hauling in more than 600 T-34s to be turned around and used against their former owners.

In the north Hitler permitted the withdrawal of two German armies behind newly prepared defenses in depth west of Moscow. Pursuing Russians blundered into thickly sown minefields and were flayed by preregistered artillery barrages. These minor successes buoyed Hitler's spirits, and when he boarded his plane on the morning of March 13 for the 500-mile flight north to Smolensk, he was in fine humor.

Despite Treskow's efforts, Field Marshal von Kluge's nerve failed him at the last minute and he forbade Treskow to initiate action against Hitler's life. The picture of the Führer's being shot out of his chair by a squad of Wehrmacht officers firing automatic pistols in the middle of lunch was more than Kluge could stomach. He further argued that "neither the world, nor the German people, nor the German soldier would understand such an act at this time." Kluge's decision meant that Boeselager's commando unit would have to stand down as well.

But Treskow was not caught short. For weeks he and Schlabrendorff had been experimenting with British plastic explosives and silently burning fuses provided by the Abwehr. The latest batch of explosives smuggled to Treskow included several metal and plastic containers known as clams: largely hollow objects measuring 5¾" x 2¾" x 1½", about the size of a thick paperback book. The British had designed these clams for use by saboteurs, and the metal bases were magnetized so that they could be slapped against anything metal and would stick. The Nobel 808 plastic explosive had the consistency of fresh taffy at room temperature; it was easy to stuff the material inside the clams, and easier still to insert time fuses of various sorts. Treskow and Schlabrendorff were delighted with the clams and planned to use them to blow Hitler out of the sky.

Kluge's headquarters, like every other German HQ, was liberally stocked with captured French wines and spirits, and it occurred to Schlabrendorff that when two clams were stuck together baseplate to baseplate, the resulting shape very much resembled a Cointreau bottle. He and Treskow got four clams and stuffed them with plastic, fashioning two bombs by mating pairs magnetically, then securing them with heavy tape. A fuse was inserted, then the devices were wrapped in kraft paper and bound with twine. The resulting package looked like and had the heft of a pair of Cointreau bottles packed and ready for travel.

Schlabrendorff hid the package in his quarters to await the coming of Adolf Hitler.

Shortly before noon on March 13, the thunder of engines overhead drew Kluge's welcoming committee outside. Three Focke-Wulf Condors, lean, elegant, four-engined airliners, banked gently into the wind with gear down and approached the airstrip. A gaggle of escorting Me.109 fighters buzzed overhead. The Condors landed first and taxied down the runway to make room for the incoming fighters, Hitler's airborne bodyguard. The exit hatch of Condor 2600 was flung open, and Hitler marched down the ladder and into a waiting car. Aides, stenographers, SS guards, staff officers, and a photographer poured out of the other planes to join the motorcade headed for Kluge's headquarters. They drove down a narrow road becoming slushy with an early thaw, past ranks of Boeslager's men, whose fingers itched for the triggers of their automatic weapons.

Following a war conference, Hitler and his entourage joined Kluge and his staff for lunch. Schlabrendorff observed the Führer's table manners: "His left hand was placed firmly on his thigh; with his right hand he shoveled his food, which consisted of various vegetables, into his mouth. He did this without lifting his right arm, which he kept flat on the table throughout the meal, bringing his mouth down to the food instead." Hitler, a few weeks away from his fifty-fourth birthday, looked older. His face was pale and drawn, his eyes protruded, he hunched forward in his chair, and tremors ran through his hands when they were at rest. Still, he remained in nervous good humor throughout the meal, prophesying great victories in Russia for the coming year.

The luncheon ended, and Hitler announced that he must be off at once for his headquarters in East Prussia. After everybody had left the table, Treskow went with Schlabrendorff to his quarters to fetch the bomb package from its warm hiding place. Then he grabbed a staff car and drove out to the airfield. Hitler was just getting ready to board the aircraft Schlabrendorff shot a glance at Treskow, standing with Kluge near the ladder. Treskow answered with his eyes. Schlabrendorff surreptitiously pressed

down on the fuse with the help of a heavy door key and handed
the package to Colonel Heinz Brandt, one of Hitler's aides, who
had agreed to deliver the "Cointreau" to General Helmuth Stieff,
a friend of Treskow's at Rastenburg. Hitler and the others
boarded the silver Condors, the hatches were slammed, and they
roared down the runway in the wake of the fighters. Treskow and
Schlabrendorff hurried back to HQ to put through a coded telephone call to Berlin that Operation Flash was under way. Treskow had selected a thirty-minute fuse, and they calculated that
Condor 2600 would be blown apart in the sky sometime before it
overflew Minsk, 200 miles southwest of Smolensk. Only charred
bits and pieces would remain, and it would seem that Hitler and
his party had met with one of those inexplicable accidents in the
air.

The Condors and their escort droned through the cold winter
sky. Inside the cockpit of 2600, Major Hans Bauer, Hitler's pilot,
kept a light hand on the wheel and his eyes on the gauges. The
fuel mixture and the throttles were set for maximum cruising
speed of just over 200 mph. Bauer had no worries about fuel; that
was the thing with these FW.200s, lean the fuel mixture right
back and you could fly 2,200 miles nonstop. This feature made
the Condors the terror of Allied Atlantic convoys trying to reach
Murmansk loaded with American tanks and trucks. Even with
the extra weight of the armor plate aboard for the Führer's protection, Bauer's Condor had more range than he would ever need.

In the Führer's compartment Hitler was conferring with General Alfred Jodl while the others in the party stretched their legs,
wishing for a smoke and hoping the cabin would not suffer its
usual failure of the heating system.

Inside the package Colonel Brandt had accepted from Schlabrendorff the corrosive acid was doing its work, eating away the
retaining wire as the Condor ate up the miles. Then the wire
snapped apart, releasing the firing pin that slammed forward into
the detonator.

Treskow and Schlabrendorff drove back to their quarters and
watched the minute hands on their watches crawl. In Berlin Gen-

eral Olbricht waited for the call that would spring his troops into action. In the Abwehr offices on the Tirpitzufer, Captain Ludwig Gehre paced the floor, his ears cocked for the ringing of the telephone and Schlabrendorff's coded message that Operation Flash was a success. Tension mounted as time ground forward. An hour passed, then two.

Finally the telephone rang in Treskow's office. The call was from Rastenburg to report the Führer's safe arrival with no incidents en route. Treskow and his aide were stunned, at a loss to understand the failure. Schlabrendorff got through to Gehre and told him Flash had failed. Schlabrendorff and Treskow were in a "state of indescribable agitation." Suppose the bomb was discovered by Brandt or Stieff, neither of whom was privy to their assassination plans. The discovery would trigger an investigation that would cost the lives of all of the conspirators, that would send their friends and families to concentration camps. Treskow risked a call to Colonel Brandt at Rastenburg and made a joke out of having sent along the wrong package for Colonel Stieff. Somebody would be along on tomorrow's courier plane to retrieve the package and exchange it for the right one.

Schlabrendorff was airborne early the next morning, praying that Brandt's curiosity would not get the better of him before he arrived with the real bottles of Cointreau. Entering Brandt's office, Schlabrendorff nearly had heart failure when he saw Brandt casually tossing the packaged bomb back and forth from one hand to the other. He quickly retrieved it and handed the colonel the other package, apologizing for the mix-up. Brandt wanted to chat, but Schlabrendorff was burning to get out of the office and away from Hitler's headquarters where he could examine the bomb in private to see what had gone wrong.

Schlabrendorff finally extricated himself and headed for the nearby railroad station at Korschen where he had reservations for a private sleeping compartment aboard a special OKW train leaving for Berlin.

Schlabrendorff entered his compartment, locked the door, and sat down to examine the bomb. Carefully removing the wrapping paper and gingerly extracting the fuse, he saw that the acid capsule had fractured, that the wire was eaten through, and that the firing pin had been activated. But the detonator had been a dud. They had come so close! Hitler owed his life to some careless British munitions worker and to some bored inspector who had stamped the detonator as operational and let it leave the factory.

The conspirators believed they were ready to strike again only a week later—this time in Berlin, and in view of ranking Nazi officials and upper echelons of the Wehrmacht. Hitler would be blown to smithereens with the arms of the assassin wrapped firmly around his Führer.

Colonel Rudolf-Christoph von Gersdorff, the Abwehr's permanent representative at the headquarters of Army Group Center, volunteered for the suicide mission to Treskow at Smolensk. He told Treskow that since his wife died a year ago life had lost much of its meaning, and he was willing to blow himself up if it meant a better future for the Fatherland.

Gersdorff planned to capitalize upon the Führer's presence at the annual Heroes Memorial Day ceremonies in the capital, an event Hitler religiously attended to pay tribute to the dead of Germany's wars. Gersdorff learned that prior to the official ceremony Hitler had agreed to visit the Zeughaus, the Berlin armory, to inspect a mass of captured Russian arms and equipment; Hitler took a keen interest in the tools of warfare and could be expected to spend at least a half-hour browsing amond the Red Army's tactical weapons. Since the various items of the exhibit were all taken from Army Group Center's front, it was only natural that an officer of Kluge's command be on hand, ready to answer the Führer's usual probing technical questions.

Gersdorff's first problem was to cope with Hitler's well-known propensity to change his mind and his schedules at the last minute; the second was the maddening quest for the right fuse to trigger the explosion. Treskow went to work on the first obstacle by calling Hitler's aide, Colonel Schmundt, who was not overly bright but was dog-loyal. He admitted that Hitler had postponed Heroes Memorial Day from March 15 to 21 for unknown reasons, but more than that Schmundt would not say. Treskow told Gersdorff to go ahead and fly to Berlin and try to prise details from

Schmundt when Hitler's party arrived in the capital. Treskow had already called Schlabrendorff with instructions to turn over the explosive-laden clams to Gersdorff.

Gersdorff arrived in Berlin on the twentieth in the company of the Ninth Army's Commander, Field Marshal Walther Model. They went straightaway to confront Schmundt, who at first bristled with arrogant self-importance. No, he could not reveal the Führer's precise schedule, and in any case Gersdorff had no need of the information because his name did not appear on the list of those permitted inside the Zeughaus at the same time as the Führer. Then Field Marshal Model unwittingly became Gersdorff's accomplice when he brought the weight of his rank to bear against Schmundt and persuaded him to spell out the day's schedule and to add Gersdorff's name to the list.

Now Gersdorff considered the question of the right fuse to set off his bombs. What he wanted were zero-delay fuses, but incredibly none could be secured. He rejected the half-hour British fuses as being impractical and, in view of the failure a week earlier, not trustworthy. Somebody suggested that the fuse belonging to the standard German potato-masher grenade might be suitable; the burning time was only 4.5 seconds, nearly ideal for the purpose, but the fuse would not fit inside the clam. Gersdorff was left with no option except to use British fuses with a ten-minute delay. He inserted these fuses into the two bombs with misgivings and set off for the armory and his rendezvous with the Führer. If things went as he planned, Gersdorff knew he had less than two hours to live.

Hitler was scheduled to arrive at the Zeughaus at 1:00 P.M. Gersdorff was there an hour earlier, a bomb on each of his greatcoat pockets. The armory was already beginning to fill. Several hundred war wounded were seated in folding chairs. A military band was turning up at one end of the hall. Gersdorff noted that SS guards and plainclothes SD were everywhere. Hitler arrived shortly before one and swept inside the armory, followed in train by several field marshals and admirals.

Gersdorff waited nervously in front of some Russian war

equipment while Hitler raced through his speech. He ran through his mind the expected sequence of events: Hitler would wind up his talk, Gersdorff would set his fuses, noting the exact time on his watch. The Führer would tour the exhibit, with Gersdorff at his heels to answer questions. When the sweep-second hand passed the ten-minute mark he would make his move: lunge forward and wrap his hands around Hitler's upper body in the clasp of death. There would be a struggle, but on this point Gersdorff had no qualms; he was not large, but lithe and toughened from a lifetime spent in the open—more than a match for the Führer, who stood but five feet seven and whose exercise was limited to walking his dog outside his bunker at Rastenburg. If the fuse worked, they would disappear in a blinding sheet of flame, and Gersdorff's mission would be accomplished.

Hitler ended his speech abruptly; the tirade had lasted less than fifteen minutes. He acknowledged the applause, then started walking toward Gersdorff, who risked placing his hand in one of his greatcoat pockets to crush the acid capsule. He shot a glance at his watch, then had to hurry to catch up with the Führer and his party, for Hitler was leading them a brisk pace. Hitler was crowded in by Göring, Himmler, Field Marshal Keitel, and Admiral Karl Donitz. If they interfered at the climactic moment, he would get them all.

Contrary to everything Gersdorff expected, Hitler fairly raced through the exhibit hall as though being pursued by demons. Gersdorff vainly tried to interest him in this Russian machine gun, that Soviet land mine, but Hitler plowed straight ahead, his eyes fixed on the exit doors now looming up. How Gersdorff wished for an instantaneous fuse! A grab at the Führer with one hand, a push with the other, and it would be all over. Hitler marched out of the armory and into the gray afternoon open air. out of reach.

Gersdorff frantically looked at his watch—two minutes had gone by, the acid was eating at the wire. He searched for a place where he could be alone to deactivate the fuse. Finally he spotted the door to a men's room and tried the handle. It was unlocked. He entered a stall, pulled the live bomb from his left-hand pocket, and hurriedly extracted the shell of the casing that held the acid. Seated in the toilet stall with the now-useless bomb in his lap, Gersdorff felt as defeated as a man could ever be.

He was on his way back to Russia the next day, and when he arrived at Smolensk he turned over the much-traveled British bombs to Treskow for possible use on another day, by another man.

10

Silent Pistol, Silent Bomb

THE ABWEHR MANAGED to keep its plans for a coup d'état secret for four years, from 1939 to 1943. But finally a chance arrest brought wreckage to General Oster's machinery of conspiracy, and the High Command had to carry on alone.

One of Oster's sidelines was funneling German Jews out of the country to Switzerland under the guise of Abwehr agents. The scheme was given Canaris's backing, and the operational details were put in the hands of Oster's chief deputy, Hans Dohnanyi, who was not only an experienced jurist but a skilled manipulator of books as well. The Jews, sometimes entire families, went on the rolls as counterintelligence agents, and money was siphoned from the Abwehr budget to recompense them partially for Nazi seizure of their homes, furnishings, and bank accounts.

One of these escapees was arrested in Czechoslovakia by a customs agent, and a search turned up $400 in American currency. The case was routinely reported to Gestapo HQ in Munich, where the victim was rigorously interrogated. He surprised his inquisitors by explaining that he worked for the Abwehr. The money, he said, had been given to him by Herr Wilhelm Schmidhuber there in Munich.

Schmidhuber, the exporter who had acted as go-between during the Vatican exchanges in 1940, quickly broke down under relentless questioning by "Gestapo" Müller and told him everything he knew, pointing the finger directly at Dohnanyi in Berlin.

Here, Müller thought, was a long-awaited opportunity to bring disgrace to the Abwehr and ingratiate himself with Himmler, who had always been jealous of Abwehr prerogatives; Himmler had been seeking ways to destroy the Abwehr for years in order to exercise absolute control over both military and political security services.

Because the Abwehr was a military agency sheltered under the army's wing, the Gestapo was powerless to move against it. This barrier was broken through when Müller turned the case over to the Reich Military Court for investigation by Judge Advocate Manfred Roeder, a fervent pro-Nazi who had recently sentenced his ninety-fifth victim to death for speaking out against the war and the Führer.

Early on the morning of April 5, 1943, Roeder and a Gestapo "observer" descended upon Canaris's office in the Tirpitzufer and confronted Oster with a warrant for Dohnanyi's arrest and a search of his office. Oster sprung to his feet and said that if any arrests were to be made they could start with him because his subordinates' Abwehr activities were carried out under his orders. Roeder answered that this was not an Abwehr affair, but a private charge against Dohnanyi for violation of currency regulations. The row brought Canaris out of his office to intervene. He looked at the warrant and, assuming that Dohnanyi had the good sense not to keep incriminating material at hand, told Roeder to go ahead.

Roeder and the Gestapo agent barged into Dohnanyi's office followed by Oster and Canaris. Dohnanyi was dumbfounded; his desk was littered with files and loose papers, and his office safe contained documents that could send him and others to a concentration camp. Roeder brusquely began to rifle the safe, grabbing papers and folders and dumping them on the desk. The others stood around as though watching an autopsy: Canaris in one corner, silver-haired, wearing his dark-blue admiral's uniform; Oster, near the desk, dressed impeccably in a civilian suit; Dohnanyi, standing by his chair, staring through steel-rimmed glasses; the Gestapo agent in a long leather coat, his eyes fixed on Oster, who seemed petrified.

Oster gazed at a file folder marked with a code letter—a file containing notes on plans for secret peace overtures to be advanced in Sweden and again in Rome, and details on Dohnanyi's Jewish operatives in Switzerland that included amounts of monies involved. Roeder's back was turned. Oster moved toward the desk to grab the folder. The Gestapo agent cried out, Roeder wheeled around, and it was all over. The investigators not only had damning evidence of Dohnanyi's currency irregularities and safe-harboring of Jews but had stumbled upon material of far-reaching political, if not treasonable, significance.

As a result of Dohnanyi's carelessness, he was thrown in prison; his wife was arrested and jailed; and Josef Müller—their man in Rome—was seized along with his wife and imprisoned, as was Dietrich Bonhoeffer, a Protestant minister working with the Abwehr to feel out peace negotiations with the Allies. The conspiracy could bear these losses, but hardly that of Oster, who was relieved of duty and later cashiered. Field Marshal Keitel, chief of staff at OKW, sent Oster a blistering letter. "I herewith expressly forbid you," he wrote, "to have any official or private contact with the Abwehr and its members, and I order you to avoid making any attempt at such approaches, either consciously or unconsciously." Canaris, for the moment, was spared suspicion.

Dohnanyi's great fear was being turned over to the Gestapo for interrogation; he knew their methods would soon break him down, force him to reveal the hiding place of even more incriminating documents—Müller's dealings with the Vatican, details of the various plans to assassinate the Führer. These papers, plus a meticulously detailed dossier of SS crimes, were stored in a cellar at army headquarters at Zossen, one of Berlin's western suburbs.

Dohnanyi used his lawyer's skills to duel with his military inquisitors inside Berlin's Tegel Prison. He stalled for time, providing false leads, creating an eccentric fabric woven of partial truths and lies difficult to check. The intense struggle lasted for months until Dohnanyi finally collapsed from the strain and from the terrible weight of the secrets he kept locked up inside. His warders confined him to a Wehrmacht hospital, and when he seemed on the verge of recovery, he decided to infect himself with a new ailment to avoid going to trial. His wife, Christine, smuggled dysentery bacilli into his room; when this failed to work she brought in diptheria cultures, which were effective.

Dohnanyi eventually wound up in the hands of the SS and was hauled off to a concentration camp, along with Müller and Bonhoeffer, but none of them ever confessed to more than Roeder and the Gestapo already knew. Ironically, the Abwehr offices on the Tirpitzufer were destroyed during a nighttime air raid not long after Dohnanyi's seizure. The Abwehr files went up in flames from British bombs, but too late to obviate Dohnanyi's initial carelessness.

Despite the attrition in the Canaris group, there still remained a tenuous line of communication open between the conspirators and the Western allies. Late in 1942 the U.S. State Department dispatched Allen Welsh Dulles, fifty, to Switzerland to head a branch of the Office of Strategic Services. Dulles's primary mission was the gathering of military and political intelligence. His superior, General William "Wild Bill" Donovan, told him to find out "if there were any underground anti-Nazi movements in Germany," and if so to get what details he could so that the situation could be exploited.

Dulles was soon in touch with Hans Gisevius, who had exiled himself in Zurich, with the Gestapo in hot pursuit, shortly after Dohnanyi's arrest. The scholarly, pipe-smoking American was impressed with the much younger Gisevius, who "looked more like a learned professor of Latin or Greek than a member of the most dangerous profession in the world—a conspirator in the German underground. He was not the type of man who could easily pass unnoticed. Six feet four and built to proportion, we called him 'Tiny.' "

Gisevius was just as taken with Dulles, "the first [foreign] intelligence officer who had the courage to extend his activities to the political aspects of the war. . . . Everyone breathed easier; at last a man had been found with whom it was possible to discuss the contradictory complex of problems emerging from Hitler's war."

Dulles and Gisevius would rendezvous either in Zurich or in Berne—the towns were less than sixty miles apart—where the German would pass along what he knew. The two men walked the blacked-out streets late at night, their conversations muted, their movements cloaked in darkness. Gisevius confided details of the abortive attempts on Hitler's life, and said he was sure the plotters within the Wehrmacht would try again. Dulles, code-naming future assassination attempts *Breakers*, related all Gisevius's information to Washington, where it created not even a flicker of interest.

Gisevius refused to become discouraged; he continued to feed updated news from inside Germany to Dulles as fast as it came in, and just as doggedly Dulles fired off one encoded cablegram after another to the United States. Gisevius turned over a 700-page manuscript to Dulles containing the history of the German underground, which was sent to Washington via diplomatic pouch. There was no response. Dulles felt that he might as well be shoveling this valuable intelligence material into the legation's furnace. Despite Washington's baffling apathy, these two men, whose goals were identical, continued their relationship throughout the war.

With the Abwehr rendered useless as a resistance tool, and with the West indifferent to Germany's underground and bent on military destruction of the Reich, a new sense of urgency seized the army High Command for Hitler's liquidation. Things started badly for the Wehrmacht in the summer of 1943 and continued to slide downhill afterward. In July, Hitler launched a great tank of-fensive, Operation *Citadel*, that turned into a costly failure. That same month saw the British and the Americans swarming ashore in Sicily, which fell within a month. In September, the Allies were ashore in Italy and could not be thrown back into the sea. Mussolini was ousted; Italy surrendered. Bomber Command con-tinued to burn German cities by night, and the U.S. Eighth Air Force stepped up its precision attacks on German industry by day, the one-two punches turning the Fatherland into a lunar-scape of ruin. Hitler's ally, the Japanese, were being beaten back everywhere in the Pacific, and the Russian steamroller was poised at the edges of East Prussia. Lookouts on the Channel coast watched for signs of an Allied armada that sooner or later would darken the horizon to disgorge British, Americans, French, Poles, Norwegians, Danes, Canadians, Belgians, and Dutch coming armed to extract vengeance on the continent. The conspirators hoped that with the liquidation of Hitler and the replacement of the Nazis by a conservative government, they might successfully conclude peace with the West and stave off the Russians before they penetrated Reich frontiers. With every day that passed, action against the Führer became more imperative.

By summer 1943 the conspiracy was a revolt looking for a leader. Henning von Treskow had taken extended leave and was living in the wreckage of Berlin to be closer to the scene of the intended action, but he was not yet a general and his weight alone could not exert enough pressure on the right levers. General Ludwig Beck was slowly recovering from a cancer operation and remained in the picture largely as an adviser. Needed was the wholehearted cooperation of an energetic frontline commander of armies. Once again an approach was made to Field Marshal von Kluge at Army Group Center. While on a visit to Hitler's HQ at Rastenburg, Kluge was cornered by Colonel Helmuth Stieff, recipient of the "Cointreau" bomb. Stieff was chief of the Organization Section of the General Staff in Berlin. His arguments were buttressed during a meeting in Berlin a short time afterward with Treskow, Beck, General Olbricht, and the indefatigable Goerdler. At last Kluge committed himself to removing Hitler by force.

Five weeks later, in the midst of planning for the takeover, Kluge's staff car was involved in a smash-up, and the general was sent to hospital with severe injuries. He lay for weeks in traction, swathed in bandages, useless to the others. They decided to go ahead anyway.

A volunteer assassin, Captain Axel von dem Bussche, was quickly located inside the command of that bastion of military conservatism, the 9th Infantry Regiment at Potsdam. A glance at von dem Bussche's tunic revealed that its wearer was unaccustomed to serving in a rear-echelon command; the field-gray cloth was festooned with decorations and wound badges earned in combat on the Russian front. A Russian bullet through the lungs had put Bussche temporarily out of action at the age of twenty-three.

Captain von dem Bussche was as determined to get rid of Hitler as he had been to kill the Fúhrer's military enemies. The motivation had been provided by an experience in Russia as a company commander. His regiment had just taken the Ukrainian town of Dubno, and Bussche was resting his men on the cratered airfield outside of town. An SS Einsatzgruppe appeared, herding a long column of shabbily dressed townspeople, many of them carrying picks and shovels. Bussche got to his feet to watch a huge pit dug by the side of the airfield. Then the civilians, all of them Jews, were forced to remove their clothing and stand uncertainly in the biting October wind. "These men, women, and children lined up naked," Bussche remembered, "and lay down in their own mass grave. There they were shot, one by one, regardless of whether the person underneath was dead or alive." Afterward Bussche was ashamed that he had done nothing to stop the wanton murders, ashamed of having sworn fealty to a mass murderer. Bussche now rejected the Führer oath because "the Führer himself had broken the oath to God a thousand times." When Bussche was approached with the opportunity to liquidate mankind's archenemy, he jumped at the chance, although he knew the attempt would claim his own life. In tyrannicide, justice; in self-destruction, expiation.

Bussche said that he was perfectly willing to gun down Hitler with a pistol, but others talked him out of the idea. For one thing, Hitler's close-in SS bodyguards would make it almost impossible to pull a handgun from his pocket, aim carefully, and fire. For another, everybody was convinced that the Führer wore a bullet-proof vest under his tunic, although the evidence for this supposition was superficial: Hitler always walked with a hunched-forward motion, as though bearing a heavy weight around the upper part of his body. The truth, known only to his personal physician, was that Hitler suffered from sciolosis, degeneration of the spine that was slowly increasing its curvature. Bussche said he would make every effort to succeed where Gersdorff had failed, using Gersdorff's own methods. He would embrace Hitler in a waltz of death with a hissing bomb in his pocket until they disappeared in a detonation.

Bussche realized that, as always, his main problem was getting close enough to Hitler to grapple with him. The mounting destruction of German cities from the air and the series of military reverses in Russia had turned Hitler into a recluse; he was almost never seen in public anymore, spending his time instead inside his bunker at Rastenburg surrounded by guards, machine guns, and barbed wire. He stayed holed up at the Wolf's Lair in East Prussia, immersed in Germany's military problems and pressing for the completion of new miracle weapons with which to overwhelm the Allies and reverse the tide of war now running against the Reich.

He appointed a new commander for the Wehrmacht in Italy, Field Marshal "Smiling Albert" Kesselring, to stave off the British-American forces readying themselves for an advance on Rome. He summoned Göring and General Adolf Galland, chief of the Luftwaffe fighter arm, and berated them for the Luftwaffe's failure to stop the marauding Allied bombers. Galland argued for stepped-up production of the sensational new Me.262 jet fighter, promising that with enough of the new jet interceptors he could create such havoc among the American B-17 daylight formations that they would soon have to cease operations. But Hitler exploded and said the Me.262s would be used for high-speed bombers only. The jets, he said, must be held in reserve against the day when the Allies decided to cross the Channel and make their move for the continent.

Hitler wrestled with the problem of reinforcements for the eastern front and reluctantly agreed that a quarter of a million German men would have to be withdrawn from industry, already short on manpower, and put into uniform. He puzzled over ways to keep neutral Turkey from falling into the Allied camp as an active belligerent, and he fretted over his inability to move heavy German forces into the Balkans following the Italian defection. He worried over the undercurrent of pro-Soviet feeling sweeping across Hungary and Rumania, and he had no answer to Goebbels's letter of November 2, 1943, which informed Hitler that "morale at the front was now lower than that at home."

By autumn 1943, Hitler could seek salvation only in the promise of a new technology. Missile technicians were at work at Peenemünde on the Baltic coast trying to make operational the short-range ballistic rocket, the A.4, with which to bombard London. Deeper inside Germany work was well along on the V.1 flying bomb, a pilotless, jet-propelled weapon carrying a one-ton warhead. These revolutionary weapons, Hitler believed, would bring British industry to a standstill, send British morale plummeting, and cause such damage to British ports that an invasion could never be mounted.

These problems, plus a great many others, kept the Führer fully occupied during his every working day, which usually began at noon and lasted until two or three the following morning. Bussche and his coconspirators wondered how Hitler could be brought into the open and his attention diverted long enough for the assassin to close in and strike. It was decided to try once again to exploit Hitler's unquenchable interest in the small details of tactical warfare.

The first years of winter war in Russia brought to light serious deficiencies in the German soldier's cold-weather combat uniform. In October 1943 the first experimental samples of new winter clothing were turned out, and the design would need the Führer's approval before general troop issue. Here, it seemed, was the perfect opportunity: Bussche would command a demonstration squad flown to Rastenburg to model the new gear for Hitler's inspection. If Hitler agreed to give even five minutes of his time, the proximity problem would be solved and Bussche's plan would stand an excellent chance of success.

While others began the wearying task of persuading Hitler to set a firm date for the modeling session, Bussche busied himself with the problem of putting together a bomb that would work without fail. He rejected the offer of British plastic and the silent ten-minute fuse, asking instead for two pounds of the more familiar German explosive. Through a Wehrmacht pioneer sergeant who asked no questions, Bussche obtained a live grenade, and he set about jury-rigging a fuse.

Bussche borrowed a small saw, a wood chisel, a pair of wire-cutters, and some pliers and in the privacy of his quarters began taking the grenade apart. German grenades were about a foot long and consisted of a cast-iron cylindrical head containing the explosive and fuse, the whole attached to a lathe-turned hollow wooden handle. In combat, one unscrewed a safety cap at the base of the handle to get at a pull cord that activated the fuse, then threw it end over end at the enemy. It would explode 4½ seconds later. When Bussche was finished sawing and chiseling, he laid bare the fuse and detonator, which fit perfectly into the explosive charge. He shortened the pull cord so that only a quick two-fingered jerk was needed to set the fuse burning. He realized that the grenade fuse burned with a clearly audible hissing noise, but counted on a simulated coughing fit to cover the sound just before he leaped upon the Führer.

Bussche gathered up his field equipment and the new bomb and left Berlin for East Prussia during the last week in November. He checked in at a subsidiary headquarters camp only ten miles distant from the Wolf's Lair, hid his bomb, and waited. He took long walks in the surrounding countryside, wondering how much longer he had to live. He later recalled, "In those sunny days of late autumn in the woods and lakeland, I had that premonition which a soldier has before the attack."

Hitler meanwhile had agreed to inspect the new uniforms, but as usual refused to be pinned down to a specific day. Colonel Stieff called up Bussche from the Wolf's Lair and told him he would have to be patient.

Back in Berlin, the harassed manager of the mill responsible for turning out the new uniforms managed to get together a dozen complete sets and find room for them aboard a train destined for Rastenburg. With the winter gear safely inside a boxcar sitting on a rail siding, and with the manifest properly rubber-stamped and countersigned, he considered his job finished. That night, along with every other Berliner, he was driven underground by the wail of sirens that heralded another saturation raid by the RAF.

High explosive and incendiary bombs rained down for hours. When the all-clear sounded, the city began counting the casualties and the damage. The railway network had been hit especially hard, and the boxcar containing Bussche's uniforms was a charred wreck resting on wheels turned orange by the fire.

There was nothing to do except to wait until the mill produced a fresh consignment. Bussche could not hang around the rear echelons while fighting raged to the east, despite his recent wound. He stowed the bomb in a musette bag, picked up his combat gear, and headed back for his old battalion. Stieff told him that when the Führer agreed upon a new inspection date, they would try to have Bussche pulled out of combat long enough to carry out the assassination.

But Bussche was never to have the chance at self-immolation. In January 1944, his battalion was caught in a tornado of Russian artillery shells and Bussche was blown into unconsciousness when an incoming round exploded nearby. He was taken to a field hospital where Wehrmacht surgeons amputated a shredded leg, leaving him alive but robbing him of his grand gesture.

To the disappointment of Bussche's failed rendezvous with Hitler was added the death blow to the Abwehr. On January 22, 1944, Hitler and his senior commanders were stunned by the unexpected landing of American divisions at Anzio, south of Rome. This end run caught the Germans flat-flooted, and Hitler flew into a rage, demanding of the Italian commander, Kesselring, how German military intelligence could be so slipshod. Kesselring defended himself by pointing out that rumors had indeed reached him of some unorthodox move by the Americans, but that Canaris had dismissed the rumors as nonsense. Hitler sharply reminded Kesselring that they "were completely surprised" by the landings in North Africa and in Sicily as well; what kind of agency was Canaris running, anyway?*

---

* A professional opinion of the caliber of Canaris's agents at this stage of the war and afterward has been given to the author by one who worked against them, then-Captain Walter Dodd Osborne, a twice-wounded field intelligence officer with the U.S. Third Army. Com-

Two weeks after the upsetting Anzio surprise, Hitler was handed a second jolt when Himmler informed him that the Abwehr's number-two man in Istanbul, Erich Vermehren, had defected to the British. Vermehen and his wife, the former Countess Elizabeth Plettenburg, disappeared into the Allied camp taking with them, so Himmler was told, the secret Abwehr codebooks. Taking a clue from Vermehen, the Abwehr agents in Sweden and Switzerland also defected. Canaris was fired on Hitler's order on February 12, and the Abwehr was wiped out of existence. Hitler ordered Himmler to absorb the Abwehr machinery into the SS, and control passed into the hands of General Walther Schellenberg. It was a clear-cut victory of the SS over the Wehrmacht, now the world's only army without its own intelligence organization.

On the morning of February 23 Hitler's special train moved ponderously onto the main tracks at Rastenburg. Two massive diesel engines in tandem pulled fifteen cars, including two special flak wagons, one forward and one aft, manned with handpicked 20-mm antiaircraft gunners. The engineers and the rest of the crew had been alerted only the night before that the Führer was leaving East Prussia, if only temporarily, and that the *Brandenburg*, as the train was now called, must be held in readiness for the 650-mile journey to Munich.

The Führer and his entourage pulled up in a convoy of sedans,

_____

mented Osborne: "The Abwehr was an old-fashioned, self-serving spy organization. Its operatives on the operational level were scummy little free-lancers. Many were pimps, burglars, forgers, and other common criminal types to whom spying was just another way of turning an illicit buck. I never ran across one who could be considered a patriot. Quite a few spied for both sides, not only because it was profitable to do so, but because it provided a sort of life insurance in that they could come up with some evidence that they were really on your side. . . . I am sure that we learned more about what was going on behind enemy lines from captured German agents than those who remained at large were able to supply to the Wehrmacht." It should not be forgotten that even when Canaris was supplied with hard intelligence that would help the Wehrmacht prolong the war, he more often than not failed to pass it along. Aside from its conspiratorial efforts to get rid of Hitler, the Abwehr was often a willing, if unpaid, tool of the Allies.

and Hitler marched across the snow and entered his private compartment. With everybody aboard, the diesels purred and the train began moving south. Hitler did not look forward to the journey, for the train would pass through one blasted German city after another—and he refused to raise the blinds to look at the damage. He was eager only to reach Munich, where his armored Mercedes would whisk him up the winding road to the still-untouched Berghof. This mountain retreat, seemingly removed from all reality, would be the site of the next assassination attempt.

This further move against Hitler was initiated by Henning von Treskow, now promoted to general and serving as chief of staff of the Second Army on the Russian front. The series of failures to liquidate the Führer, beginning with the "Cointreau" attempt the year before, in which Treskow had participated, only determined Treskow to try again, but this time with his own hand. Hitler no longer visited advanced headquarters in Russia, and Treskow could find no legitimate reason to visit the Wolf's Lair at Rastenburg. He repeatedly tried to arrange transfer to Führer headquarters, where he planned to execute Hitler with a pistol, but he was considered too valuable where he was, and his requests were denied. Kluge's replacement as commander of Army Group Center, Field Marshal Ernst Busch, was one of the few Wehrmacht senior commanders still fiercely loyal to Hitler, and any attempt to win him over to a conspiracy was out of the question.

Treskow was frustrated at every turn until he discovered that he had an ally in Busch's camp, Captain Eberhard von Breitenbuch, the field marshal's personal aide. On March 9, 1944, Busch summoned Breitenbuch and told him to prepare for a flight to Berchtesgaden; the Führer, Busch said, had ordered him to put in an appearance at the Berghof for a command briefing on the deteriorating conditions facing Army Group Center. Breitenbuch sought out Treskow and gave him the news, affirming that he stood ready to assassinate Hitler inside his own home. Treskow said that Breitenbuch "had it in his hands to spare Germany endless suffering at home and senseless sacrifice at the front." Treskow offered Breitenbuch a new kind of bomb with a one-second fuse, but the young officer declined, explaining that he was a crack shot with a pistol and wouldn't miss a head shot even at ten or fifteen meters *if* he could smuggle a handgun into the Führer's presence, and *if* he could clear the weapon from his pocket and hold it long enough to take aim.

Because Breitenbuch's assassination plan was simple and direct, no elaborate preparations were necessary. He checked a 7.65-mm automatic, which he slipped into a trouser pocket, but some personal effects into an envelope for delivery to his wife should his mission be successful, then gathered up the papers Field Marshal Busch would need for the Führer conference.

Busch and Breitenbuch flew to Germany and were picked up and chauffeured to the Obersalzberg by Hitler's driver. They reached the Berghof shortly before noon on March 11, 1944, and were kept waiting in the anteroom adjoining Hitler's sprawling reception room. Breitenbuch was already in a state of high nervousness, and wondered if the pistol, heavy in his pocket, was not obvious to even the most cursory glance. He placed his cap on a table put there for the purpose, where it joined the more spectacular caps belonging to Busch and Field Marshals Keitel and Jodl.

Finally as SS major appeared and said that the Führer would now receive the visitors. Breitenbuch took his place at the end of the queue, clutching the field marshal's heavy briefcase under one arm. Any second now he would be inside the great hall, in the presence of the Führer himself. Breitenbuch intended to make his move after the conference was well under way, when Hitler and the others were engrossed in conversation, when the SS guards were perhaps lulled by Hitler's inevitable monologue. In thirty minutes or an hour the course of history might be changed, if only Breitenbuch had a little luck.

But Breitenbuch's luck deserted him even before he got through the final door. Just as he was about to enter, the SS major held up his hand and said, "Today, please, no aides de camp." It was a clear command. Breitenbuch protested, and Field Marshal Busch explained that his aide was needed at his side. The SS major explained that it was a Führer order, not subject to question. Grumbling, Busch took his briefcase from Breitenbuch and walked through the heavy double doors, which were closed firmly behind him.

Breitenbuch now passed the most uncomfortable time of his life. He waited alone in the empty anteroom, feeling horribly conspicuous. Terrifying thoughts raced through his head. *Had Treskow's phone been tapped? Was the scheme known? Perhaps even now Treskow was arrested.* Breitenbuch jumped every time one of the SS guards passed through the room; he felt he was under surveillance, that he would be seized at any moment. He wondered frantically how he could get rid of the pistol in his pocket. Breitenbuch, a veteran of the Russian front for more than two years, had never felt more endangered. He was afraid he would fall to pieces.

His agony ended when the conference broke up early in the afternoon and the great doors swung open to allow Busch and the other field marshals to fan out into the anteroom for a round of farewells. Busch was in a pressing hurry to get back to Russia, and he and Breitenbuch paused in Germany only long enough for a hasty dinner before boarding a four-engined Condor that roared off the runway at Salzburg and headed east.

Neither Breitenbuch nor Treskow ever discovered why Hitler refused Breitenbuch's presence at the briefing. Obviously, had the assassination plan somehow been revealed, then Breitenbuch would have left the Berghof manacled to join Treskow in the dungeons. Was Hitler's action a fluke, or was it born of a premonition? They would never know. In any case, Breitenbuch later said he would rather face Russian divisions than undergo another afternoon like the one he had just spent.

But the plotters still doggedly kept on trying; and now the planning of Hitler's assassination would be taken over by a Wehrmacht officer of resource and determination.

11

Finis Initium

IN TUNISIA ON April 6, 1943, a small Volkswagen scout car bounced over the winding valley road leading to Sidi Mansour, a haphazard collection of Arab mud huts not far behind German lines and the temporary headquarters of the 10th Panzer Division. The car's only passenger, Lieutenant Friedrich Zipfel, twenty-two, clung to the edge of the metal seat with one hand and to part of the fold-down windshield with the other while the hard-sprung vehicle fought its way forward over the primitive road surface made slippery with spring rains. Zipfel and his driver could hear the whine and crash of incoming artillery rounds up ahead, and Zipfel guessed correctly that the remnants of the 10th were being shelled by American guns.

Zipfel ordered the driver to half in the lee of a hill until the shelling stopped, then they drove the remaining few hundred yards to reach an olive grove east of the village where the divisional command post was located. Zipel dismounted, observed by Afrika Korps veterans who were climbing out of holes, brushing dust from their uniforms. Zipfel approached a caravan under the olive trees, knocked on the door, and went inside.

He was greeted by the 10th Panzer's senior staff officer for operations, Lieutenant Colonel Count Claus Philipp Maria Schenk von Stauffenberg, who was thirty-five but looked younger. Stauffenberg casually acknowledged Zipfel's salute and continued sweeping glass splinters and fresh dollops of mud off the maps stretched across the trestle tables inside the caravan. Stauffenberg led Zipfel to a blown-out window and pointed outside to a pair of foxholes. "If that starts again," he said, "you take the right one and I'll take the left."

Zipfel noted that Stauffenberg was tall and lean, not robust but with an equestrian's build; he had an air of youthfulness imparted by short, thick, metallic black hair and a firm mouth seemingly on the verge of rippling into laughter. Heavy brows shaded dark-blue eyes alive with intelligence. With his firm jaw, straight nose, and small ears, Stauffenberg looked like the aristocrat he was, although he was indifferently uniformed in loosely fitting American-style slacks and a faded khaki shirt adorned only with badges of rank.

When Zipfel observed that he had arrived in Tunisia just in time to be taken prisoner, Stauffenberg laughed and said, "That's it. That will be the end of the war for us." Stauffenberg spoke realistically: 300,000 fighting men and support troops of the Afrika Korps and the Italian First Army were penned in an enclave sixty miles wide and barely twenty miles deep, their backs to the sea. Field Marshal Erwin Rommel was gone, invalided back home with jaundice, and Hitler's orders remained firm: they must hold out to the last man, the last bullet.

Stauffenberg and his commander, General Friedrich von Broich, had watched their division grind itself to pieces in two fruitless and costly attacks against the U.S. 1st Armored Division southeast of El Guetter. The 10th Panzer Division had been fighting its way backward ever since.

By daybreak of April 7 the division was disengaged from the Americans and was making its way slowly northward along Gumtree Road, which led to Tunis. Stauffenberg and Broich stood by their command cars near a hillside watching what was left of the division move down the road in a parade of defeat. When the greater part of the division had rolled past, the general turned to Stauffenberg and said it was time to head back and prepare for the next probing American attacks. They would travel in separate vehicles, Broich said, in the interest of the division; Broich's predecessor and the division's deputy commander had both been maimed when their command car struck a British mine.

Stauffenberg and his driver climbed into their car and disappeared in the rolling country beyond. An hour later Broich swung himself into his own vehicle and started north. He left behind him only empty hills.

At Sbeitla, sixty miles to the southeast, a gaggle of American P-40F fighters roared down the runway, climbed into the air, and flew north. The 33rd Fighter Group, under the command of Lieutenant Colonel William W. Momyer, had been in action since the first days of the North African invasion. For five months Momyer's pilots had been bombing and shooting up ground targets in support of their own armor and infantry, and they were experts in search-and-destroy missions.

The 10th Panzer Division was caught strung out on the road where it crossed an open plain. The fighters fell on the column in a cab-rank of destruction. The pilots were down so low they could make out facial details of the Germans who fled left and right like flushed quail. Some of the German tank crews fired back with light machine guns, but the P-40s whipped overhead at better than 400 feet per second, and the fire was ineffective.

General von Broich flung himself out of the car and zigzagged away from the column. Heavy .50-caliber slugs tore into the thin-skinned trucks, ricocheted in singing straight lines of flight off the German tanks, and tore up cupfuls of dirt where they slammed into the road. The fighters came again and again until they had expended approximately 30,000 rounds of ammunition; they they wheeled in the sky and disappeared. Broich got back on his feet and hurried back to his car. He ordered the driver forward to see what damage had been done to the rest of the column. He found Stauffenberg's Volkswagen leaning askew at the side of the road with both doors flung open. The car was heavily punctured with half-inch holes and smelled of raw fuel. Congealing blood covered the front seat and was splashed against the dashboard and the shattered windscreen.

It seemed unlikely that Stauffenberg could have survived the machine gunning. Even so, Broich surmised, Stauffenberg's services would be lost to him for the rest of the campaign, which Stauffenberg referred to as "another of the Führer's lost causes."

Broich got back in his car and drove off down the road to Tunis.

Stauffenberg survived the American guns, but barely. He was hurried to a military hospital at Carthage, and when he was wheeled out of surgery he was missing his left eye, his right hand, and the third and fourth fingers on his left. The doctors held little hope that Stauffenberg would ever be fit for duty again, especially since vision in his right eye was also threatened. When the immediate crisis passed, Stauffenberg was airlifted to Munich, along with other badly wounded troops, and hospitalized. The wounds became infected, and he remained delirious for weeks; doctors told his wife, Nina, he might not pull through. When the fever lapsed, Stauffenberg began to mend and was able to withstand the surgical shocks of successive head and leg operations. Vision to his remaining eye returned, and the day came when he sat up in bed and asked for pen and paper to learn to write with the two fingers and thumb on his left hand.

Stauffenberg stayed in the military hospital until early summer, more than three months after the strafing attack. It was the longest period of idleness in his career. A staunch Catholic, Stauffenberg reached the conclusion that his life had been spared to fulfill a mission of critical importance to mankind: destiny had chosen him as the prime mover in Hitler's overthrow by assassination, while Germany's frontiers were still unviolated, while there was still time to salvage the vestiges of honor rightfully belonging to a once-great Fatherland. He told his fellow officers, "As General Staff officers we must all share the burden of responsibility . . . I could never look the wives and children of the fallen in the eye if I did not do something to stop this senseless slaughter."

Stauffenberg, who could trace his Swabian ancestry back for nearly seven centuries, had not always wanted to be a professional soldier—but he had wanted to excel at whatever he put his hand to. Raised in a towering Renaissance castle near Stuttgart, the young count at first considered architecture, but he felt that his drawings were not good enough. He took up the cello; he was talented enough to perform in salons but realized he could never become a virtuoso. He was a passionate reader of classic literature but had no wish to become an academician, explaining, "I am interested in men—not ideas." He was too forthright in manner and careless of external trappings to be a diplomat, which left soldiering as the only worthwhile alternative. In 1926, when he was nineteen, he joined the elite 17th Cavalry Regiment, where he first began earning a reputation for astuteness, diligence, a penetrating curiosity, and arrogance mitigated by a deep sense of *noblesse oblige* toward noncoms and fellow officers less gifted than himself.

Initially, like 95 percent of Germans his age, he greeted Hitler's rise to power with a certain enthusiasm. The new Führer promised a resurgence of national pride, an elevation of the economy, and a Wehrmacht capable of dealing with Germany's natural enemies to the east. Stauffenberg had respect for Hitler's seeming military genius during the Polish and French campaigns, but he held the low intellectual capacity and bourgeois behavior of the Führer and his entourage in contempt. While serving in Russia in 1942, Stauffenberg finally realized that Hitler was leading them all to perdition. He turned to another staff officer, Lieutenant Colonel Burkhart Müller-Hillebrand, and cried out, "Is there no officer over there in the Führer's headquarters capable of taking his revolver to the brute?" Müller-Hillebrand was startled; he had never heard Stauffenberg speak that way before.

The military surgeons wanted Stauffenberg to remain on extended leave so they could fit him with a glass eye and a carefully wrought artificial hand. Stauffenberg was not interested in these cosmetic touches, wanting only to involve himself in direct action against Hitler as quickly as possible. He settled for a traditional black eye patch and a pinned-up sleeve, and learned to dress himself using three fingers and his teeth. He wore on the third finger of his left hand a broad gold ring embossed with the legend, *Finis Initium* (Finish What You Begin), which summed up his credo.

Stauffenberg secured a posting as chief of staff of the General Army Office in Berlin, working under General Friedrich Olbricht, who was already committed to the conspiracy. Olbricht's organization was part of the Home Army, commanded by General Friedrich Fromm, a fat, indolent man not inclined to risk his neck so long as Hitler remained in power. Stauffenberg's job was to find replacements for the troops being chewed up in Russia and in Italy and to somehow dredge up the manpower to create new battalions and regiments. His office in the Bendlerstrasse was at the heart of the Wehrmacht's planning and operations, and within easy reach of his older brother, Berthold, a lieutenant commander in the navy and also dedicated to the overthrow of the Nazis.

During late fall 1943 and spring 1944, Stauffenberg, Beck, Treskow, and Olbricht wrestled with the problem of how to eliminate Hitler and his régime while keeping Germany capable of action as a political and military power. The mere liquidation of Hitler and his top henchmen was not enough; they would have to be replaced overnight by a responsible government the Allies could not ignore. Otherwise, Germany would face internal chaos—possibly a civil war—as well as swift invasion from across the Channel; and nearly 8 million troops would be left in the lurch.

Stauffenberg first drew up an abbreviated list of conditions as a basis of negotiations with the Allies predicated upon a successful coup d'état. The conditions were hopelessly unrealistic, especially in view of the unconditional-surrender doctrine implacably laid down by Allied leaders at Casablanca early in 1943. Stauffenberg wanted the Allies to agree to:

1. Cessation of the bombing offensive against Germany
2. Abandonment of plans to invade the continent
3. Avoidance of further bloodshed
4. German evacuation of all conquered territories in the north, south, and west—but with Germany continuing to

function defensively in the east, i.e., to keep the Red Army at bay

5. A freely elected German government under a constitution chosen by Germans themselves
6. No Allied occupation of Germany
7. Full cooperation by Germany in fulfilling armistice conditions and in preparing the peacetime order in Europe
8. German withdrawal to the Reich frontiers of 1914; autonomy for Alsace-Lorraine; but retention of Austria and the Sudetenland within the Reich
9. Energetic reconstruction in Germany, with German help in the restoration of the rest of Europe
10. Germany to deal with her own war criminals
11. Restoration of German honor and self-respect, and restoration of Germany's standing in the world of nations

The cover plan for the seizure of Berlin by Wehrmacht forces within and near Berlin was a perversion of a plan originally drawn up by Olbricht and Canaris during the winter of 1941–42 and given Hitler's stamp of approval. Codenamed *Valkyrie*, the plan provided for activation of the Home Army to put down what Olbricht termed "internal unrest." Olbricht pointed out to Hitler that by the end of 1942 more than 4 million foreign workers and enemy prisoners of war would be within Reich frontiers, and that number would double by 1944, if the war lasted that long. He persuaded the Führer that this mass of aliens presented a possible source of danger to the Reich and could only be dealt with at short notice by whatever troops were available at the moment any uprising would take place. Olbricht updated Valkyrie to meet the constantly changing conditions, and when Stauffenberg arrived to help put the finishing touches to the plan, they believed they had just enough troops to occupy ten SS centers, ten government offices, and nine Party offices. Telegraphic centers and all broadcasting facilities would be seized at once. Skilled Wehrmacht broadcasters, chosen by Olbricht, would flash the startling message: "The Führer Adolf Hitler is dead! An unscrupulous clique of Party leaders, remote from the fighting front, has tried to exploit the situation, stab the struggling army in the back, and usurp power for their own selfish ends."

With the Wehrmacht declared executor of the Reich, an additional thirty-two objectives would be secured by the Valkyrie forces, the new provisional government installed, and the Stauffenberg armistice plan presented to the Allies. Stauffenberg agreed that Ludwig Beck should be named provisional head of state upon Hitler's death, but he quarreled with the notion that Goerdler should be the new Reich chancellor. In his opinion Goerdler was too middle-class, too conservative, a politician who would lead Germany back to the Weimar Republic days of splinter parties and lack of firm leadership, a period that set the stage for Hitler's sudden rise to the pinnacle. Stauffenberg commented that Goerdler was leading a "revolution of the graybeards"; for his part Goerdler thought the fiery younger officer was "arrogant, cranky, and pig-headed," and, being a military man, had no business meddling in political decisions. After several initial clashes, Stauffenberg had to concede that Goerdler had the depth of political experience that he himself lacked, and Goerdler realized that the conspiracy needed Stauffenberg's single-minded drive and capacity for making decisions. "After all," Beck explained to Goerdler, "Stauffenberg is our trigger."

General Fromm was so impressed with the organizational work Stauffenberg was doing for Olbricht that he pirated him away from Olbricht and appointed Stauffenberg as his own chief of staff. Stauffenberg at once saw the advantages in the new post: Fromm was frequently summoned before the Führer for conferences, which meant that Stauffenberg's presence would also be required. It was now becoming clear to Stauffenberg that the ultimate dirty work would be left in his hands. Crippled as he was, the use of a pistol against Hitler at close quarters was out of the question. He reached General Stieff at Rastenburg and asked that the British plastic explosive and fuses secreted there be smuggled to Berlin, where Stauffenberg would have it at hand, just in case.

Stauffenberg reported for duty with General Fromm on June 1, 1944, and at once made clear his attitude toward Hitler and his cohorts, hinting strongly that he and certain others planned drastic action to save what they could of Germany. Fromm only nodded, neither offering to help nor threatening to stand in the way. He did comment, however, "For God's sake don't forget that fellow Keitel when you make your putsch."

Four nights later swarms of American and British paratroopers and infantry-laden gliders descended upon France, and on the following morning, June 6, some 5,000 Allied ships stood off the coast of Normandy loosing a thunderous barrage to cover the assault on beaches named Utah, Omaha, Gold, Sword, and Juno. While D-Day was taking shape, Hitler was sound asleep in the master bedroom at the Berghof, his aides seeing no point in awakening the Führer until the situation had cleared later in the morning. By the time Hitler was up and dressed for the noon situation conference, the invaders had chewed their way inland two miles on a front fifteen miles wide. They kept coming ashore in the face of heavy small-arms fire, bothered only briefly by a pair of German Me. 109 fighters, all that the Luftwaffe could send them during the entire day.

The conspirators were caught as flatfooted as Hitler and the rest of the Wehrmacht; not one of them expected the invasion until July at the earliest. Before Stauffenberg had time to reflect upon what the invasion would mean to the plans for Hitler's overthrow, he found himself on the way to the Berghof in a converted He. 111 bomber with General Fromm to brief Hitler on the condition of the Home Army. They were ushered into the great hall, where Stauffenberg got his first close-up look at Hitler. He saw a man of fifty-five who looked much older; a man with a stooped back, sallow complexion, graying hair, whose right hand shook uncontrollably. Hitler now struck Stauffenberg as "a nothing"—yet the blue eyes still blazed with the fire of confidence born of the belief that he could push the Allies back into the sea, make them sue for peace when the perfected V.1 and V.2 rockets began raining down on England. Stauffenberg looked with distaste at the rotund Hermann Göring, whose face was made up with rouge and lipstick, and with revulsion at weak-chinned Heinrich

Himmler, whose eyes stared blankly from behind pince-nez glasses. To Stauffenberg, only Hitler's minister of armaments, Albert Speer, seemed normal. He later told his wife that the atmosphere generated by Hitler and his satraps was "rotten and degenerate," that Hitler and the others were "patent psychopaths." However, Stauffenberg came away from the Berghof encouraged by how easy it was to gain access to Hitler on official business; moreover, he was not searched, nor did the SS pry into the contents of his heavy pigskin briefcase.

Fighting raged deeper inside Normandy, and it was obvious that the Americans and the British were ashore in overwhelming strength that sooner or later would swamp the Wehrmacht. The Allies held absolute mastery of the air, so much so that desperately needed reinforcements could venture toward the beach only under cover of darkness. Later in that month of June the Russians surged out of their trenches behind a devastating bombardment and rolled through the creaking defenses of Army Group Center. Twenty-seven German divisions were smashed—350,000 men swallowed up in that Slavic wasteland. Rome had already fallen to the victorious American Fifth Army, and the Wehrmacht was everywhere in retreat.

Stauffenberg wondered what use it was to implement the Valkyrie plan now. He thought of General von Treskow, who had devoted heart and soul to Hitler's overthrow for so long, and got a message to him asking if the liquidation of the Führer could now serve any practical purpose.

Treskow sent his answer back from Russia immediately. He wrote: "The assassination must take place, cost what it will. Even if it does not succeed, the Berlin action must go forward. The point now is not whether the coup has any practical purpose, but to prove to the world and before history that German resistance is ready to stake its all. Compared to this, everything else is a side issue."

With this persuasive answer, the colonel went ahead with plans for Valkyrie. He enlisted the support of more than a hundred officers of all ranks into the conspiracy, largely through his own infectious enthusiasm and ability to make those in his company feel perfectly at ease.*

Treskow still clung to the hope that an accommodation could be reached with the Western powers. He urged Stauffenberg to hurry to France and persuade the senior commanders there to open the floodgates and let the Americans and the British pour through, all the way to the Reich forntiers, if necessary, anything to end the war in the west, to prevent additional hundreds of thousands of casualties, to bring an end to the ordeal by fire of German cities, to stop the chimneys at Auschwitz, Dachau, and Treblinka from belching their dreadful smoke.

Stauffenberg flew to Paris and saw an old friend, Colonel Eberhard Finckh, deputy chief of staff for Field Marshal Rommel's Army Group B. Stauffenberg laid out the details of Valkyrie, urging Finckh to confer with Rommel, who, Stauffenberg be-

---

*This charisma is revealed in the impressions of a young lieutenant of artillery, Urban Thiersch, who met Stauffenberg for the first time in the colonel's office in Berlin on July 1.

Thiersch found Stauffenberg "radiantly alive, and so self-assured that it made one think his serious mutilations did not handicap him in the least. . . . I was fascinated by his appearance. His complexion was fresh and healthy, his sound eye flashed unimpaired as if kindled by some fire from within. The other half of his face, with the black patch, was less active—yet it had peculiar power. Looking at him from that angle, only this part of his face gave Stauffenberg something remote, something monumental."

During their meeting, the telephone on Stauffenberg's desk rang; when Stauffenberg had dealt with the caller, he replaced the receiver in the cradle, turned to Thiersch, and said, "Let's get straight to the point. I am committing high treason with every means at my command." Then he explained to the awestruck lieutenant what was in the wind, pointing out that the chances for a successful coup were doubtful, but that passive acceptance of disgrace and paralyzing tyranny were far worse than simple failure.

Thiersch was converted on the spot. He felt that although "there was nothing hypnotic or mystical about Stauffenberg, he nevertheless had some unassailable power of genius which made one want him to be the leader, made one feel sure it would be wonderful to work with him, and for him."

lieved, was the exception to his conviction that "We have no real field marshals anymore—they all shake in their shoes and stand to attention when the Führer gives an order."

Finckh went straightaway to Rommel's HQ at La Roche-Guyon, west of Paris, and repeated Stauffenberg's words. Rommel said he could not abet in Hitler's assassination, but if he could not persuade the Führer that the game was up for Germany, then he would lend himself to Hitler's arrest and trial.

Rommel and Field Marshal Gerd von Rundstedt, who had befriended General von Fritsch in 1938 and who was commander-in-chief, West, and Rommel's superior, reached the Berghof on June 29 after an exhausting drive, mostly by night to avoid Allied fighter-bombers. Their attempts to point out the hopeless situation in Normandy were fruitless, however. Hitler fantasized about the new miracle weapons, and reminded them of how Frederick the Great held out to the last moment during the Seven Years' War. They must be firm, he said, they must have faith, they must not give way to pessimism. Rundstedt, sixty-eight, an aristocrat of the old school who always referred to Hitler as "that Bohemian corporal," wondered if Hitler was not going to bring up the story of Robert the Bruce and the spider to bolster their flagging spirits. Hitler dismissed both field marshals without even asking them to dinner before starting the long drive back to the front.

General von Rundstedt accepted a phone call the next day from the bewildered Field Marshal Keitel at the Berghof who asked Rundstedt what he should do about the conflict between Hitler and his generals. Rundstedt replied in his usual acerb manner, "What shall you do? You should put an end to the war, your idiots!"

Twenty-four hours later Rundstedt was sacked by Hitler, his job taken over by Field Marshal von Kluge. Primed by Hitler, Kluge stormed into HQ of Army Group B and engaged in an acrimonious exchange with Rommel over his pessimism and "willfulness." Rommel's deputy, General Hans Speidel, heard Kluge say: "You, too, Field Marshal Rommel, must obey unconditionally from now on. I give you fair warning!"

Walter Schellenberg, who
played a decisive role in the
abduction of British agents,
and whose marksmanship
was much in demand

Reichsführer SS Heinrich
Himmler, the chicken farmer who
became one of the most dreaded
men in the Third Reich

Himmler's extermination squads in Russia wantonly gunned down
civilians. Actions of these Einsatzgruppen hardened resistance
of Wehrmacht officers to Hitler and his policies.

Professor Kurt Huber, who committed treason with a hectograph machine and paid for his actions with his life

Sergeant Hans Scholl, whose pamphlets led to a students' revolt—and to his own execution

Sophie Scholl, beheaded at twenty-two for daring to oppose Hitler and his war

Roland Freisler, infamous judge of the People's Court, sent the Scholls and thousands of others to their deaths for raising voices against the policies of the Third Reich.

Hitler (*below*) was fascinated by war's tactical tools. At Rastenburg, he examines a new flame-thrower. Colonel Rudolph-Christoph von Gersdorff (*left*) went for the Führer with fused bombs in his greatcoat pockets during one such tactical-weapons display, but Hitler's uncanny instinct for survival saved both their lives.

Colonel Georg von Boeslager (*top left*) waited in vain for the order to machine gun the Führer and his entourage deep inside Russia. Field Marshal Hans von Kluge (*bottom right*) blew hot and cold toward assassination plans, while Rommel, the Desert Fox (*bottom left*), was put out of action at a critical time in history.

Hitler's shredded trousers testify
to the narrow brush with death
on July 20, 1944.

Count Claus von Stauffenberg
spurred the opposition
to its greatest attempt
on Hitler's life.

Stauffenberg's bomb demolished the interior of the briefing hut at Rastenburg;
Göring, in white uniform, gestures toward the point where
Hitler had been standing when the bomb exploded.

Helmuth von Moltke faces his accusers at the People's Court.
Sentence: death by hanging.

Field Marshal von Witzleben faced
Judge Roland Freisler and
the hangman with equal dignity.

Hans von Donanyi endured agonies
at the hands of the Gestapo
but kept silent.

In one of the last pictures taken of Hitler, he congratulates
a youthful soldier outside the bunker in Berlin where,
not long afterward, the Führer's body was consumed by fire.

The room inside Plötzensee prison in Berlin where conspirators
were hung from meat hooks is now a permanent memorial
to those who opposed Adolf Hitler.

Rommel blew up and demanded apologies, both oral and written, for Kluge's "Berchtesgaden-style" tirade. He then suggested that since Kluge had been so long in Russia, he should visit the front in Normandy and see for himself what the troops were up against there. Kluge hastened off to the battlefields and returned forty-eight hours later a changed man. He apologized to Rommel, explaining that he had been taken in by Keitel and Hitler, "who exists by wishful thinking, and when the dreams fade he looks for scapegoats"—the quintessence of what had happened in the east.

Rommel and Kluge now agreed that they must persuade the Führer to halt the fighting; if they failed, there was nothing left to do except to take matters into their own hands and, as Rommel put it, "seek an independent solution in the west." Once again Rommel drove up the narrow, hedgerow-lined Normandy roads to canvass opinions from his subordinate commanders. General Graf Schwerin, commanding the 116th Armored Division, and General Freiherr von Lüttwitz, commanding the 2d Armored Divison, told Rommel that the war must be ended and the Nazis deposed; their divisions were at his disposal for action against the enemy within. But what of the fanatical SS forces fighting alongside the Wehrmacht? Rommel conferred with Obergrüppenführer Sepp Dietrich, once commander of Hitler's own Life Guards and now commander of the First SS Armored Corps. Dietrich, who had once been on the Oster study list of Hitler cohorts to be liquidated, was now infuriated with the contradictory and largely idiotic orders issued from the Führer's HQ; he had already demanded "independent measures in case the front crumbles," which he thought likely to happen at any moment. Rommel drove back to La Roche-Guyon convinced that he had the necessary backing for the move he contemplated and that internicine warfare would not erupt between the Wehrmacht and the SS.

On July 9, Rommel received Stauffenberg's cousin, Cäsar von Hofacker, at his headquartes at La Roche-Guyon. Hofacker, a reserve lieutanant colonel in the Luftwaffe, was the only German air force officer involved in the plot on Hitler's life. He was the trusted aide of the military governor of France, General Karl-

Heinrich von Stülpnagel, a bitter opponent of Hitler from the beginning. It would be up to Stülpnagel to seize Paris in the name of the new provisional government when the time came, and keep it secure pending Allied reaction to Valkyrie. Hofacker's mission was to sway Rommel to action and to obtain a military appreciation of the Normandy front to carry back to Stauffenberg and Beck. "How long can the invasion front hold?" he asked Rommel.

"Fourteen days to three weeks at the maximum," Rommel replied, "and then a breakthrough must be reckoned with. We have nothing to put up against it anymore." Hofacker returned to Paris to brief Stülpnagel, then flew to Berlin to report to Stauffenberg.

By July 10 the southern end of the front in Russia faced the same caving-in process just undergone by Army Group Center, and Russian armies in the far north were poised to cut off German armies there, threatening another Stalingrad-type fiasco. Although Rommel and Kluge had not yet firmly committed themselves in the west, they seemed on the verge of doing so, and Stauffenberg decided to make his move against Hitler the instant an opportunity arose. The bomb and fuse were prepared and at hand.

Stauffenberg's first chance presented itself on Tuesday, July 11, when he was summoned suddenly to the Berghof to report personally to the Führer on the progress being made in creating the new so-called grenadier divisions for emergency use. Stauffenberg stuffed the bomb inside his briefcase under a shirt and some documents. He and an aide, Captain Friedrich Klausing, were driven to the airfield for the ninety-minute flight to the small airfield at Freilassing, just above Berchtesgaden.

They got into a staff car waiting for them at Freilassing and left the summer heat of the valley for the cooler air of the nearby mountains. The Berghof and the other buildings were now hidden from view from the sky above by camouflage netting that cast splotchy shadows on the earth when bathed in the noonday sun. Having reached the Berghof, Stauffenberg climbed out with his briefcase and told Klausing not to leave the vicinity of the car; he might be out sooner than he expected, this time without his briefcase. Klausing was ordered to stand by, ready for a breakneck drive back to the waiting airplane. Klausing leaned against the car and watched Stauffenberg swiftly mount the terraced steps and disappear inside Hitler's house. He looked at his watch. It was shortly before 1:00 P.M. Twenty minutes passed, then thirty, then an hour. Klausing wondered if anything had gone wrong inside.

When Stauffenberg entered the anteroom, he placed his cap, belt, and revolver on the usual table. At 1:07 he was ushered into the main conference room. His eyes swept the room, and his heart fell: the Führer was there, along with Keitel and some other senior officers, but Himmler and Göring were not. Stauffenberg had agreed with Rommel and Kluge that he should try for a clean sweep. Thus, when his turn came to brief the Führer on how matters stood with the new divisions, all he did was to withdraw the papers shielding the still-inert bomb and read off what Hitler wanted to hear.

At 3:30 Klausing looked up to see Stauffenberg coming back down the staircase, still carrying the bulging briefcase, and he knew the mission had failed.

Back in Berlin, Stauffenberg and Hofacker, fresh from the Normandy front, paid a call on General Beck that same evening. The discussion swayed back and forth, but they could not agree that Stauffenberg should loose his bomb the next time he saw the Führer, whether Himmler and Göring were present or not.

Two days after Stauffenberg's abortive trip to the Berghof, Hitler summoned nearly 200 generals and staff officers to address them on the heavy duties that lay ahead. These were the officers chosen to command the fifteen new infantry divisions and ten Panzer brigades being raised by Stauffenberg and Olbricht in Berlin for defense of the Reich. When they had gone, Hitler told his entourage he would be rising earlier than usual on the following morning, for he had decided to return to Rastenburg and conduct the war from there, despite the latest intelligence report indicating Russian divisions were only sixty miles from the outer periphery of his heavily defended enclave.

Stauffenberg's next attempt, on Saturday, July 15, was plagued with uncertainty and confusion. That morning he, General Fromm, and Captain Klausing boarded a Ju.52 that rose in the heavy summer air shrouding Berlin and lumbered toward East Prussia. Only Stauffenberg and Klausing knew what rested at the bottom of the colonel's briefcase.

They were driven to the Wolf's Lair, where they were informed that the Führer had decided upon three individual conferences that afternoon, the length to be determined by Hitler himself. The first meeting started at 1:10, and once again Stauffenberg was disappointed not to find Himmler or Göring present. Stauffenberg was in a quandry. Should he blow up just the Führer or not? He excused himself from the droning voice of Fromm and the sharper retorts of Hitler and made his way to a telephone to call Berlin.

He got through to his balding replacement, Colonel Albrecht Mertz von Quirnheim, and reported his dilemma. Mertz cupped his hand over the receiver and talked to Olbricht and to Beck, who was standing by to take over the government once Valkyrie was set in motion. They argued back and forth, then told Mertz to tell Stauffenberg not to set his bomb.

Exasperated, Stauffenberg said to Mertz, his voice tinny and riddled with static over the long-distance line, "When we get right down to it, this is a matter between you and me. What do *you* say?"

"Do it," answered Mertz.

Stauffenberg hurried back to the conference hut only to find that the meeting had already broken up. It had lasted thirty minutes, most of which Stauffenberg spent on the telephone waiting for Olbricht and Beck to make up their minds. He frantically began searching for his briefcase, but it was nowhere to be found. It was returned to him a few minutes later, having been removed by General Stieff during Stauffenberg's lengthy absence. By the time he had the bomb back in his hands it was too late to take action: the second conference of the day had already started, Stauffenberg had no idea whether it would last ten minutes or an hour, and he was working with a ten-minute fuse.

One of Hitler's aides approached Stauffenberg and told him he would be required to attend the third and final conference of the afternoon, which meant that the last chance was gone. Stauffenberg rushed out and telephoned Berlin, then hurried back to the hut in time to present his briefing to the Führer. The meeting lasted five minutes, then Stauffenberg was dismissed to return with the others to Berlin. In all, they had spent seventy minutes with the Führer with nothing accomplished.

That afternoon at La Roche-Guyon a military typist was at work on a corrected copy of a three-page memorandum drafted by Field Marshal Rommel and addressed to the Führer directly. This "Blitz" message, when approved by Kluge, would be sent to Führer HQ by teleprinter on priority status. Rommel said that the situation in Normandy was approaching a major crisis, and he criticized the paucity of replacements: 6,000 men for 97,000 casualties, 17 tanks to replace 225. He criticized the greenness of the new divisions, the overwhelming superiority of matériel used by the Allies, the shortage of artillery and mortar ammunition. He took a swipe at Göring, pointing out that Allied aircraft roamed freely behind German lines, while "the enemy's supply system is undisturbed by our Luftwaffe."

Rommel concluded: "Our troops are fighting heroically everywhere, but the unequal contest is drawing to an end. I must ask you to draw the conclusion from this situation without delay."

Rommel signed the finished typescript and handed it to Kluge, saying, "Now I have given him his last chance. If he does not draw the right conclusions we shall act." After Rommel left, Kluge read the blistering ultimatum and set it aside. Rommel expected the teletype to be in Hitler's hands that same afternoon, but Kluge fell into another crisis of vacillation and hid Rommel's message for more than a week, by which time events had overtaken them all.

Rommel spent all of Monday, July 17, touring the front lines and combat command headquarters in his open staff car. He visited Sepp Dietrich of the 1st Armored SS Corps and told him of the ultimatum, which Rommel assumed was already on Hitler's desk. At four that afternoon Rommel climbed back into the rear seat of his car and told the driver to hurry back to La Roche-Guyon. The solitary vehicle speeding along the road from Livarot to Vimoutiers churned up summer's dust in its wake. Three Allied fighters sweeping low over the Norman countryside spotted Rommel's wake and peeled off to line up their sights on the black sedan, now accelerating, for a line of poplars lining the road. The machine-gun slugs reached the car before it reached the trees. Rommel's driver was killed on the spot. The speeding car careened wildly and smashed into a ditch. The fighters swept by overhead looking for other targets. Rommel lay unconscious, bleeding, and with a cracked skull. He was rushed to a nearby hospital, where doctors said the field marshal would live but would be out of action for months to come.

Rommel's misfortune could not have happened at a worse time. Everywhere Stauffenberg and the others looked on that Monday, July 17, the horizons were bleak. Only hours before Rommel's car was strafed, he had told Military Governor von Stülpnagel that he was ready to act "openly and unconditionally" on behalf of the revolt whether Kluge went along with it or not. Now, with Rommel out of the picture, who would be on hand to stiffen Kluge's spine as the final countdown began? It was on Monday that the dreaded Russian offensive in the south began, and it was on Monday that the bastions of Caen and Saint-Lô fell to the British and the Americans, respectively. The plains leading to the greater Paris area were now open to the enemy. At this rate, the projected new German provisional government would have nothing left to trade with the Allies in exchange for halting the fighting on any of the fronts.

More disquieting news followed. Stauffenberg learned that "Gestapo" Müller had issued a warrant for Carl Goerdler's arrest and that Goerdler was on the run. Was the ring tightening around the Wehrmacht conspirators as well? "There is no longer any alternative," Stauffenberg remarked. "The Rubicon has been crossed." He made up his mind to carry the bomb with fuse burning into Hitler's presence, cost what it would, kill whom it might.

On Tuesday the eighteenth Stauffenberg received a teletype from Führer HQ requesting his presence at yet another briefing at the Wolf's Lair at midday, Monday, July 20.

On Sunday evening Stauffenberg held a final conference with the active members of the plot, then ordered his driver to take him home. It was shortly after eight, and there was a vestige of twilight left in the summer sky as the driver picked his way through the ruined city. Stauffenberg noted a Catholic church up the street and ordered the driver to pull over to the curb. Stauffenberg spent several minutes in the church, alone with his thoughts, then was driven to his brother's home by Lake Wannsee.

He was ready to pull the trigger.

12

Explosion at Rastenburg

SHORTLY BEFORE SIX on the morning of Thursday, July 20, Stauffenberg threw aside the bedcovers with the stump of his right arm and headed into the bathroom to shave. In the four-teen months since his wounding in the hills of Tunisia, sheer will and nature had combined to force two fingers and a thumb to replace the dexterity of two hands, and the colonel shaved himself quickly and expertly. Then, with the help of strong teeth, Stauffenberg dressed himself for the day in dark slacks and a white tunic. Properly uniformed and with briefcase in hand, Stauffenberg left the house with his brother, Berthold. They were driven through nearly deserted streets to the center of Berlin, where they picked up Stauffenberg's ebullient aide, Lieutenant Werner von Haeften, thirty-five. He carried a briefcase similar to Stauffenberg's.

Twenty minutes later they were at Rangsdorf airfield, due south of the city, where a Ju.52 transport plane waited with its trio of engines ticking over. Berthold Stauffenberg wished his brother and Haeften good luck, then got back into the car for the drive back to his office in Berlin. Stauffenberg and Haeften boarded the corrugated metal Junkers and soon were airborne, flying east to carry out their planned day's work.

Not all of the army units involved in Operation Valkyrie would be aware that they were taking part in a coup d'état; that

182

knowledge would come after the coup was accomplished, when there was no longer any need for a cover. Many of the unit commanders would be acting in the belief that they were helping to put down an insurrection, to prop up the cracking edifice of National Socialism. Exceptions were the Armored Troop School at nearby Krampnitz and the Infantry School at Doberitz, whose commanders had enthusiastically embraced the real purpose of Valkyrie. Units earmarked for action by Stauffenberg and Olbricht included combat groups to be organized from replacement and training units, officer and noncom training battalions, units of the field army then in the zone of the interior for refitting and rehabilitation, plus signal corps, motorized, motor-maintenance, medical, and administrative troops. Stauffenberg had qualms about the crack Grossdeutschland Guard Battalion, scheduled to surround the key government buildings in the heart of Berlin. The battalion's new commander, Major Otto Ernst Remer, a tough frontline officer who had received the Knight's Cross from Hitler personally, had not been let in on the Valkyrie secret, and no one was sure how he would react when he discovered he was being used to help overthrow the Führer's government.

Stauffenberg and the others knew that the key to the success of the entire operation, once the bomb had exploded, was in the hands of General Erich Fellgiebel, chief of Wehrmacht communications. Fellgiebel, fifty-eight, a rangy outdoorsman and horse enthusiast, had been involved in the opposition to Hitler for the past six years. His office and private telephone at home were tapped by the Gestapo; yet he remained in one of the top ten posts in the Wehrmacht because his incisive communication skills and organizational abilities were considered indispensable to the German army.

Fellgiebel discussed again and again with Stauffenberg and Olbricht the formidable problems of controlling communications once Valkyrie was launched. He stressed that he did not control the communication facilities of the SS, the Party, the Luftwaffe, or the navy—but he did control army communications and, to some extent, those originating from Führer HQ at Rastenburg. Fellgiebel promised to seize enough network to enable the conspirators to issue Valkyrie orders once Hitler was dead, while blocking selected incoming and outgoing traffic between Führer HQ and Berlin so that orders issued by the hastily installed new government could not be countermanded by Himmler, Göring, or Goebbels.

The complicated communications network at the Wolf's Lair was dispersed inside separate bombproof bunkers scattered widely throughout the compound, complete with back-up systems that included linkage with the Reich's post office, another communications outlet over which Fellgiebel had no control. Fellgiebel was sure he could block communications between exchange *Anna* there at Rastenburg an exchange *Zeppelin* at army HQ at Zossen, twenty-eight miles west of Berlin, long enough for the other conspirators to consolidate the first phase of the coup in Berlin and elsewhere in the Reich. He was ready to move to execute his assignment the moment Hitler vanished in the explosion. There was, he said, no possibility of blowing up the entire communications system inside the Wolf's Lair—and such action was not desirable anyway because it would create chaos among the fighting divisions engaged in heavy combat in Russia and in France.

Rastenburg appeared off to the left of the Ju.52 a few minutes past ten, and the pilot let down for a landing at the airfield sited near the hamlet of Wilhelmsdorf. A car was waiting to drive them six miles to the Wolf's Lair, a 625-acre tract deep inside a forest, cut off from the rest of the world by miles of barbed-wire fencing 7½ feet high. Stauffenberg noted broad stretches of level green fields that seemed an invitation to enemy paratroopers, but the fields were thickly sown with mines against just such an eventuality. The car passed through three checkpoints and entered the inner compound where the main HQ bunkers and huts were located. The place swarmed with foreign workers, captive labor of the Todt Organization, who had been busy all that spring and summer pouring concrete to strenthen bunker walls and roofs, some of which were twenty-two feet thick. Hitler feared bomb-

ing raids that never came. Stauffenberg also took in the flak tow-
ers, machine-gun nests, and slit trenches. The heat was oppressive even under the canopy of trees, and the air was alive with
singing mosquitoes bred in nearby marshes. Stauffenberg could
only agree with General Alfred Jodl that the place was "part
monastery and part concentration camp."

Stauffenberg reported to the camp commandant, and then was
offered breakfast *al fresco* at a table set for officers beneath a tree
outside of the stifling mess hut. The colonel took his time over
coffee, not leaving the table until eleven and his first meeting with
one of Hitler's generals. The Hitler briefing was scheduled for
1:00 P.M. He had two hours to go.

Stauffenberg met next with General Keitel to discuss his pre-
sentation concerning the new reserve divisions. Keitel told Stauffenberg they had to hurry because the Führer conference had
been moved up to 12:30; the deposed Italian dictator, Benito
Mussolini, was coming to the Wolf's Lair that afternoon to see
Hitler. The meeting with Keitel broke up a few minutes past
noon, and Stauffenberg went outside to get Captain von Haeften,
who was pacing up and down carrying a briefcase loaded with
high explosives.

Stauffenberg summoned Keitel's aide and asked where he
could wash his hands and change his shirt; he wanted to appear
immaculate in the presence of his Führer, he explained. He was
directed to the men's room, but instead he and Haeften disappeared into an empty office where they hurriedly unlatched both
briefcases. Stauffenberg pulled out a clean shirt and some papers,
and Haeften removed two packages of plastic explosive wrapped
in heavy brown paper. Stauffenberg picked up one of the two-
pound packages and put it on the table before him. Then he
gripped a pair of pliers with his mutilated left hand and crimped
down hard on the capsule, hearing the tinkle of broken glass. He
put the triggered bomb inside his briefcase. Outside the door
somebody was calling out for Stauffenberg to hurry—the conference was about to begin. Stauffenberg shoved the fresh shirt and
the papers back inside his briefcase. Haeften put the second

bomb, unfused, back in his own case and snapped it shut. Then they straightened up and walked through the door, down the corridor, and out of the building.*

With the acid now eating at the wire, Stauffenberg had less than fifteen minutes to reach the briefing hut, place the charge, and get clear before the bomb detonated. He and Haeften walked briskly through the compound, Haeften in the direction of the waiting staff car and Stauffenberg in the direction of the hut. He reached it in three minutes and was ushered inside. Keitel introduced Stauffenberg and Hitler, who had never formally met, and Stauffenberg shook hands with the man he hoped to kill.

The conference room measured fifteen by thirty-five feet, and Staufenberg noted that all ten windows were wide open and the red-and-white checkered curtains were drawn back; open windows would lessen the effect of the blast, but he hoped that he could place the briefcase near enough to the Führer so that this would make no difference. Hitler was seated on a wicker stool at the center of a massive oak table nineteen feet long, four feet wide, and four inches thick. The surface was covered with war situation maps, all of them indicating doom for the Wehrmacht.

Including Hitler, there were twenty-three men in the crowded conference room; there were representatives of each branch of the service, including the SS, but Göring and Himmler were not present. Moving to the other side of the table, Stauffenberg jostled his way to the right of General Adolf Heusinger, who was standing next to Hitler holding forth on the situation along the Russian front. Engrossed in Heusinger's report, the others at that end of the table paid no attention when Stauffenberg leaned down and set his briefcase on the floor, where it protruded partway under the table. He waited a moment, then excused himself, whispering that he needed to telephone Berlin.

Stauffenberg walked straight out of the building without even

---

* Whether Stauffenberg intended to use both bombs but did not, either because only one would fit inside his already crowded briefcase or because of the interruption from outside, is an unsolved mystery.

pausing to pick up his belt and cap and kept going until he reached the signals bunker 200 yards away. There he met General Fellgiebel and Haeften, who were pacing nervously back and forth. They all kept glancing anxiously at their wristwatchs. Then the crack of an explosion jerked their heads to the west, across the road that led to safety, in the direction of the briefing hut. The three conspirators jumped in a reflex action as though electrified, but an officer standing nearby said to pay no attention: wild boars and other animals were forever making their way through the fence and into the minefields.

A car and driver were standing by, and Stauffenberg and Haeften climbed in and told the driver to head straight for the airfield because they had urgent business back in Berlin, as indeed they had: Stauffenberg had assumed the role not only of executoner but as leader of the revolt in Berlin as well. From the road, the briefing hut was visible in the distance off to the right. A cloud of smoke was rising slowly in the still, warm air, doctors and orderlies were rushing about, and it seemed that bodies were being pulled from the hut. Stauffenberg was convinced that the bomb had done its work. The car drove on.

Stauffenberg managed to bluff his way past the three checkpoints, but there were anxious moments. The driver thought the beltless, bareheaded, mutilated colonel was acting strangely, but he was only a lieutenant and kept his opinion to himself for the time being. He risked glances at Haeften in the back seat through the rear-view mirror, and saw him pull a paper-wrapped parcel from his briefcase and fling it outside into a ditch while the car sped down the road leading to the airfield. He watched the two officers hurry over to a waiting He.111 and get aboard. The engines roared, and the plane cleared the runway and flew off to the west. Thirty-three minutes had passed since the explosion of Stauffenberg's bomb.

When Stauffenberg precipitately left the conference, General Heusinger's chief assistant, Colonel Heinz Brandt, moved forward so as to see the maps spread out on the table more clearly. His boot encountered Stauffenberg's briefcase, which Brandt shoved farther under the table so that it rested against the heavy slab of oak that supported the table at that end. Heusinger was winding up his analysis of the desperate situation facing Army Group North. "West of the Dvina, strong Russian forces are driving northwards. Their spearheads are already southwest of Dvinsk. Unless, at long last, the army group is withdrawn from Lake Peipus, a catastrophe will . . ." At 12:42, Heusinger's words were obliterated by a shattering explosion. A blinding sheet of yellow flame filled one end of the room. The supersonic pressure wave smashed against the table, wrecking the support and blasting one end to splinters. It boomed against the thin walls separating the conference room from adjoining rooms, staving them in. It roared down the narrow corridor to the opposite end of the hut and wrecked the rooms there. It flew upward, bringing down much of the ceiling, and it flashed outward through the open window, splintering glass and taking the facings with it. All this happened in microseconds.

To those inside the crowded conference room, it was like being in the center of the detonation wrought by the crash of a heavy artillery shell. The pressure wave lifted SS General Hermann Fegelein and SS Colonel Otto Günsche and hurled them through the windows to land unconscious on the ground outside. Others were blown backward against the crumpled wall facing Hitler. Lath, plaster, and timber rained down from the shredded ceiling. Blinded by smoke and deafened by the cataclysmic cracking of the bomb, men staggered outside, beating at the flames that were scorching their hair and licking at their torn uniforms. The screams of the badly wounded lying in the rubble sounded far away.

At the moment of the explosion Hitler was leaning over the table, propped on his right elbow staring at the map. He was hurled to the left and crashed to the floor, partially buried by debris. Both eardrums had burst, and his legs and elbow hurt him terribly. He lurched to his feet and was led out of the shambles of the conference hut through a dense cloud of smoke by Keitel, who was beside himself with relief. "The Führer is alive! The Führer is alive!" he called out.

"Some swine has thrown a grenade!" Hitler cried, believing one of the foreign workers to be responsible for the outrage. He was helped to his quarters forty yards away where the doctors saw to his injuries. His black trousers were slit front and back as though by razor blades, and the legs underneath were filled with wooden splinters and splotched red from superficial burns. His face was cut, his elbow badly bruised, and there was blood in his right ear, but he was in no way incapacitated. With his injuries dressed, his hair combed free of plaster, his hands and face washed and outfitted in a fresh uniform, Hitler at first appeared years younger. One of his aides who saw him shortly afterward remarked that the Führer "had the lively, almost cheerful expression of a man who had been expecting something terrible to happen, and now luckily survived it." At 1:15—just as Stauffenberg's plane was lifting off the runway for Berlin—Hitler, limping slightly, but otherwise not impaired, emerged from his bunker followed by the usual entourage.* Fellgiebel, standing just outside the wire surrounding the inner compound, could see Hitler walking in the sunshine and knew that Stauffenberg's bomb had missed its target. Fellgiebel managed to put through two telephone calls, one to General Stieff's HQ at Maurerwald not far from Rastenburg, and the other to General Fritz Thiele, his chief of staff in Berlin. His message was cryptic, seemingly ambiguous, so that eavesdroppers on the line could not interpret it. He said only, "Something terrible has happened. The Führer is still alive." What he meant was that Stauffenberg had gone into action, but the attempt had failed. He expected that Phase II of Valkyrie, the seizure of the reins of power in Berlin and else-

---

*Others were less fortunate. The recording secretary, Heinrich Berger, had both legs blown off and died that same afternoon. Colonel Brandt, whose action in shoving the briefcase forward probably saved Hitler's life, lost part of one leg and an eye and died in the Rastenburg hospital two days later, as did Luftwaffe General Gunther Korten, whose abdomen was impaled by a jagged shaft of wood wrenched from the table. General Rudolf Schmundt, Hitler's dog-faithful adjutant for many years, sustained vicious thigh wounds and died of infection three months later.

where, would be launched without delay, and that his subordinates would shut down outgoing communications from Berlin. To Fellgiebel, the fact that Hitler was still alive was almost irrelevant; Valkyrie must go forward at all costs. As for blocking unrestricted signals traffic at Rastenburg, that had already been accomplished by one of Hitler's aides, Colonel Nicholaus von Below, to keep news of the assassination attempt from leaking out. Communications would be restored on the Führer's orders when Hitler was ready to inform the world. Since there was no more Fellgiebel could do for the moment, he returned to his own headquarters to await developments.

Revitalized by his narrow brush with death, Hitler began issuing a fresh series of commands forty-five minutes after the explosion. He ordered a thorough search of the buildings inside the compound against the likelihood there were more bombs hidden away, ready to go off. He sent pioneer troops scurrying around in the vicinity of the conference hut to seek the detonating wire that must have exploded the bomb there, still in the belief that the bomb had been placed underneath the hut by disgruntled foreign workers. He summoned Ernst Kaltenbrunner and a team of Gestapo specialists from Berlin to the Wolf's Lair to conduct a thorough investigation. He ordered Grand Admiral Karl Dönitz to fly to Rastenberg from Berlin so as to be on hand if he needed him. Then, at 2:30, he and his followers went to the small railway station just outside the compound to meet Mussolini's train.

A gray drizzle began, and the train made its way into the station under towering pine trees whose branches glistened with rain. Hitler, wearing a dark cape, greeted Mussolini effusively, and they walked together to the car for the 400-yard ride to the briefing hut, where Hitler explained in detail what had happened. Mussolini seemed horrified. His German was fluent, and he caught Hitler's meaning when the Führer said that a miracle had saved him—he was standing six feet away when the bomb went off—because "Providence still had a task" for him.

A closer look at the area where the bomb detonated revealed that the eighteen-inch hole in the floor had been blow downward, not upward as first assumed. This could only mean that the bomb had been carried inside by one of the conferees. The log was gone over once again, and a name jumped out: Colonel Claus von Stauffenberg. Where was Stauffenberg anyway? In the half-hour of chaos following the explosion, his absence had been over-looked. Now the signals sergeant on duty stepped forward and reported that the one-eyed colonel had departed from the hut—leaving cap, belt, and briefcase behind—several minutes before the bomb went off. At first the officers found outrageous the suggestion that the heroic combat officer could be involved in an attempt on the Führer's life. Then the outlying guard posts were checked, and somebody got through to the operations officer at the airfield, who reported that Stauffenberg and his aide had taken off in haste with Rangsdorf as their destination. It was suggested that Stauffenberg had flown behind Russian lines, less than twenty minutes away, to seek asylum, but Himmler, discounting the idea, got on the telephone and ordered the SS in Berlin to rush to Rangsdorf and arrest Stauffenberg and Haeften the moment they stepped off the plane. At this point, Hitler and the others assumed that Stauffenberg had gone mad and had acted on his own.

By now Göring, Dönitz, and Joachim von Ribbentrop were in tow, and Hitler led them to the tea house for refreshments and discussions with his Italian guests. The conversation quickly degenerated into a row, and Mussolini and his aides were treated to the spectacle of the leaders of the Reich engaged in petty squabbling. Irritated in the first place at having to leave Berlin on short notice, Admiral Dönitz turned his wrath on the army, which had been against the Führer from the beginning, and now was involved in active treason. One had only to point to Stauffenberg for the proof. Göring, seizing the opportunity, agreed with the admiral—but Dönitz, lean of figure and acerb of tongue, lashed out against the poor showing of the Luftwaffe for the past four years: See how Germany's beautiful cities were being destroyed one after another from the air, he said; recall the Luftwaffe's failure to supply the doomed men at Stalingrad.

Ribbentrop agreed with Dönitz; the Luftwaffe had failed all

along the line. Göring blew up. His corpulent body, stuffed inside a dazzling white uniform, advanced toward the startled diplomat. Göring had always loathed Ribbentrop personally and was contemptuous of his false pretensions to nobility. Raising his gold-and-white field marshal's baton as though to strike, he roared, "Shut up, you champagne salesman!"

"I am still foreign minister," Ribbentrop primly replied, "and my name is *von* Ribbentrop."

The quarrel died away as quickly as it had begun. Hitler remained silent throughout it all, sitting and staring moodily into space.*

With Hitler's approval, the security blackout at the Wolf's Lair was lifted by Himmler shortly after 3:00 P.M., and normal traffic resumed. Hitler ordered a recording van dispatched from Konigsberg, sixty miles to the north, so that he could record a message to the German people to be broadcast throughout the Reich assuring them that he was perfectly all right and still capable of leading them to victory. With communications fully restored at Rastenburg, backed-up messages flooded in. At 4:20, General Keitel was summoned to take an urgent call from Berlin. General Fromm, the commander of the Home Army, was at the other end of the line, exasperated.

"What on earth is going on at headquarters? The wildest rumors are afloat here in Berlin."

"What is supposed to be going on?" Keitel asked. "Everything here is perfectly all right."

"But I've just received a report that the Führer has been assassinated," Fromm said.

"Nonsense!" replied Keitel. "There *was* an attempted assassination, but fortunately it failed. The Führer is alive, and received

---

*Hitler's thoughts were put into words less than six weeks later. On August 31 he discussed the assassination attempt with Keitel and confided: "If my life had been ended, I think I can say that for me personally it would only have been a release from worry, sleepless nights, and a great nervous suffering. It is only a fraction of a second, and then one is freed from everything and has one's quiet and eternal peace. Just the same, I am grateful to Destiny for letting me live. . . ."

only superficial injuries. By the way, where is that chief of staff of yours, Colonel von Stauffenberg?"

"He's not here," said Fromm. "I thought he was still at Rastenburg."

When other calls came in from various commanders asking about the Führer's death, and when the teleprinters began clattering automatically to repeat messages sent out from the Zeppelin exchange at Zossen ordering Phase I of Valkyrie, it became clear for the first time that Stauffenberg's act was not that of a lone wolf, but part of a conspiracy to take over the government. Outraged, Himmler called Gestapo HQ in Berlin and ordered a squad to the Bendlerstrasse to find out what was going on. The question uppermost in his mind was, *Where is Stauffenberg?*

13

Fateful Hours

THE BOMBER CARRYING Stauffenberg and Haeften reached Berlin two hours after takeoff from Rastenburg—two hours during which Stauffenberg could only wonder what he had left behind at the Wolf's Lair; two hours in which General Olbricht could have Valkyrie launched and well on the way to completion in Berlin, Vienna, Prague, Paris, and in the provinces of the Reich. Two hours in which each minute counted, but events were entirely beyond the colonel's control.

As a precaution against encountering an unwelcome reception committee at Rangsdorf, Stauffenberg ordered the pilot to land elsewhere. They let themselves out of the airplane, and Haeften rushed to call Olbricht's office to get a progress report on the revolt. He returned incredulous; no orders had been issued, no troops were on the move, no buildings seized. Indeed, Olbricht had just returned from a leisurely lunch, still undecided what to do. Olbricht was the victim of a glaring oversight in operational planning: they knew to take no action if Stauffenberg failed to place the bomb, and they knew what action to take if the bomb exploded and killed the Führer, but no contingency plan existed in the event Hitler survived the blast. Nearly three hours wasted. Stauffenberg was furious. He got on the telephone and declared that Hitler could not have survived the terrific explosion. Set Valkyrie in motion without losing another second, he demanded.

Because his own driver was still futilely waiting for him at Rangsdorf, Stauffenberg had no transportation to the Bendlerstrasse, and his dynamo presence was obviously required if the revolt was to get off the ground. He and Haeften scurried around the airdrome, where fuel was at a premium, and finally secured a Luftwaffe car and driver. He did not arrive at the scene of inaction until 4:30.

By then, things were moving, but slowly. Olbricht's deputy, Colonel Mertz von Quirnheim, had prodded the general into a semblance of activity. The first orders began to move through the complicated and time-consuming teleprinter system. General von Witzleben, who had been active in guiding the resistance all along, arrived in full uniform. General Beck, who would head the provisional government, appeared in a conservative gray suit. General Erich Hoepner, who was to replace General Fromm, arrived with a full-dress uniform which the Führer had forbidden him ever to wear again. Hans Gisevius appeared, bearing false identity papers supplied by Allen Dulles in Switzerland. To Gisevius, Stauffenberg, bathed in sweat, seemed "more spiritualized. There was a smile of victory on his face; he radiated the triumph of a challenge successfully met."

Beck and Hoepner, whose lives were at stake along with almost everybody else's in the room, needed reassuring that Hitler was indeed dead. To quell their doubts and to help stiffen Olbricht's resolution, Stauffenberg declared, "I saw the entire thing from outside. It was the same as if the hut were struck by a six-inch shell! It is unlikely that any of them could have survived." Now Olbricht urged Stauffenberg to confront General Fromm with his eyewitness account.

They entered Fromm's office, and Stauffenberg told him the Führer was dead. Fromm, indignant, said that it was impossible: "Field Marshal Keitel himself assured me that it is not so."

"Keitel is lying as usual," Stauffenberg replied. Then, lying himself, he added, "I saw Hitler being carried out dead."

Olbricht spoke up and told Fromm, "We have already issued the code word for internal arrest to the commanding generals."

Fromm leapt from his chair and slammed his fist on the desk.

"That is sheer disobedience!" he shouted. "What do you mean, *we?* Who gave such an order?"

"My chief of staff, Colonel Mertz von Quirnheim," replied Olbricht.

"Send him in here at once!" Fromm bellowed.

Mertz walked into the supercharged atmosphere and freely admitted sending out the Valkyrie commands, whereupon Fromm shouted that he must consider himself under arrest. Stauffenberg moved closer to the desk and told Fromm that he himself had set the charge that killed Hitler. "In that case," said Fromm, "you must shoot yourself at once."

Stauffenberg said that he would do nothing of the kind, and when Olbricht admitted to Fromm that he, too, was taking an active role in the revolt, Fromm raised his voice even higher and said, "I hereby declare all three of you under arrest!"

Olbricht replied, "You cannot arrest us. You do not realize who holds the power here. We arrest *you.*" Fromm came out from behind his desk and started to grapple with Olbricht, but the others interceded to disarm Fromm and lock him in an adjoining room. The telephone wire was ripped out and the room put under guard.

Back at the Wolf's Lair, Himmler had ordered a small unit of the SS to locate the traitor Stauffenberg and make a discreet arrest. Accordingly, Oberführer (Colonel) Humbert Piffrader of the Berlin Reich Security Office gathered up a few plainclothesmen and headed for the Bendlerstrasse. Had Piffrader had any idea what was going on inside those offices, he would not have acted as he did. He approached the main entrance and boldly asked to see the Colonel Count von Stauffenberg. He was escorted under armed guard to Stauffenberg's presence. "Heil Hitler!" Piffrader cried out. Then he and the others were disarmed and locked in an empty office. Gisevius complained that Piffrader should have been shot out of hand.

The next captive was General Joachim von Kortzfleisch, commander of the Berlin Military District, who steamed into the Bendlerstrasse offices to find out what was going on. When Beck demanded to know why Kortzfleisch had not deployed his troops as ordered, Kortzfleisch drew himself up and said that the Führer still lived, and it was to the Führer that he and the rest of the Wehrmacht had pledged a sacred oath. "Oath?" said Beck. "How dare you talk of oaths? Hitler had broken his oaths to the constitution and to the people a hundred times over. How dare you refer to your oath of loyalty to that perjurer?"

Kortzfleisch's response was to bolt from the room in an undignified gallop down the corridor, but he was grabbed before reaching a stairwell exit. His pistol was removed from its holster, and he joined the others in captivity.

An hour and a half later, at 6:30, the Grossdeutschland Guard Battalion arrived from south of Berlin and smartly deployed to surround the area containing the partially destroyed government buildings. No one could enter the Bendlerstrasse building where the revolt was being guided without an orange pass signed by Stauffenberg. All traffic, including public streetcars, was cut off. It was late, but Valkyrie orders were now being carried out in Berlin, and Stauffenberg's confidence grew. He now turned his attention to France. If Stülpnagel's forces nullified the SS and the Gestapo in Paris, and if Field Marshal von Kluge swung immediately to their side, an armistice could follow, and the war in the west would be over. Kluge's decision was crucial.

The revolt in France began to gather momentum in Paris at 2:30, when Colonel Finckh of Rommel's Army Group B received a call from General Eduard Wagner at Zossen. Wagner said simply, "Finished," the code word indicating that the attempt on Hitler's life had been carried out. Finckh locked up his office and summoned his car for the half hour drive to Kluge's HQ at Saint-Germain-en-Laye, an ancient and somnolent village whose old houses had been surrounded with bunkers and barbed wire and converted into headquarters buildings.

At the two-story, gray-stone country house that served as Kluge's operations center, Finckh was greeted by Kluge's chief of staff, General Günther Blumentritt, a plump, jovial Bavarian wearing pince-nez. Blumentritt later recalled, "I expected Finckh to inform me about the supply situation, but instead he reported an insurrection of the Gestapo in Berlin, an attempt on the Führer's life, and that Witzleben, Beck, and Goerdler had formed a provisional government. I was completely surprised, but felt [the new government] would send out peace feelers at once."

Blumentritt asked where Finckh had heard the startling news, and was told that it came from Zossen and had been confirmed by Lieutenant Colonel Hofacker in Paris. Kluge, said Blumentritt, had moved his HQ only the day before to La Roche-Guyon, where he could better command Rommel's leaderless Army Group B. Blumentritt reached for his telephone and asked to be put through to La Roche-Guyon. The call was taken by Kluge's chief of staff, General Hans Speidel, who said that Kluge had been away from HQ since nine that morning and was not expected back until early in the evening. The field marshal was in a wood east of Saint-Pierre-Dives conferring with SS and Wehrmacht operational commanders about how best to shore up their sagging defenses on the eastern part of the Normandy front. His job done, Finckh drove back to Paris, while Blumentritt ordered his own car and headed for La Roche-Guyon to wait for Kluge's return.

Meanwhile, Stülpnagel and Hofacker waited nervously in their offices at the Hotel Raphael on the rue Kléber. Shortly after 4:30, Stauffenberg rang through and told Hofacker what had happened at the Wolf's Lair, that the way to action was now open. Hofacker hung up the receiver and said thoughtfully to one of the office officials, Friedrich Teuchert, "If this thing goes wrong, it will certainly be the hangman for us."

Back at Rastenburg, Hitler had approved the draft of a radio communiqué to be broadcast throughout Germany to inform the people that their leader was alive and well. The text was sent off to Goebbels in Berlin under the assumption that the propaganda minister would get it on the air at once. Sixty minutes passed, then ninety, and still the radio blared with routine programming. Irate, Hitler got on the telephone and asked Goebbels to explain the delay. Goebbels said that he was working on the text of a preface and a postscript. Hitler, furious, ordered Goebbels to stop meddling with the copy and to get the message broadcast.

At 6:28 the following bulletin went on the air: "Today an attempt was made on the Führer's life with explosives. . . . The Führer himself suffered no injuries beyond light burns and bruises. He resumed his work immediately and, as scheduled, received the Duce for a lengthy discussion. The Reich Marshal [Göring] joined the Führer shortly after the attempt was made." The message was rebroadcast at frequent intervals on varying frequencies throughout the rest of that afternoon and evening, spreading the word throughout Europe and the Near and Far East.

Stauffenberg at once utilized the communications network at his command in the Bendlerstrasse to issue denials, thus starting a teleprinter and telephone war waging between Berlin and Rastenburg.

Kluge returned to La Roche-Guyon at six to find Speidel waiting for him with the news of Hitler's assassination, or attempted assassination—even now no one in France could guarantee which. Kluge remained calm. The telephone jangled; it was Beck calling from Berlin, urging Kluge to throw his armies into the revolt. A typed copy of Goebbels's first radio broadcast had just landed on Kluge's desk, but he did not mention this fact to Beck. "Kluge," Beck asked, "do you approve of our action and will you place yourself under my orders?" Kluge hedged; when Beck pressed him, he said that he could not say no and he could not say yes until it was certain that the Führer was dead. Beck said that the consideration was not relevant; what mattered was to act together to create a *fait accompli*. Kluge hesitated, then told Beck he would have to think it over and would call back in thirty minutes. Then he hung up. Knowing that Kluge would never call back, Beck put the receiver down and said to those around him, "That's Kluge for you!"

Kluge now told Speidel to contact Paris and request that Stülpnagel and Hofacker report to La Roche-Guyon at 8:00 P.M. for a command meeting. Stülpnagel hoped that Kluge had made up his mind to back the revolt; in any event he had, an hour earlier, already alerted the First Garrison Regiment on his own initiative to stand by to move against the SS and the Gestapo in Paris.

While the regiment was making their way carefully cross-country under the threat of Allied fighters, Kluge was handed a long teleprinter message originating from the Bendlerstrasse over the signature of Field Marshal von Witzleben, who had apparently been called from retirement. The message delivered to Kluge at 7:28 began:

I. The Führer Adolf Hitler is dead.
II. An irresponsible gang of Party leaders, men far from the front, has tried to exploit this situation to stab the hard-pressed army in the back and seize power for its own ends.
III. In this hour of grave danger the Reich government, in order to maintain law and order, has declared a state of military emergency and entrusted to me full powers of supreme command of the armed forces and executive power in the Reich.

This general order, drafted weeks earlier, turned Kluge completely around. So Hitler was not alive after all; his oath to the Führer could no longer be binding. Blumentritt and Speidel waited for Kluge's first reaction. It was this: he decided the first move must be to order the cessation of the bombardment of England by the V.1 buzz-bombs, which were only killing civilians anyway and having no effect on the course of the battle in Normandy. This gesture, Kluge believed, would convince the Allies of the new government's sincerity and would persuade them to call off their own campaign of extermination of German cities and industry from the air. After this, an armistice should be easy to arrange in the west.

Twenty-eight minutes after Kluge received Witzleben's message, he was handed another, this one from Rastenburg and signed by Keitel. "The Führer is alive! In perfect health!" it began. Keitel said that Heinrich Himmler was the new commander of the Home Army in Berlin and that any orders issued by Fromm, Witzleben, or Olbricht were to be disregarded. Understandably perplexed, Kluge's newfound enthusiasm for the putsch lunged to zero. He ordered Blumentritt to get on the telephone and solve the mystery of the conflicting signals. Blumentritt finally reached General Stieff, himself a hesitant conspirator in faraway East Prussia, and Stieff said that Hitler still lived. Had Stieff told Kluge otherwise, Kluge might have disregarded Keitel's order and plunged ahead on his own. Now, only the persuasive powers of Stülpnagel and Hofacker could prod Kluge to action.

They arrived shortly after eight; the medieval castle of the dukes of La Rochefoucauld that served as Kluge's HQ was still bathed in midsummer light. Hofacker delivered an impassioned address, pointing out that the hour of destiny for the field marshal was at hand. He described Stauffenberg's own heroic efforts to bring German honor back from the brink of ruin. Then Kluge told Blumentritt to read Keitel's signal aloud. When he finished, the field marshal said, "Yes, gentlemen, it has been a bungled affair."

Kluge asked them to stay for dinner, a candlelight-and-wine affair that only Kluge pretended to enjoy; he had left the burning issue of the revolt against Hitler in the other room, and talked instead of the battles fought for Normandy all that day, less than sixty miles from where they sat. Seething with an anger born of disappointment, Hofacker and Stülpnagel maintained a hostile silence. It seemed to Speidel that they were "sitting in the house of the dead."

Now Stülpnagel put his napkin aside and butted at Kluge without restraint. "I thought you knew about [the conspiracy] all along," he said.

"I had no idea," Kluge replied. He said that to act as Stülpnagel suggested with Hitler alive would be irresponsible. Stülpnagel retorted that failure to act would be a greater irresponsibility. He added that he had already set in train an action in Paris to arrest all of the SS and Gestapo; therefore Kluge would not have to worry about initiating a civil war involving the Wehrmacht.

Hofacker interrupted to remind Kluge that he had seemed willing enough to cooperate with the conspiracy the year before while in Russia. Kluge admitted this, but in turn reminded Hofacker that his willingness was predicated on the removal of the Führer. He added that he might be willing to act even now "if only the swine were dead."

"Herr Field Marshal," Hofacker said, "the fate of millions of Germans and the honor of the army lies in your hands."

"No!" said Kluge, and the dinner ended.

Stülpnagel expected Kluge to have him arrested on the spot for initiating Phase II of Valkyrie in Paris without permission, but Kluge ordered him instead to return to Paris and call off his men, after which he should consider himself relieved of duty as military governor. Then Kluge suggested to Stülpnagel that he change into civilian clothes and go underground. Stülpnagel shook his head, and he and Hofacker got into the car to drive back to the capital.

As the exhausting evening wore on in Berlin, it became clear that Olbricht's failure to act decisively right at the beginning had been calamitous. The lost hours were not merely crucial, they were fatal. The first teleprinter messages sent to each of the Reich's twenty-one military districts did not begin arriving until after 5:00 P.M., when most of the offices were closed for the day and only lesser duty officers were on hand to deal with the momentous news. Vienna did not learn of the activation of Valkyrie until six, and Prague only at seven. The commands directed at the military district commanders over Witzleben's signature were lengthy and complicated, and time could have been saved had the orders been put in code beforehand. Since they had not been, the laborious process had to be carried out on the spot by the sender at the Bendlerstrasse. The conspirators also overlooked the fact that whatever went out over the wire to the military district HQs was automatically fed into the Rastenburg teleprinters. Thus Hitler and Keitel had their hands on Stauffenberg's commands as fast as they could be issued. Moreover, Keitel's disclaimers arrived at the various provincial headquarters long before the encoded Valkyrie orders did. Adding to the confusion, later editions of the Valkyrie order omitted the opening phrase about

Hitler's death, substituting instead the cryptic phrase, "internal disturbances." Although a few district commanders knew what was in the wind, most did not. The consequent chaos resulted in a flurry of telephone calls to Rastenburg and Berlin.

Stauffenberg fielded these calls, using both telephones in Fromm's office; Fromm, he explained, was not available. An observer noted Stauffenberg's clarity and decisiveness in dealing with the perplexities streaming into his ear:

"This is Stauffenberg . . . yes, all orders from the commander-in-chief of the Home Army . . . yes, of course . . . that's right . . . all orders to be carried out immediately. You must occupy all transmitters and signals centers. . . . All resistance must be crushed. . . . It's likely that counterorders will be handed out by Führer HQ . . . don't believe them . . . no . . . the Wehrmacht has taken control . . . only the commander of the Home Army is entitled to give orders . . . do you understand? . . . yes, the Reich is in danger, and always in times of danger the soldiers take charge. . . . Yes, Witzleben has been appointed Supreme Commander. . . . Do you have that? Heil!"

Stauffenberg's strenuous efforts largely came to naught. A few temporary arrests were made in Prague, and in Vienna the Guard Battalion was called out to surround the district HQ, after which a dozen SS and Party leaders were taken into custody for two hours. But elsewhere in the Reich commanders came to the conclusion that the uncertainties equaled the risks involved, and nothing came of Stauffenberg's fiery pleas. Only from Paris was there real encouragement: Finckh rang up Mertz von Quirnheim and said excitedly, "Tanks on the move. Carry on."

Although General Ludwig Beck had not issued an operational command since 1938, he intended to now. More than 200,000 German troops of Army Group North were in danger of being hopelessly trapped in Kurland (Latvia-Estonia) by overwhelming numbers of Russians driving to cut off their rear. Beck told Stauffenberg to get General Eberhard Kinzl, the group's chief of staff, on the telephone. Stauffenberg got through at 7:55 and explained the situation in Berlin, then handed the receiver to Beck, who ordered Kinzl to disengage from the Russians and prepare to fall back before a Stalingrad-type disaster overcame them. Kinzl said that he would like nothing more than to extract his men and save his armies for the battles that lay ahead in East Prussia, but he would have to check with Führer HQ first in view of the extraordinary situation.

Kinzl rang up the Wolf's Lair and asked for the Operations Branch. Since General Heusinger and Colonel Brandt had been knocked out of action by Stauffenberg's bomb, the call was taken by Colonel Johann von Kielmansegg. Kinzl said, "You know this is the only sound solution—we've discussed this often enough—but we simply can't obey Beck without knowing what's going on. What are we to do?" Kielmansegg had no intention of broaching the subject to Hitler or Keitel—certainly not on orders from a renegade general. He told Kinzl he had better forget the whole idea, unless the Führer changed his mind.

A few minutes after Beck's futile call, Field Marshal von Witzleben swept into the Bendlerstrasse offices in full uniform, carrying his marshal's baton in one gloved hand. His first words to Stauffenberg, who stood at attention in the center of the room, were, "A fine mess, this!" Witzleben then motioned for Beck, Olbricht, Hoepner, and Stauffenberg to join him in Fromm's spacious office. The sliding doors were closed, but from outside it was clear from the pitch of the voices that Witzleben was furious. The arguments raged for a half-hour, then the doors were shoved open and Witzleben strode out of the building and into his car to be driven home. He saw that the revolt was crumbling; the coup d'état was a failure.

Among the uninterrupted stream of telephone calls was one for Gisevius from Berlin's police president, Count Wolf von Helldorf, who, true to his word, had kept the entire corps of police immobilized during the afternoon of the putsch. Helldorf seemed excited and wanted Gisevius to come at once. A car was somehow located and Gisevius was driven a circuitous route to reach police HQ at the Alexanderplatz on the eastern part of the city. Helldorf told Gisevius that it was all over; the Guard Battalion commanded by Major Remer and posted in front of the Bendler-strasse was pulling out. Remer, Helldorf said, had gone over to the enemy. He urged Gisevius to run, but some quixotic streak prompted the ex-Gestapo officer to return to "the doomed circle inside the Bendlerstrasse."

Gisevius and his police driver started back for the Unter den Linden but were stopped repeatedly by armed troops, who diverted them this way and that. Gisevius later recalled that as the car moved closer to the Bendlerstrasse a refrain ran through his mind, *I am riding to suicide, I am riding to suicide . . .* Finally the driver pulled up and said he would go no farther. Gisevius got out and stood uncertainly in the street near the Chancellery. He tore up Stauffenberg's pass and walked a short distance to the cellar apartment of Theodor Strünck, where he would hide from the Gestapo before starting on the long underground road back to Switzerland.

Major Otto Ernst Remer had been uneasy about his assignment ever since he had posted his battalion around the bomb-damaged government buildings. But for Remer, thirty-two, a serving officer in the German army for the past twelve years, following orders was an automatic response. Several times wounded and heavily decorated, most recently by the Führer himself, Remer's personal courage was unquestioned. These qualities, combined with his zeal for his job and his admiration for his Führer, made Remer an ideal officer of the Wehrmacht.

Remer's first qualms about the action he was ordered to take were brought on by Lieutenant Hans Hagen, a liaison officer between Remer's battalion and Goebbels's propaganda ministry. At 2:45 that afternoon, near the Wintergarten, Hagen observed an open Mercedes rolling down Friedrichstrasse. As the car flashed by, Hagen mistakenly thought he recognized the uniformed figure of Field Marshal Walther von Brauchitsch sitting in the back seat. Brauchitsch had been fired as commander-in-chief of the Wehrmacht three years before, and Hagen wondered why he should be back in Berlin, and in uniform. Then Hagen hurried off to deliver a lecture on leadership and political motivation to a

205

gathering of noncoms. After the lecture ended, Remer invited Hagen to his apartment to discuss battalion morale. At 4:10 Remer was ordered to report to the city commandant, General Paul von Hase. Remer told Hagen to wait for his return.

Remer was back thirty-five minutes later, "his face as white as chalk" as he snapped out that somebody had tried to kill the Führer, and that the Wehrmacht now held the reins of government. Remer summoned the battalion officers and noncoms and briefed them on the forthcoming exercise. While the briefing was in progress, Hagen recalled the picture of the ousted Brauchitsch wheeling through the capital. Hagen pulled aside the lieutenants standing nearby and whispered forcefully, "Boys, I have a terrible suspicion. Something stinks. I've seen Brauchitsch. I hope a putsch isn't in the works."

The briefing over, Hagen approached Remer and blurted out his suspicions. "I feel uneasy about the whole thing myself," Remer said. It bothered him that General von Hase had given him only oral, not written, orders. "We've got to keep clear heads, maintain our calm, and not be taken advantage of in any way," he told Hagen. Hagen asked to be released from Remer's command long enough to go to Goebbels directly and find out the real story. Concurring, Remer provided him with a motorcycle and sidecar with driver, and they roared up the street to find Goebbels. Meanwhile, orders were orders, and Remer set to work to deploy his battalion expertly as required. General von Hase had mentioned to him that there was a strong possibility that one of Remer's companies might be called upon to seize the propaganda ministry and arrest Goebbels himself, an event that Remer simply could not envision.

Hagen reached the ministry, but Goebbels wasn't there. He explained the urgency of his mission to some of the minister's underlings, and they arranged for an audience with Goebbels at his private residence without going through further bureaucratic channels. The motorcycle soon screeched to a stop in front of number 20 Hermann Göringstrasse.

"Well," Goebbels said airily, "what are you bringing me now, Lieutenant Hagen?" When Hagen outlined the situation outside and said that one of the Wehrmacht's elite units was about to seize the heart of the government there in Berlin, Goebbels was aghast. "But that's impossible!" he cried. Hagen assured him it was so, and Goebbels gathered his aides around to ask them what he should do. Hagen suggested that Goebbels talk face-to-face with Major Remer who, after all, held the trump cards. Suspicious, Goebbels asked, "Is he reliable?"

"On my head," answered Hagen.

The motorcycle blasted through the streets in a search for Remer. He was tracked down at his command post on the Unter den Linden, but was in conference with General Hase, whose interest in Hagen's lectures on National Socialism was only perfunctory. "I shrank from entering the general's room," Hagen said later. Instead he told another lieutenant what was afoot and urged him to pass the word to Remer when he came out, stressing that it was vital for Remer to see Goebbels as soon as humanly possible.

When Remer received Hagen's message, he went right back inside Hase's office and asked permission to go see the Reich minister. Hase, not at all sure that Goebbels was innocent of the plot to overthrow the government—after all, the provisional government in the Bendlerstrasse was ordering his arrest, and as yet he had not heard from anybody at the Wolf's Lair—turned down Remer's request. "You stay here," he ordered. Remer saluted and walked out, but he decided to put his neck on the block and go see Goebbels anyway. He confided in several of his officers, then climbed into his car; a few minutes later he was ushered into Goebbels's presence. Goebbels limped over to welcome the martial figure towering over him, and asked Remer if he were a convinced National Socialist. "Herr Reich Minister, that is self-evident," Remer replied. "I am with the Führer 100 percent." Whereupon Goebbels grasped Remer's hand in both of his own, and was gratified to hear Remer promise "as an honest National Socialist officer to perform my duty under any circumstances, true to my oath of loyalty to the Führer."

Releasing his hold on Remer, Goebbels picked up the telephone and asked for a blitz (lightning) connection with the Führer

207

at the Wolf's Lair. Hitler was on the line almost immediately and spoke to Remer. "Major Remer, can you hear me? Do you recognize my voice? They tried to kill me—but I'm alive! I'm speaking to you as your supreme commander. Only *my* orders are to be obeyed. You must restore order in Berlin for me. Use whatever force you find necessary. Shoot anybody who refuses to obey my orders!"

Remer's elation at being handed this major responsibility by the Führer himself can be imagined; he, an infantry major, given carte blanche to put down a revolt of the generals. Hitler's tactic in handling Remer was shrewd; Goebbels had already alerted the fanatically loyal SS Life Guards at Lichterfelde, but sending the SS against the Wehrmacht could only result in a bloody clash between these two natural enemies, with God only knew what consequences to the political structure at home. Now, the Wehrmacht would deal with its own.

Remer ordered his driver to hurry back to the command post. En route he noted with alarm unfamiliar armored and infantry units moving into position only several blocks west of the government quarter. Were they part of the Valkyrie forces? They were, but Remer did not pause to investigate. He continued to his command post and, without consulting General von Hase, ordered his junior officers to begin withdrawing the Guard Battalion from the extended periphery of the government quarter and assemble the units in the sprawling garden that fronted Goebbels's residence. He ordered Lieutenant Rudolf Schlee to the Bendlerstrasse, two miles away, to gather in the regular headquarters guard there and have them marched back to Goebbels's garden to join the others.

Schlee, accompanied by Lieutenant Herbert Arnds, took off for the Bendlerstrasse. When they arrived Schlee was told by the captain in charge to go up and see General Olbricht about removing the High Command's guard unit. "In spite of my reservations," Schlee later recalled, "I did this, for I wanted to know what was going on up there." Schlee told Arnds to form a combat patrol and come after him if he were not back within twenty minutes.

Schlee was directed to Colonel Mertz von Quirnheim, who exploded in anger when he heard Schlee's message. Telling Schlee to forget about removing the guard, he ordered him not to leave the room. But when Mertz von Quirnheim left the room to find Olbricht, Schlee opened a door leading to the main corridor and quick-marched down the staircase and outside the building, passing a huddle of generals on the way. Schlee was excited because he was sure he had found the seat of the entire conspiracy. He rushed back to report to Remer.

Remer had been kept busy rushing back and forth between his command post and Goebbels's house, and it was there that a breathless Lieutenant Schlee caught up with him. When Goebbels heard Schlee describe how the revolt was being run from the Bendlerstrasse, he got another blitz connection to the Führer. Schlee wanted to form an assault force and seize army headquarters. Hitler agreed at once, and Remer told Schlee to get his men together, head back for the Bendlerstrasse, and arrest them all, including the generals. Schlee lost no time in assembling more than 200 heavily armed men, including a bicycle platoon, and moving them off in the fading twilight to deal the final blow to the revolt in Berlin.

In Paris, that same twilight covered the preparations for the assault Stülpnagel had ordered before he left the city for the showdown with Kluge. The army commander for Greater Paris, General Hans von Boineburg-Lengsfeld, mustered the greater part of the 1st Garrison Regiment inside the Bois de Boulogne, that 2,500-acre forest on the western edge of the city. More than 2,000 of his troops, loaded aboard trucks and personnel carriers, were ready to debouch from the park. There were two objectives: the SS barracks on nearby boulevard Lannes, and the Gestapo headquarters on the avenue Foch, the broad thoroughfare running eastward to the Arc de Triomphe. Boineberg-Lengsfeld had fought at Stalingrad, and moving troops around in large cities was one of his specialties. He did not expect much trouble from the SS and the Gestapo, who for the past four years had busied themselves with arresting and torturing French civilians, but he told his battalion commanders to have their men open fire on anybody who resisted.

At 10:30 P.M. whistles blew, and the raiding force moved out of the park and rolled through the streets of Paris. Lieutenant Colonel Kurt von Kräwel's troops piled out of their trucks on the Avenue Foch, half of them deploying smartly in the street while Kräwel led the others bursting inside the building brandishing rifles and Schmeisser machine pistols. The Gestapo agents were caught flatfooted; only a few of them managed to scramble through windows half-dressed to flee down darkened streets. Kräwel ordered the rest outside and into waiting trucks.

The SS were taken equally unawares. Leading the assault on the Boulevard Lannes was General Walther Brehmer, a grizzled tough who had marched with Hitler down the streets of Munich in 1923; his chest blazed with decorations, including the rare medallion of the Blood Order conferred by the Führer himself, but Brehmer had lost his illusions and his enthusiasm long ago. He crashed into SS barracks with drawn pistol and shouted *Hande hoch!* The astonished SS slowly raised their hands, wondering at the intrusion. They, too, were hustled outside and ordered aboard Wehrmacht trucks for the ride to prison.

General Brehmer next swooped down on the SS commander in Paris, Gruppenführer Carl-Albrecht Oberg. When the door burst open, Oberg was seated at his desk talking on the telephone with the German ambassador, Otto Abetz. The SS general shot to his feet and asked what was the meaning of this outrage, but Brehmer motioned to him with his pistol to hang up the receiver, surrender his sidearm, and follow him outside the building.

It was a copy-book exercise, flawlessly executed, and went off without a shot being fired. More than 1,200 SS and Gestapo were put behind bars at the Wehrmacht prison at Fresnes and inside the stone casemates of the old Fort de l'Est. Oberg and other ranking SS and Gestapo officers were held captive at the Hotel Continental.

At the three-star Hotel Raphael, Stülpnagel's deputies waited for word from Berlin. Inside room 405, Friedrich von Teuchert and another war ministry official,. Walther Bargatsky, suffered through a Wagnerian opera blaring on the radio; they were waiting impatiently for Carl Goerdler's voice to break through the music to announce that he had just taken over as Germany's new chancellor. Paris trailed far behind events in Berlin, and no one there knew that the revolt was on the point of collapse in the German capital.

At 10:45 the door was flung open from the outside and Stülpnagel's chief of staff, Colonel Hans-Ottfried von Linstow, appeared, leaning heavily against the frame. Bargatsky knew that Linstow was a heart patient, and he thought the colonel was having an attack. Linstow gasped out, "All is lost. The struggle in Berlin is nearing an end. Stauffenberg has just telephoned. His executioners are raging around the corridors outside his office."

Bargatsky later recalled: "Only at that moment did we experience the terrible emotions of the conspirator, the certainty that we were outcast, the fear that we would be condemned by history. I cannot say why, after a silence a minute long, we each arrived at that diabolic calmness that was so necessary for an objective look at our predicament."

By nine-thirty that night Lieutenant Arnds had cleared the Bendlerstrasse of the members of the First Guards Battalion, and when General Olbricht looked out of the second-floor window he could see only a handful of his own sentries remaining. Alarming telephone calls were coming in to the effect that SS and Wehrmacht troops were assembling to storm the Bendlerstrasse. Olbricht realized that they would have to defend themselves if they could. There were six entrances to the building, and Olbricht ordered a half-dozen staff officers to arm themselves with submachine guns and take up their posts. Lieutenant colonels and majors hurried off to carry out orders usually handed to privates.

Incredibly enough, not all of Olbricht's staff officers realized they were taking part in a putsch; many still believed that the SS or the Gestapo was trying to take over the government. The disappearance of the guard and Olbricht's unprecedented action in ordering General Staff officers to man the barricades triggered suspicion among those still ignorant of the real purpose of the confused Valkyrie operation. Lieutenant Colonel Franz Herber, who wondered "what the real game was," called a quarter of equally baffled officers into another room and said they were being duped. After heated discussion, they decided to crush the revolt themselves without waiting for help from outside. Herber told Olbricht's ordnance officer, Major Herbert Fliessbach, to call up the arsenal at Spandau and have them deliver submachine guns and hand grenades as quickly as possible. After a while a truck pulled up at the rear entrance and offloaded the arms to be taken up to the second floor; Olbricht's officer posted at that entrance thought the weapons were for defense of the building and let them pass. Herber distributed the arms to six or eight officers and noncoms and told them what to do.

At 10:50, Stauffenberg heard a commotion outside in the corridors. Herber and the others burst inside Olbricht's office and covered him with cocked weapons. When Herber demanded the truth, Olbricht said he had nothing more to add to the general picture. "Why not ask General Fromm?" he suggested. Stauffenberg opened Olbricht's door to find the general facing armed and angry men. He wheeled around and fought his way through restraining arms, hurtling through the anteroom and Mertz von Quirnheim's office to reach the corridor.

Olbricht's secretary, Delia Zeigler, heard shouts and the cracking sounds of firing. "This is against the Führer! We stick to our Führer!" Frightened, she hurried down the corridor to reach another office and the companionship of another secretary, Anni Lerche. She was brushed aside by Stauffenberg and Lieutenant Haeften who were rushing pell-mell down the corridor. More firing erupted from behind her, and she dropped to the floor. She looked up and saw Stauffenberg wince, probably hit in the upper left arm. Behind her, two pistol shots rang out, fired by somebody at Herber's group.

Outside, Schlee's assault force had just arrived. He flung a seventy-man cordon around the entrance to the building and set up light machine guns at the entrances. "Things were really hectic," he recalled. "Officers armed with machine guns were running about, shouting orders. . . . We used no half-measures, arresting those who offered resistance and locking them in the doorman's alcove." Schlee sent twenty men upstairs; they collared everybody they encountered, barking out, "For or against the Führer?"

Schlee's men arrived inside the building at about the time Herber's group unlocked Fromm's door and escorted him upstairs to confront the conspirators. The shouting died down, and Fromm, flushed and angry, began to speak. Beck, Olbricht, Hoepner, Stauffenberg, and Haeften stood before him. "Well, gentlemen, now I am going to do to you what you wanted to do to me this afternoon."

Beck, looking suddenly old, told Fromm that he still had his pistol and wanted to use it on himself. Fromm told him to hurry up. Beck raised the gun to his head, closed his eyes, and squeezed the trigger. The pistol roared, but the slug only creased Beck's scalp. He reeled, blood spilling down his face and onto his gray suit. "Help the old fellow," Fromm said. Two officers approached Beck, who had slumped in a chair still gripping the pistol. They tried to wrench it away, but Beck said he wanted to try again. Fromm turned away from the scene and told the others to write their last letters. Olbricht asked for pen and paper, but Stauffenberg and the rest remained standing and silent.

Beck fired again, and again the wound was not mortal. Sick of this bungled self-butchery, an officer ordered a noncom to haul the former chief of the German General Staff into another room and finish the job. A single shot rang out; Beck finally was dead.

Fromm took it upon himself to order the execution of the ringleaders without first asking Hitler what he wanted done. He ordered Schlee to detail a firing squad and muster them in the courtyard behind the building. Schlee had Lieutenant Werner Schady of the Guard Battalion choose ten men and marched them outside. It was too dark to see, so Schady ordered a Wehrmacht truck driven into the courtyard, ready to turn its lights on when the time came.

Fromm gave Hoepner the choice of execution on the spot or imprisonment and trial later on when the Führer decided what he wanted done with the putschists. Hoepner decided to face Hitler's wrath and was taken away to prison. Then Fromm ordered Stauffenberg, Olbricht, Mertz von Quirnheim, and Haeften taken outside and shot.

At 12:21 A.M. the condemned men stood in a line in front of a sand embankment put in the courtyard for use on incendiary bombs. The courtyard was closely confined, and it seemed as though the firing squad was almost on top of them. Stauffenberg stood out from the rest because of his height and the white tunic he wore, now dirty and sweat-stained. It was almost exactly twelve hours since he had placed the bomb near Hitler's feet, and he was ready to pay the price for failure. The truck lights were switched on, blinding them. The firing began; those who watched heard Stauffenberg shout above the din, "Long live our sacred Germany!" Then he was knocked backward against the embankment and slumped dead.

The bodies lay sprawled unattended in the darkness before Fromm ordered them carted away. Beck's lifeless form was added to the four others, and they were flung into the back of a truck and driven to the Matthäus churchyard cemetery two miles away in south Berlin. They were hastily buried in unmarked graves, but the next morning Himmler ordered them dug up and cremated and their ashes scattered to the winds.

At 1:00 A.M. in Paris, Stülpnagel, Hofacker, Bargatsky, and the other French-based conspirators were gathered around radios to listen to the words of the men they had tried to overthrow. Recordings from the Wolf's Lair had been flown to Berlin, where Goebbels aired them on local and shortwave frequencies.

Hitler began by saying, "I don't know how many times by now assassinations have been planned and attempted against me, and I am speaking to you now so you will hear my voice and know that I am unhurt, and so you may know the details of a crime without equal in German history!" He referred to the conspirators as "a very small clique of ambitious, unscrupulous, and at the same time criminal and stupid officers," and accused them of trying to stab the army in the back, just as in 1918. He promised that those involved in trying to take the Führer away from the German people would be ruthlessly exterminated. He concluded his eight-minute address by saying that his survival was "a sign from Providence that I must, and therefore shall, continue my work."

After another military fanfare, Göring was heard from, lashing out at Stauffenberg and the other "cowards" and ordering his Luftwaffe people to apprehend and shoot down anyone trying to win them over to their abominable schemes. Admiral Dönitz spoke of "righteous wrath and boundless fury" at the plot to take the life of the beloved Führer. He called conspirators "dastardly cowards . . . stooges of our enemies whom they serve with unprincipled and false cleverness."

Stülpnagel, Hofacker, Finckh, and the rest of the staff huddled over the radio listened in silence, then switched off the receiver. The word of the night arrests of the Gestapo and SS had spread quickly, causing a brief moment of joy among Parisians, but causing indignation elsewhere. The Paris naval commandant, Admiral Theodor Krancke, was livid and ordered a thousand sailors armed and formed into companies to assault the prisons and free the captives. This word reached Stülpnagel at the Raphael shortly before he learned that SS Obergruppenführer Sepp Dietrich was threatening to disengage part of his armored corps from the Normandy front and fall on Paris. Everyone in Berlin was now dead or jailed; Kluge had failed them; what more could he do? Stülpnagel realized he was beaten, so at 2:00 A.M. he regretfully ordered Boineburg-Lengsfeld to spring all 1,200 prisoners and truck them back to their quarters. Then he sent a staff car to fetch SS commander Oberg from his hotel room.

Oberg entered the lobby of the Raphael in a white heat of rage, and when he saw Stülpnagel rising to meet him it seemed to those present that the SS general was ready to attack. Ambassador Abetz intervened and said, "Oberg, what happens in Berlin is one thing; here what matters is that the battle in Normandy is raging . . . here we Germans must show a united front." Oberg was persuaded to join the others who took seats in plush chairs arranged in a circle. Glancing at Stülpnagel, he said, "Herr general, you have backed the wrong horse." Stülpnagel showed Oberg the conflicting teleprinter messages, and Oberg calmed down. Champagne and brandy were ordered, and coaxed by Abetz, Oberg agreed that no real harm had been done, and perhaps there was a way out for Stülpnagel and his staff. Even the senior Gestapo officer, Helmut Knochen, chimed in with a proposal that a cover story be presented to Himmler claiming that the arrests were merely a preplanned exercise agreed to by all parties and that Stülpnagel was blameless for the putsch.

By now General Blumentritt had driven up from La Roche-Guyon, and he said he would do what he could to shield the military governor and the others from Hitler's wrath. The strange conclave in the lobby of the Raphael broke up toward four that morning after an exhausting day. Stülpnagel began to believe that he might not have to die after all.

In this he was mistaken, for with the sunrise on Friday, July 21, Europe would see the beginnings of Hitler's terrible revenge.

Part 3

Calvary

14

Vengeance

A LIGHT RAIN fell on Paris throughout Friday morning, July 21, a rain that brought with it sobering realities. Blumentritt had returned to his headquarters at 4:00 A.M. to find a teletype from Keitel ordering Stülpnagel to Berlin to explain his outrageous action of the night before. It was a fantasy to think that Stülpnagel could be shielded from the consequences. Blumentritt reluctantly passed the order along to Stülpnagel at nine. By now, Himmler was in Berlin to take over from Fromm as the new commander-in-chief, Home Army. Stülpnagel was repelled to think of the SS in charge of an important Wehrmacht post. He decided he would not accept a meeting with Heinrich Himmler, and declined the offer of a Luftwaffe courier plane to Berlin. Instead, he ordered his car prepared for the road.

The car, with Stülpnagel and two sergeants aboard, left the rain-slicked, cobbled streets of Paris and headed east through the open, rolling country of the Marne. The engine quit thirty miles out, and while the driver called for another car from the motor pool in Paris, Stülpnagel found a mattress in the corner of a garage and fell asleep. By 3:00 they were on their way again, and soon they reached the somber region of the Champagne. The general directed the car northward, over a narrow and little-used road above Verdun. The road ran through withered country where all the villages had been flattened during the war before this one—a desolate region where the topsoil had been blown away and where no birds sang. Stülpnagel had fought here as a captain of the Darmstadt Grenadiers in a consuming battle that was the Stalingrad of 1916: more than half a million men had lost their lives there.

He ordered the car stopped, explaining he was going for a little walk up forward. The sergeants protested, pointing out that the place was infested with armed French *Maquis*, but Stülpnagel waved them off and started walking across the old battlefield. When the car was out of sight below a fold of earth, Stülpnagel walked until he reached the bank of a canal filled with sluggish green water. He removed his cap, belt, and Knight's Cross and laid them on the bank. Then he pulled his pistol from its holster, placed the muzzle against his right temple, and fired. The impact tumbled him into the canal, where the sergeants found him a few minutes later floating face up in a reddening pool of water. He was dragged out of the canal still breathing, and rushed to the Wehrmacht hospital at Verdun.

Skilled surgery and transfusions saved Stülpnagel's life, but he was permanently blinded, and sightless he went to the gallows a few weeks later, along with Colonels Finckh and Linstow.

At about the same time that Stülpnagel was on his way to Verdun, General von Treskow was readying himself for his own rendezvous with death in Russia. When word came through that Valkyrie had failed, Treskow told his aide Schlabrendorff that since his name would turn up on the list of conspirators sooner or later, he had no option except to kill himself to prevent giving away others under torture.

"Schlabrendorff," he said, "God once promised to spare Sodom should there be found ten just men in the city. He will, I trust, spare Germany for what we have done, and not destroy her. None of us can complain of his lot. Whoever joined the resistance movement put on the shirt of Nessus. After all, the worth of a man is established only if he is ready to give his life for his convictions."

Treskow walked off toward a forest fronting the lines of the

28th Rifle Division and disappeared in the trees. He fired his pistol into the air to create the illusion of combat, then activated the fuse of a grenade and placed it against the side of his head. Treskow was listed as killed in action, and Schlabrendorff was detailed to escort the body back for burial in the family plot in Brandenburg.

When, as he had prophesied, Treskow's name surfaced as a key conspirator, the SS disinterred the remains and reviled them in front of Treskow's relatives, an act of barbarism indicating Hitler's insensate fury at those who betrayed him. Hitler's rage was tempered with political considerations. Wanting the German people to believe in an indispensable leader threatened by a small body of traitorous madmen, he insisted that terrible examples be made of the conspirators. But, as a tirade at the Wolf's Lair shows, he feared that the culprits' brief day in open court might prove more of an indictment of himself than of those in the dock.

"This time I'll make short shrift," Hitler rasped. "These criminals are not going to be put before a court-martial where their accomplices sit and where the trial is dragged on. They will be kicked out of the Wehrmacht and put before the People's Court. They are not to get an honest bullet, but they are to hang like common traitors! A court of honor will expel them from the Wehrmacht, then they can be tried as civilians and won't sully the name of the Wehrmacht. They've got to be tried at top speed. They mustn't be given a chance to say too much. And sentence must be carried out within two hours after the judgment is handed down. They must hang at once, without mercy, and, most importantly, they must not be given time for long speeches. Freisler will see to that."

On August 3, Himmler summoned all of the Reich's district party chiefs at Posen to reiterate what the Führer meant by vengeance, and he added a legal concept of his own, an outrage to the precepts of law and justice that he resurrected from the time when Germans still wore bearskins. In his high-pitched voice Himmler told the Party faithful:

"All you have to do is to read up on the old Germanic sagas.

When they proscribed a family and declared them outlaws, or when they had a vendetta, they went all the way. They had no mercy. They outlawed the entire family and proclaimed, *This man is a traitor, there is bad blood in that family, the blood of traitors, the whole lot must be exterminated.* In the case of vendettas, that is exactly what they did, down to the last member of the clan." What Himmler proposed was to install "a system of absolute liability on the grounds of kinship." This idea of justice was so novel that the word for it could not be found in any dictionary and one had to be created: *Sippenhaft*, literally, "tribe liability." To start with, Himmler proclaimed, "The Stauffenberg family will be exterminated root and branch!" At this, noted an observer, the chiefs burst into wild applause.

Even Hitler thought this was going too far, but he authorized Sippenhaft in a modified form: the Gestapo fell upon the Stauffenberg family and scattered it to the winds. Stauffenberg's wife was thrown into prison along with a newborn child, and his other four children were taken from the mother and sent to distant foster homes where they were forced to assume new names. A dozen women over the age of seventy were arrested, as were pregnant younger women, whose babies had to be born in prison hospitals. It was only a beginning; puzzled and terrified relatives, most of whom had no knowledge of their kin's involvement in the conspiracy, were dragged from their homes in the dead of night and flung in jail. "Sippenhaft" soon became one of the most dreaded words in Germany.

The first trials of the July 20 conspirators were held in the so-called People's Court in Berlin on August 8. The principal victims were Witzleben, Hoepner, Stieff, and General von Hase, the city commandant of Berlin who only unwittingly carried out the Valkyrie orders. Roland Freisler, who had dealt such summary justice to the clandestine White Rose group seventeen months earlier, dominated the proceedings with unusual vindictiveness and histrionics because he knew he was on camera: the Führer had ordered the courtroom proceedings to be filmed with synchronized sound. One of the top newsreel cameramen of the *Deutsche Wochenschau*, Erich Stoll, has described how they installed more powerful bulbs in the existing light fixtures and drilled holes in the doors to poke the lenses through so as to be as unobtrusive as possible. Freisler, again flamboyant in a scarlet robe and black hat, sent the recording-level needle bouncing to the end of the scale each time he spoke.

When the accused were pulled inside the courtroom by uniformed bailiffs, Stoll's cameras revealed men stripped of all dignity. Continuous interrogation had left them sleepless and dispirited. They entered the courtroom unshaven and dressed in ill-fitting, unpressed civilian clothes that better suited mendicants. Witzleben was not permitted to wear his false teeth, and jailers had taken away his belt and suspenders, forcing him to grasp the front of the baggy trousers to keep them up. Freisler badgered and taunted these former Wehrmacht generals and field marshals, referring to them as cowards, knaves, and traitors. To a court stenographer named Peter Vossen, Freisler seemed to wear "a theatrical, merciless expression on his face—obviously practiced in front of a mirror—like a second Robespierre."

Witzleben refused to be intimidated. Freisler lashed out at him for a conversation he had with Beck in 1943, when they discussed the Führer's tendency to elevate political reliability above strategic and tactical capability in choosing field commanders. "Did you think on that occasion who could do it better?" Freisler yelled.

"Yes!" replied Witzleben.

"Who, then, could have done it better?"

"Both[of us]," said Witzleben.

"Both! Both of you! This is an outrage that has never before been perpetrated here. A field marshal and a general declare that they could do things better than he who is the Führer of all of us, who had made the borders of the Reich the borders of Europe. . . . You profess to having said this?"

"Yes!" Witzleben shot back.

When any of the defendants tried to inject into the record their motivations for wanting Hitler removed, Freisler shouted them down in a voice "that must have been heard like a trumpet in the surrounding streets, violating all the rules of secrecy."

The results of the trial were a foregone conclusion; all those who stood before Freisler were condemned to death by hanging, as Hitler ordered.

Then, with the knowledge that the sound cameras were running, Freisler stood to his feet and cried, "We return to life, to the struggle. Our people have freed themselves from *them*. We fight on. The Wehrmacht voices its salute, *Heil Hitler!* We all voice our salute, *Heil Hitler!* We struggle together with our Führer, following him for Germany. We have cast out the danger. With full strength we march toward the final victory."

The condemned men were handcuffed and taken across the railroad tracks to Plötzensee Prison, facing the Lehrterstrase, where they were put to death one by one on the afternoon of the trial. The execution chamber looked like the abbatoir it was: a single door led inside a high-ceilinged chamber with dirty gray paint peeling from the brickwork. A guillotine stood in the center of the room, lighted only by the pale rays of sunlight admitted through two narrow windows. A steel I-beam ran the twenty-six-foot length of the chamber, from which hung hooks used to suspend the carcasses of beef. Witzleben went first, his hands tied around his back, his ankles roped together. A hemp rope was placed around his neck, then he was lifted from the stone floor by two executioners who attached the loop at the other end of the rope to one of the hooks, then let him drop.

The cameras invaded even here, and one of the newsreel men described how "a narrow black curtain was drawn in front of the hanged man so the next one could not see the man who had gone before him. . . . Each doomed man walked his last steps erect and manly, with no words of complaint." After each corpse dangled for twenty minutes, as laid down by Reich law, the curtains were drawn back and the bodies stripped for exposure to film whirring through the motion picture cameras. Only then were the bodies lifted from the hooks and carted away to the Berlin Anatomical Institute for cremation and secret burial.

The negatives were rushed through processing, and 35-mm prints were flown out to the Wolf's Lair for those who had the stomach to sit through the screening. Some of Freisler's later trials were filmed in the same way as the first, but the staff of the *Deutsche Wochenschau* refused to a man to bring their cameras to subsequent Plötzensee executions.

That evening Carl Goerdler boarded a train on the outskirts of Berlin to begin a final pilgrimage to West Prussia. He was dressed in a suit of rough material and carried a rucksack and a heavy walking stick, as though bound for a carefree walking tour in the mountains. Goerdler, anything but carefree, was a man crushed by the failure of a dream: instead of sitting in the chancellor's chair trying to work out a peace with the Allies and planning for a new Germany, he was a fugitive who had been on the run for twenty-three days. Hitler had put a price of 1 million marks on his head for his part in the overthrow plot, and his picture was being circulated throughout the Reich like a common criminal's. He had passed his sixtieth birthday the week before, but he was a man without hope, and he doubted he would live to be sixty-one.

For the past three weeks Goerdler had been sheltered by one friend or relative after the other, seldom sleeping in the same place twice. Without passport, travel permit, or ration cards, escape was impossible; he could only move peripatetically from one Berlin suburb to the other—waiting, as did his hosts, for the Gestapo's knock at the door. Goerdler realized that his presence was no longer an honor but a liability, and that those who shared their slender rations with him were risking a trip to Dachau. Goerdler knew that eventually he would wind up in the hands of his pursuers, but first he wanted to visit his parents' graves at Marienwerder, not far from his birthplace.

Goerdler reached Marienwerder two days later, after switching from one local train to another, sleeping when he could on hard coach benches and in waiting rooms. On the morning of the eleventh he started walking to the cemetery; just as he reached the gate he was recognized. Goerdler quickly turned away and hiked off through fields and woods. After several hours of heavy going in the summer's heat, he reached the shores of a lake and eased himself down to sleep on the ground.

He awoke with hunger pangs, and decided to risk having breakfast at a *Gasthaus* at Konradswalde, a way from the place where he had been recognized. While waiting for breakfast, he looked up to see a table filled with Luftwaffe personnel. Goerdler had forgotten about the airfield nearby. Staring at him was a young female Luftwaffe auxiliary who had known the Goerdlers from before the war. Goerdler hurriedly left the table and set off across open country to reach the cover of some woods. Helene Schwaerzel excitedly told the two Luftwaffe paymasters sitting at the table that she recognized Carl Goerdler, and they took off in hot pursuit, easily catching up with the older man to make Helene Schwaerzel a quarter of a million dollars richer.

Under intense interrogation by the Gestapo in Berlin, Goerdler revealed a wealth of information about the plans to overturn the Nazi régime, but he was careful to shield those who had given him shelter while he was a fugitive. As he had done all along, Goerdler vehemently disavowed participation in any of the plans for the Führer's assassination. He poured out his soul to the Gestapo, and indeed wrote fresh drafts of how Germany could be idealized under another system of government. He freely admitted his distaste for National Socialism, and he named a host of minor philosophers and economists who had worked with him to transform Germany. A month after Goerdler had been pumped dry of information, he was turned over to Freisler's court and swiftly condemned to death.

Now Heinrich Himmler entered the scene and stayed the execution. Himmler knew the war was lost and desperately wanted to open a dialogue with the Allies to end the war. He thought the best route lay through neutral Sweden. Goerdler's sympathetic SS guard, Wilhelm Brandenburg, recalled: "Himmler invited him to use his close personal and political contacts with the Swedish banker Jakob Wallenberg in Stockholm, and with the Zionist leader Chaim Weizmann, and through them the King of Sweden. In short, he was to do what he and his circle would have done had the coup d'etat succeeded, that is, pave the way for contact with Churchill and end the war on acceptable terms."

Goerdler seized the opportunity to realize his original ambition and to free the noose from his neck. From his cell he laid down his terms to Himmler: free Goerdler unconditionally and provide him safe conduct to Stockholm where he would plead the case in person, he hoped with the king himself. Himmler pondered and stalled, but finally got word to Goerdler that what he proposed was impossible. Undaunted, Goerdler now had the wild idea of putting the same proposal to Hitler, an even more hopeless undertaking. Goerdler stayed busy to the last, writing out political manifestos and outlines for economic reform on paper smuggled into his cramped cell by the guard. Five months after his arrest he was taken to the meathooks at Plötzensee.

By August 15 the crucial battle for Normandy was being fought inside a pocket twenty miles wide and more than thirty deep. Field Marshal von Kluge had recklessly flung his armor and infantry in a drive for Mortain, and within hours the flanking American and British armies threatened to slam the door shut in the German rear, putting a quarter of a million German troops in the bag. Back at the Wolf's Lair Hitler frantically waited for Kluge's report on what was to become known as the battle of the Falaise gap. But Kluge could not be reached by Keitel from East Prussia, and commanders in Normandy replied that the field marshal had been incommunicado for several hours. A wild thought flew to Hitler's mind: Kluge was dealing with the enemy in the hopes of ending the war. The Führer straightaway ordered Field Marshal Walter Model to fly to Normandy from Russia to replace Kluge and to extract the irreplacable Wehrmacht and SS armor.

Kluge, in fact, was inside the Falaise pocket in a command car trailed by his communications trailer trying to salvage the rapidly deteriorating battle. There was no sign of the Luftwaffe, but the air was alive with strafing Spitfires and P-51s. It was a fighter that howled down to shoot Kluge's communications to pieces, accounting for the extended silence.

Kluge turned over his armies to Model on August 17 and departed for Germany. The next day he composed a letter to Hitler in which he praised Hitler's "greatness" and "genius," then closed by begging the Führer to exhibit a higher level of greatness by putting an end to the hopeless struggle because "the German people have endured such unspeakable agonies that it is time to end this horror."

Kluge's car continued across France, and it was nearly noon on the nineteenth before they reached the neighborhood of Verdun. Kluge and his aides paused for lunch before going on to Germany, and after lunch Kluge said he wanted to take a short walk. When Kluge failed to return, his aides began a search that ended with the discovery of his body. Kluge had bit down on a small glass vial of cyanide and had died instantly.

Hitler reacted by saying to Keitel and some others, "There are strong reasons to suspect that had he not committed suicide he would have been arrested anyway. I am bitterly disappointed! I personally promoted him twice, gave him the highest decorations, gave him a large estate so he could have a permanent home and gave him a huge supplement to his pay . . . Freisler wanted to question the field marshal, but then he was no longer alive. I don't want this to leak out, I don't want this business talked about . . . it would certainly foster contempt for the army." Hitler ordered Kluge buried without fanfare in his native village; heart failure was given as the cause of death.

Ernst Kaltenbrunner, head of the special commission to investigate the events leading up to the twentieth of July, sent his ferrets into every likely office and archive in the Reich, a paper chase joined in relentlessly by the SS security network. In September investigators came across a heretofore-overlooked safe in the basement in the headquarters at Zossen. There they discovered the meticulously kept notes jotted down by Beck and parts of a diary with entries made in Canaris's hand. For the first time Hitler was made aware that officers in his own High Command had plotted against him since 1938. Details of the Vatican exchanges were spelled out, as was the shocking revelation that Oster and the others had betrayed his plans for the invasion of France and the Lowlands. These revelations added to the incriminating evidence already extracted during sessions at the People's Court and from

Goerdler's exhaustive confessions, providing Hitler with a picture of treason not only among the military hierarchy, but among former labor officials, intellectuals, and the religious and industrial communities.

The pace of arrests was stepped up, and soon more than 700 Germans suspected of even peripheral complicity in the plot were languishing behind bars waiting for Gestapo interrogation.* Fabian von Schlabrendorff was seized in his quarters near the front lines in Poland on August 17, and his recounted experiences as a prisoner in the cellars of the Prinz Albrechtstrasse speak of the agonies endured by the hapless victims of Hitler's rage and Gestapo methods.

Direct interrogation failed to draw from Schlabrendorff any information about himself or others. The next stage was the employment of obvious psychology: one official would threaten him with physical terror, another would slide in with the offer of cigarettes and confidential chats, another would appeal to his code of honor as an officer in the Wehrmacht. Schlabrendorff remained silent.

Then he was dragged from his cell in the dead of night and shoved into a room with his hands chained behind his back. His fingers were spread apart and fitted with steel cylinders lined with needle points. A guard turned handles, driving the sharp pins into Schlabrendorff's flesh, causing the blood to squirt. Through the exquisite pain Schlabrendorff refused to confess. Then he was thrown down on an iron frame, a rough woolen blanket dropped on his face to muffle his screams. This time both legs were given the Iron Maiden treatment, punctured in dozens of places from ankle to thigh. When this brought no results, his bleeding body was strapped to a rack designed in the Middle Ages and his limbs nearly wrenched from their sockets. When he regained consciousness, his tormentors roped him in a bent kneel-

---

*It is a testimony to the courage shown in Gestapo cells that four of the Wehrmacht officers who planned to liquidate Hitler—Gersdorff, von dem Bussche, Breitenbuch, and Boeslager—were never picked up, their names never revealed by others. Boeslager was killed in action in Normandy; the others survived the war.

ing position; "then the Police Commissioner and the sergeant fell on me from behind and beat me with heavy clubs. Each blow caused me to fall forward, and because my hands were chained behind my back I crashed full force on my face." Unable to walk, Schlabrendorff was dragged back to his cell and dumped on a pallet, wearing only his bloody underwear.

The next morning Schlabrendorff had a heart attack, from which he recovered only to be subjected to a second round of torture more brutal than the first. He decided that he either must kill himself or feed the Gestapo some harmless bit of information. Yes, he said, he did know of Treskow's plan to persuade the Führer to step down in favor of one of his field marshals and put an end to the war. This simple confession put an end to the torture, but not to his confinement. Schlabrendorff spent the next four months locked up, first inside the concentration camp at Sachsenhausen, then back to cell 24 at Gestapo HQ in Berlin.

On December 21 Schlabrendorff and five others were put in the dock at the People's Court. Schlabrendorff watched while Freisler sentenced all the others to death by hanging, one after the other, but he was reprieved when the court adjourned before his own case could be called. Six weeks went by before Schlabrendorff was again handcuffed and driven through the rubble of Berlin to face Freisler for what he was sure would be the last time.

Schlabrendorff was forced to sit through the trial of another defendant on the morning of February 3, 1945, wondering when his own long ordeal would be over. Freisler was suddenly stopped in midsentence by the dreaded sound of Berlin's air raid sirens winding up all over the city. Wave after wave of silver-glinting American B-17s were streaming toward the battered capital, more than anyone had ever seen before. The courtroom was quickly emptied as everyone crowded down the stairs to seek safety in the basement.

The heavy bombs began walking through the city, and the earth heaved under Schlabrendorff's feet. Then the sky seemed to explode. The basement ceiling flew apart; timber and bricks cascaded down. To Schlabrendorff it seemed "as though the end of the world had come." When the choking dust had cleared enough to see, those uninjured began pulling others from the debris. They found Freisler dead in one corner, his skull crushed by the fall of a heavy beam, one hand clutching Schlabrendorff's file. It seemed to Schlabrendorff that justice had indeed come from the heavens.

He was tried again a month later, this time before Freisler's successor, Wilhelm Krohne, who surprisingly allowed Schlabrendorff to speak in his own defense. The prisoner cited the fact that his confession had been extracted under torture, although "Frederick the Great had abolished torture in Prussia two hundred years earlier." Krohne dismissed the charges, but Schlabrendorff nonetheless found himself on the way to the extermination camp at Flossenburg near the Czech border. Here, part of the remaining drama of the seven-year-old conspiracy against Adolf Hitler would be played out.

Despite the overwhelming problems closing in on Germany from every side, Hitler continued to devote a part of each day to reading fresh reports of the arrests, trials, and executions of those who had plotted against him. When Stülpnagel's Luftwaffe aide, Colonel von Hofacker, was run to ground, he signed a statement that Field Marshal Rommel had stood ready to end the war in the west once Hitler had been disposed of. This revelation shook Hitler to the core; Hofacker was later hanged like all the rest, but Hitler could not envision this treatment being meted out to Germany's most popular soldier; the damage to the reputation of the army would be irreparable. On the other hand, Rommel had recuperated from his injuries, and who knew what he might be capable of?

Hitler ordered Rommel to appear at the Wolf's Lair, but the "invitation" was turned down. On October 14, Generals Ernst Maisel and Wilhelm Burgdorf appeared at Rommel's home in Ulm with an ultimatum: suicide or a trial in Berlin with the attendant disgrace to his name and his family. He had only a few minutes to think it over. Rommel spoke privately with his wife and sixteen-year-old son, Manfred, telling them he was taking a ride with the generals and would not be coming back. Twenty minutes later he was dead, having bitten down on a vial of cyanide Burgdorf had brought along for the purpose. Hitler kept his promise of a state funeral befitting one of Germany's great heroes, and it wasn't until after the war that Rommel's part, however small, in the conspiracy became known.

By April, Allied armies were across the Rhine and fighting their way through Germany town by town, while the Russians in the east were overrunning Poland and East Prussia. Hitler finally had to abandon the Wolf's Lair and return to the underground bunker deep in the earth below the ruins of the Chancellery. When the time came, he said, he would emerge from the bunker and "die fighting at the head of his troops."

As the American and British armies swept down on the concentration camps scattered throughout Bavaria and in northern Germany, the ovens were kept going twenty-four hours a day. The discovery of the rest of Canaris's diary sealed the fate of many of those conspirators still left alive. Hans von Dohnanyi, Oster's assistant, was carried to the gallows on a stretcher, propped up, and hanged. On April 8, 1945, guards at Flossenbürg pulled Oster and Canaris from their cells and led them nude to the executioner's rope, after which they were put in wheelbarrows, trundled to the crematory, and burned. Schlabrendorff thought he might be next, but four days later he and several others—including General Franz Halder, former chief of staff, and economist Hjalmar Schacht—were put aboard trucks for transfer to Dachau on orders from Himmler.

Those same orders, dated April 5 in Berlin, contained instructions to the Dachau camp commandant to liquidate Georg Elser, executor of the attempted beer-hall assassination, now a prisoner for nearly five years. For reasons he kept to himself, Himmler wanted the master cabinetmaker's death to appear accidental. He wrote: "During the next air raid, that is to say, the next terror bombing, see to it that Elser is mortally wounded. . . . Destroy this order when the deed has been executed." American bombers were over in force on the morning of April 9, and Elser was led

232

unprotesting from his cell and shot dead in a remote area of the compound.

During the final week of April it was clear even to the prisoners still lodged in Berlin jail cells that it could be only a matter of days before the Russians swamped the ruined capital, ending the war for all practical purposes. Surely the executions would stop. They did not, however; Hitler and Goebbels were still functioning in their burrow beneath the earth, still giving orders.

At 1:00 A.M. on April 23, sixteen prisoners condemned by the People's Court were taken from their cells at Moabit Prison and told they were being removed from Berlin and taken to Potsdam. Leading the column of prisoners was Herbert Kosney, a young Berliner who felt far from reassured by the sight of their SS escort walking on either side of the column with unslung submachine guns. They were led outside into the rain and darkness and marched through streets littered with rubble to reach a nearby bomb-cratered park. An SS Sturmführer barked at them to halt, and Kosney knew that none of them would reach the station. Fiery blasts from the gun muzzles suddenly lighted up the night, and Kosney was knocked forward by a slug that tore through his neck. He lay still on the ground, listening to the firing, hoping the SS would not bother making the rounds to deliver the *coups de grâce*. The SS went away, and after a few minutes Kosney crawled away to find medical attention. He was the only survivor.

The SS indulged in a final paroxysm of killing early the following morning at Plötzensee and in the cellar of the Gestapo headquarters. Then they began to disappear, shedding their uniforms and weapons before falling into the hands of the Russians.

Adolf Hitler's last ten days were spent underground in an atmosphere of unreality and desperation. April 20 was the Führer's fifty-sixth birthday. The Allies celebrated the occasion with a heavier than usual plastering of Berlin with high-explosive bombs delivered by high-flying B-17s of the U.S. Eighth Air Force. When the Fortresses droned away from the shattered capital and headed back for England, Hitler made his way up from the bunker to award Iron Crosses to a waiting rank of Hitler Youths standing at attention in the ruined Chancellery garden. These uniformed boys, thirteen to fifteen years old, had been fighting Russian tanks that had broached the Oder River only forty-five miles east of Berlin. Hitler chatted briefly with the awestruck child warriors, then turned and made his way slowly down the spiral staircase leading back to his underground shelter.

Berlin was all but surrounded—only a narrow corridor leading southward toward Bavaria was open—and others in Hitler's entourage joined Field Marshal Keitel in urging him to flee to the Obersalzberg while there was still time. Hitler looked at Keitel and replied, "I know what I want. I'm going to go down fighting either inside or outside of Berlin!" Göring, whom Hitler blamed for failing to stop the cascade of bombs that were falling on the Reich, asked the Führer if *he* could leave Berlin for the Obersalzberg. Hitler coolly gave his permission, and the fat field marshal hurried away from the bunker.

Although even a cursory glance at the military situation maps provided glaring proof that Berlin was doomed, Hitler nevertheless radiated confidence that the Russians would suffer their greatest defeat when they reached the gates of the capital. This confidence sustained Hitler throughout the rest of his birthday, even when a new series of air raids began that night. At dinner that evening—the usual vegetarian repast shared with his mistress, Eva Braun, and his two secretaries—he once again listened to pleas that he fly south and direct the final struggle from the Berghof. Once again he refused, saying, "I must force a decision here—or perish."

The American Ninth Army, under General William Simpson, had reached the Elbe River five days earlier and stopped there. Simpson's infantry and tanks were only forty miles from the western outskirts of Berlin, and the general predicted that the Ninth could launch an arrow thrust at the heart of the capital and be inside the city within twenty-four hours. Simpson's divisions were eager to continue their pell-mell dash for Berlin, but their hopes were extinguished when the supreme commander, General Dwight D. Eisenhower, ordered them to halt along the Elbe; the

Russians, Eisenhower had decided, could have the capital of the Reich. Now Berliners, totally unprepared for organized defense, girded themselves to face the onslaught of the Red Army.

Hitler's hopes for the salvation of the city lay in the belief that the Americans and the British would have a disastrous falling-out with the Bolsheviks and begin fighting among themselves; until this happened, the Führer depended upon the fighting qualities of General Walther Wenck's Twelfth Army, then hemmed in with the Elbe at its back and elements of the Red Army at its front. Hitler was sure Wenck could fight his way through the Russians and raise the siege of Berlin. North of the capital was SS General Felix Steiner's combat reserve, two depleted divisions lacking ammunition, fuel, and even motivation. Hitler's eyes brightened at the thought of these Wehrmacht and SS veterans fighting their way south and east to turn back the Bolshevik hordes, and he issued orders for the counterattacks to be launched at once. Hitler warned Steiner that any officer of his command who refused to join in the attack was to be shot out of hand.

Steiner, however, had no intention of sacrificing his worn troops in an attempt to carry out what he considered insane and suicidal orders. Berlin was only twenty-five miles to his south, but the country between the Führerbunker and his divisions swarmed with Red Army tanks, infantry, and artillery, and any movement in that direction could only mean captivity or death. When it became clear that Steiner was not going to budge, Hitler sagged visibly, then flew into a rage, screaming that he was surrounded by "traitors and liars." He realized that even SS generals could disobey his orders with impunity, and he stormed, "The war is lost—hopelessly lost." His rage spent, Hitler fell heavily into an armchair, the pallor of death on his face, his arms and right leg jumping uncontrollably.

Göring, safe in Berchtesgaden, was told that the Führer, in a state of collapse, was speaking of killing himself. Göring at once composed a radiogram that began, "My Führer, is it your wish, in view of your decision to remain in Berlin, that I take over complete control of the Reich in accordance with the decree of

29 June 1941?" He went on to say that if he had received no answer from Hitler by ten that night he would take over the reins of government himself on the assumption that Hitler had been deprived of his freedom of action. The result of the message was predictable: Göring was stripped of all official powers and placed under house arrest by the SS.

Where is Wenck? The question was repeatedly posed by Hitler in the following days. Wenck had in fact turned his corps around and was trying to fight his way to Berlin, but his attack stalled south of Potsdam, twenty-five miles west of the center of Berlin. By April 27, Berlin was completely encircled by the Red Army, and house-to-house fighting was going on in the suburbs. One of Hitler's secretaries, Traudl Junge, recalled that she and the others "expected some sort of decision, but nothing happened. Maps were spread out on tables, all the doors were left open, nobody could sleep any more, nobody knew the date or the time. Hitler could not bear to be alone; he kept walking up and down through the small rooms and talking with everybody who remained. He spoke of imminent death and the end which was coming."

Hitler still clung to the hope that Wenck's command would somehow smash through the ever-tightening Russian ring of steel that surrounded Berlin, but as the hours dragged by the hope was finally abandoned. Berlin was an inferno: fires blazed everywhere; buildings were being methodically reduced by Russian shellfire. Grimy bands of German defenders—young boys and old men of the *Volkssturm*, the Home Guard, leavened with a scattering of Werhmacht veterans, fought behind barricades and from house to house against the swarms of fur-hatted Red Army troops, who advanced against the heaviest fire without regard for casualties. German females from the ages of twelve to seventy were dragged from hiding places and raped repeatedly. An eerie orange haze hung over the city: the sun was blotted out by brick dust and rising clouds of smoke in the warm spring air.

On April 29 Hitler was dealt two more blows: word reached him that Heinrich Himmler had flown to the port city of Lübeck to discuss ways of surrendering unconditionally to the Western powers with the Swedish nobleman, Count Folke Bernadotte, who had agreed to act as a middleman. Now "Faithful Heinrich," as Hitler used to call him, had become a traitor as well. Then Hitler learned that Benito Mussolini, whom he had last seen at Rastenburg on the day Stauffenberg's bomb went off, had been seized by Italian partisans, shot, and strung up by his heels along with his mistress outside of a gas station in Milan. Hitler told the others that he would never allow the Russians to take him alive, that he had no intention of being led in a cage through the streets of Moscow or preserved as a stuffed figure in a communist wax museum. There was no other course, he said, except to die by his own hand and have his body consumed by flames.

With the bunker trembling from the impact of shells falling in the Chancellery area, Hitler summoned Traudl Junge and asked her to take dictation. "Begin," he said, "with the heading, 'My Political Testament.' " Hitler's last words included the expulsion of Göring and Himmler from the Nazi party and the appointment of Admiral Karl Dönitz as successor to the Führer; he blamed "the political clique in England" and "international Jewry" for causing the war. Hitler left his personal possessions to the National Socialist party, "or if this no longer exists, to the state." Then Hitler surprised everyone by announcing his intention to marry at last his mistress of many years, Eva Braun, who had refused to leave the bunker although her safety was at stake. The civil ceremony was performed almost immediately afterward.

Now Hitler turned his thoughts to how and when he and his wife would kill themselves. The bunker was amply supplied with cyanide capsules, which Hitler ordered passed all around—including eight vials for Goebbels, his wife, and their six young children. But would the things really work? Hitler ordered one of his assistants to fetch his aging companion, the German shepherd named Blondi. The dog's jaws were prised open, and the glass capsule was broken with pliers. A strong smell of bitter almonds quickly filled the room. Blondi jerked in agony and fell over dead.

On the morning of April 30 heavy combat flamed through the Teirgarten only a few hundred yards from the bunker, and the earth continued to heave with a succession of explosions from the rain of mortar and artillery shells. Hitler shaved and dressed himself as usual, having already made up his mind to kill himself that afternoon: the cyanide capsule and a 7.65-mm Walther automatic were already in his pocket. After a light lunch of spaghetti and sauce, washed down with tea, he began making his farewells to those who had remained behind with him in the bunker.

At 3:30 P.M. Hitler and Eva Braun entered the small sitting room that adjoined his spartan bedroom and closed the door behind them. A few moments later those standing outside heard a shot, then Sturmbannführer Otto Gunsche rushed inside to find both Hitler and Eva Braun sprawled dead on a faded, blue-and-white settee. They were carried upstairs in blankets, doused with gasoline, and set blazing. The bodies burned most of the afternoon.

On May 4 Schlabrendorff and many others were in the village of Niedernhausen, south of the Brenner Pass. When Dachau was about to fall in the hands of the Americans, the camp was broken up and the prisoners marched eastward into Austria. The departure was so hurried that the corpses of Jews were still stacked up waiting to be shoveled into the ovens. The prisoners, including a French bishop, two Greek generals, and the former Wehrmacht commander in Belgium, General Alexander von Falkenhausen, were joined in Innsbruck by more prisoners before continuing the trek south. They were later joined by a company of German infantry driven out of Italy, and in the uncertain circumstances Schlabrendorff asked himself: *Will the SS shoot the prisoners? Will the regular troops shoot the SS? Or will the Italian partisans shoot the whole lot of us?*

It was at Niederhausen that the SS guards simply took off, leaving the mixed bag of prisoners to shift for themselves. Schlabrendorff and the others were still wondering what to do when the decision was taken out of their hands by the unexpected arrival of an advance party of Americans, who wheeled into the town square aboard Jeeps. Schlabrendorff felt ashamed of his filthy uniform issued at Dachau: when an American brigadier got out of his Jeep and walked over to Schlabrendorff's group, the

German officer's first thought was, "How beautifully tailored his uniform is, what an elegant figure he cuts."

He thought next that he would soon be free. He was thankful to be one of the few who had opposed Hitler who would survive to tell about it.

Appendix I

_____

KNOWN VICTIMS OF HITLER'S VENGEANCE FOLLOWING THE ASSASSINATION ATTEMPT OF JULY 20, 1944

Beck, General Ludwig	Suicide
Bernadis, Lieutenant Robert	Executed
Bernstorff, Count Albrect von	Executed
Blumenthal, Major Hans Jürgen von	Executed
Boehmer, Lieutenant Colonel Hasso von	Executed
Bolz, Eugen	Executed
Bonhoeffer, Claus	Executed
Bonhoeffer, Pastor Dietrich	Executed
Breidbach-Bürresheim, Randolph	Executed
Brucklmeir, Eduard	Executed
Caminecci, Oscar	Executed
Canaris, Admiral Wilhelm	Executed
Cramer, Walter	Executed
Delbrück, Justus	Died in camp
Delp, Alfred, SJ	Executed
Dieckmann, Wilhelm	Executed
Dohnanyi, Hans von	Executed
Dohna-Tolksdorf, Count Heinrich	Executed
Dorsch, Lieutenant Hans Martin	Executed
Drechsel, Count Max von	Executed
Elsas, Dr. Fritz	Executed
Engelhorn, Lieutenant Colonel Karl-Heinz	Executed
Erdmann, Lieutenant Colonel Hans Otto	Executed
Fellgiebel, General Erich	Executed

APPENDIX I

Finckh, Colonel Eberhard	Executed
Fleischmann, Max	Suicide
Frank, Reinhold	Executed
Freytag-Loringhoven, Colonel Wessel von	Suicide
Frick, Walter	Executed
Gehre, Captain Lugwig	Executed
Gloeden, Elisabeth Charlotte	Executed
Gloeden, Erich	Executed
Goerdler, Dr. Carl Friedrich	Executed
Goerdler, Fritz	Executed
Groscurth, Colonel Helmut	Died in camp
Gross, Nikolaus	Executed
Guttenburg, Karl Ludwig von	Executed
Habermann, Max	Suicide
Haeften, Hans Bernd von	Executed
Haeften, Lieutenant Werner von	Executed
Hagen, Albrecht von	Executed
Hahn, Colonel Kurt	Executed
Halem, Nikolaus von	Executed
Hamm, Eduard	Suicide
Hansen, Colonel Georg	Executed
Harnack, Ernst von	Executed
Hase, General Paul von	Executed
Hassell, Ulrich von	Executed
Haubacu, Dr. Theodor	Executed
Haushofer, Albrecht	Executed
Hayessen, Major Egbert	Executed
Helldorf, Count Wolf von	Executed
Herfurth, General Otto	Executed
Hoepner, General Erich	Executed
Hofacker, Lieutenant Colonel Cäsar von	Executed
Hösslin, Major Roland von	Executed
Hübener, Otto	Executed
Jaeger, Colonel Friedrich	Executed
Jennewein, Max	Executed
Jessen, Jens	Executed
John, Hans	Executed
Kaiser, Hermann	Executed
Kempner, Franz	Executed
Kiep, Otto	Executed

Kissling, Georg Conrad	Executed
Klamroth, Lieutenant Colonel Bernhard	Executed
Klamroth, Hans-Georg	Executed
Klausing, Captain Friedrich-Karl	Executed
Kleist-Schmenzin, Ewald von	Executed
Knaak, Major Gerhard	Executed
Koch, Dr. Hans	Executed
Koerner, Heinrich	Executed
Kranzfelder, Lieutenant Commander Alfred	Executed
Kuenzer, Richard	Executed
Kutznitzki, Elise Auguste von	Executed
Lancker, Lieutenant Colonel von der	Executed
Langbehn, Carl	Executed
Leber, Dr. Julius	Executed
Lehndorff-Steinort, Count Heinrich von	Executed
Lejeune-Jung, Dr. Paul	Executed
Leonrod, Major Ludwig von	Executed
Letterhaus, Bernhard	Executed
Leuninger, Franz	Executed
Leuschner, Wilhelm	Executed
Lindemann, Else	Executed
Lindemann, General Fritz	Executed
Linstow, Colonel Hans-Ottfried von	Executed
Lünick, Ferdinand von	Executed
Lynar, Count Wilhelm	Executed
Maass, Hermann	Executed
Marcks, Karl	Executed
Marogna-Redwitz, Colonel Rudolf von	Executed
Matuschka, Count Michael von	Executed
Mertz von Quirnheim, Colonel Albrecht	Executed
Moltke, Count Helmuth von	Executed
Müller, Dr. Otto	Died in Prison
Mumm von Schwarzenstein, Herbert	Executed
Munzinger, Lieutenant Colonel Ernst	Executed
Nebe, Arthur	Executed
Nieden, Wilhelm zur	Executed
Oertzen, Major Ulrich von	Suicide
Olbricht, General Friedrich	Executed
Oster, General Hans	Executed
Perels, Friedrich Justus	Executed

Planck, Erwin	Executed
Plettenberg, Kurt von	Suicide
Popitz, Johannes	Executed
Rabenau, General Friedrich von	Executed
Rathgens, Lieutenant Colonel Karl Ernst	Executed
Reichwein, Adolf	Executed
Roenne, Colonel Alexis von	Executed
Rommel, Field Marshal Erwin	Suicide
Sack, Dr. Karl	Executed
Sadrozinski, Lieutenant Colonel Joachim	Executed
Salviati, Major Hans-Viktor von	Executed
Schack, Count Akfred Freidrich von	Executed
Schleicher, Rüdiger	Executed
Schneppenhorst, Ernst	Executed
Scholz-Babisch, Friedrich	Executed
Schöne, Colonel Hermann	Executed
Schrader, Lieutenant Colonel Werner	Executed
Schulenburg, Count Fritz-Dietlof von	Executed
Schulenburg, Count Werner von der	Executed
Schultze-Büttger, Lieutenant Colonel Georg	Executed
Schwamts, Lugwig	Executed
Schwerin von Schwanenfeld, Count Ulrich Wilhelm	Executed
Sierks, Hans-Ludwig	Executed
Smend, Lieutenant Colonel Günther	Executed
Sperr, Franz	Executed
Staehle, Colonel Wilhelm	Executed
Stauffenberg, Lieutenant Commander Berthold von	Executed
Stauffenberg, Colonel Claus von	Executed
Steinaecker, Colonel Hans-Joachim von	Executed
Stieff, General Helmut	Executed
Strünk, Theodor	Executed
Stülpnagel, General Carl-Heinrich von	Executed
Thadden, Elisabeth von	Executed
Thiele, General Fritz	Executed
Thoma, Major Busso	Executed
Thüngen, General Karl	Executed
Treskow, Lieutenant Colonel Gerd von	Suicide
Treskow, General Henning von	Suicide
Trott zu Solz, Adam von	Executed
Üxküll, Colonel Nikolaus von	Executed

Voss, Lieutenant Colonel Hans-Alexander	Suicide
Wagner, General Eduard	Executed
Wagner, Colonel Siegfried	Suicide
Wehrle, Chaplain Hermann	Executed
Wentzel, Carl	Executed
Wiersich, Oswald	Executed
Wirmer, Joseph	Executed
Witzleben, Field Marshal Erwin von	Executed
Yorck von Wartenburg, Count Peter	Executed
Ziehlberg, General Gustav von	Executed

Total: 154

Appendix II

GENERAL ORDER NUMBER 1 DISPATCHED
BY THE CONSPIRATORS IN BERLIN ON
THE AFTERNOON OF JULY 20, 1944

Teletype Message 1
—FRR—HOKW 02150 20.7.44, 16:45
FRR to Corps Area HQ XII—Secret—

I. The Führer Adolf Hitler is dead. An unscrupulous clique of non-combat party leaders has tried to exploit the situation to stab the deeply committed front in the back, and to seize power for selfish purposes.

II. In this hour of highest danger, the Reich government has proclaimed a state of martial law, and has at the same time delegated supreme executive power of the armed forces to me.

III. Accordingly I order the following.

1. I delegate the executive power—with the right of further delegation by those named to the Territorial commanders—in the Zone of the Interior to the commander of the replacement army, appointing him at the same time commander-in-chief in the Zone of the Interior.

In the occupied West areas, to the commander-in-chief West (commander-in-chief of army group D), in Italy to the commander-in-chief Southwest (commander-in-chief of army group C), in the Southeast area to the commander-in-chief Southeast (commander-in-chief of army group F), in the occupied East areas to the commanders-in-chief of army groups South Ukraine, North Ukraine; to the Middle, North, and the armed forces East commanders for their respective command areas; in Denmark and in Norway, to the commanders of the armed forces.

2. To the holders of executive power are subordinated:

(a) All offices and units of the armed forces, including the armored SS, the Reich Labor Service, and the Organization Todt, that are within their command area.

(b) All public authorities (of the Reich, the states, and the communities), in particular the entire police forces, including forces for keeping order, for security, for administration.

(c) All office-holders and formations of the National Socialist party and its affiliated units.

(d) Traffic and supply organizations.

3. The entire armored SS is incorporated into the army, with this order to take effect immediately.

4. The holders of executive power are responsible for maintenance of order and public safety. In particular they are charged with:

(a) The security of the signal installations.

(b) The elimination of the SD. Any resistance to the military executive supremacy must be broken regardless of consequences.

5. In this hour of highest danger for the fatherland, solidarity of the armed forces and maintenance of full discipline is the highest order.

Therefore I charge all commanders in the army, the navy, and the air force with supporting the bearers of executive power in carrying out their difficult task with all means at their disposal, and with ensuring obedience of their orders by subordinate offices. The German soldier is facing a historic task. On his determination and bearing will depend wether Germany is to be saved.

The same responsibilities apply to all territorial commanders, the commanders-in-chief of the segments of the armed forces and the command authorities of the army, navy, and air force that are directly subordinate to the commanders-in-chief.

The commander-in-Chief of the armed forces.

signed: v. Witzleben, Field Marshal

Appendix III

GENERAL ORDER DISPATCHED
FROM THE BENDLERSTRASSE TO
MILITARY DISTRICT HQS

Teletype Message 2
—Kr—HOKW 02155 20 July 1944, 18:00
To Corps Areas HQ I—XIII, XVII, XVIII, XX, XXI, Government-General
(Poland), Bohemia-Moravia. Secret!

   I. Under the authority given to me by the commander-in-chief of the armed forces, I transfer the executive power in the corps areas to the deputy commanding generals and corps area commanders. Together with the executive power, the authority of the Reich defense commissioners passes over to the corps area commanders.

   II. The following direct measures are to be taken:

(a) Signal installations: The principal buildings and installations of the post and armed forces signal net (including radio installations) are to be made militarily secure. The forces assigned to this task must be strong enough to prevent interference and sabotage. Principal signal installations are to be occupied by officers. These in particular are to be made secure: amplifying stations, communications exchanges of the army operations network, high-power transmitters (broadcasting stations), telephone and telegraph officers insofar as major telephone lines run through them, amplifier and battery rooms, antennas, emergency power supplies, and operating rooms. The communication net of the railways is to be protected in agreement with the transport offices.

248

Radio network is to be kept operative from own resources.

(b) Arrests: The following are to be removed from their posts without delay and are to be held in individual arrest: all district (Gau) leaders, Reich governors, ministers, chief presidents, police presidents, senior SS and police leaders, Gestapo leaders and chief of SS officers, chief of propaganda offices and area leaders. Exceptions are to be ordered by me.

(c) Concentration camps: The concentration camps are to be occupied speedily, the camp commanders arrested, the guards disarmed and confined to barracks. The political prisoners are to be informed that they must abstain from all rallies and individual measures until their discharge.

(d) Armed SS: If doubts exist as to the obedience of leaders of armed SS units or of senior armed SS officers, or if they seem unsuitable for further command, they are to be taken into protective custody and replaced by officers of the army.

Units of the armed SS whose unlimited obedience is in doubt are to be disarmed ruthlessly. This is to be accomplished energetically with superior forces, to avoid bloodshed as far as possible.

(e) Police: The offices of the Gestapo and of the SD are to be occupied. Regular police are to be utilized for relief of the armed forces.

Police orders are to be issued through the chief of German police via police command.

(f) Navy and air force: Connection is to be established with commanders of navy and air force. Common action is to be achieved.

III. For the administration of all political matters that arise under the state of martial law, I appoint a political commissioner for each corps area. Until further notice he is to discharge the tasks of the chief of administration. He is to advise the commander of the corps area in all political matters.

IV. The staff for domestic operations is the executive authority of the commander-in-chief in the Zone of the Interior in all executive matters. He appoints a liaison officer to the corps commanders for the purpose of mutual information about the situation and intentions. (VO OKH).

V. No arbitrary actions or actions based on vengeance are to be tolerated in the exercise of the executive power. The population must be made aware that the executive power distances itself from the arbitrary methods of the previous rulers.

APPENDIX III

The commander-in-chief in the Zone of the Interior
No. 31 160/44, secret.
signed: Fromm, General.   Graf Stauffenberg, colonel.

Appendix IV

A RADIO APPEAL TO THE WEHRMACHT
THAT WAS NEVER BROADCAST

Soldiers!

You have fought unfailingly for four years. You have been brave, have defied death. You have been impervious to danger, unconcerned about your troubles and sufferings. You have been motivated by an iron sense of duty, a glowing love of people and fatherland. No task was too hard for you, no sacrifice too great. You were imbued with the belief that the war was just and necessary to make good for the injustices your country incurred after the first World War. To secure our freedom, you moved into battle. On the land, in the air, and on the sea, you performed enormous feats. Your victories affixed the laurel of invincibility to your flags. And in spite of all that—an end of the war is not in sight. Your return to wife and children, to house and farm, to peaceful jobs, seems to have receded into the far distance. You have already asked yourselves often enough: Why is this so? You did not find answer. You did not find it, because a propaganda that balks at no lie, that plays with your courage, with your life itself, has obscured our view of things. Actually, the answer is clear and simple. Behind the mystery is a state that no longer considers politics as the art of the possible. That state does not try to attain its goals with the most economical use of its forces. Instead, it revels in fantastic plans for boundless conquests. These war aims ignore moral obligations both to other peoples and to our own. That is why such war aims can never bring about peace with other peoples. Your military leaders cannot do anything to change this situation; in fact, they only awaken in the régime more immoderate wishes as the war continues. The rulers of the state were not wise enough to limit themselves in their aims to our people's true necessities. Instead, the submission of almost the entire continent was undertaken. The excuse they gave was the "new-ordering" of Europe. The defeated people were enslaved and exploited. This was done instead of winning them over, with a sensible consideration for their national pride. Neither was proper use made of their will for freedom and their life-interests: a policy that might have built bridges of permanent understanding. In other words, your state leadership has disregarded the clear teaching of history, which says such enterprises as the one you were committed to are doomed. This war policy has sown hate everywhere instead of trust. By so doing, it has barricaded the road to an early and lasting peace.

We do not want to enslave other peoples. We concede to all other peoples the same freedom that our fathers won for Germany in the last century, and that we have to guard with the same dedication. Such freedom is the most precious asset a nation can have, and we do not deny it to others. Only this attitude can repair the rift that has been torn by a policy engineered by men who were intoxicated with power. And there is something else that threatens to deprive you of the fruits of the victories that you have won under the leadership of experienced and skilled men. That is the "strategic genius" of Hitler. He claimed this genius for himself. Boot-lickers have played up to him by gushing about his "genius" in the most nauseating way. A man who wants to sole a boot has to have learned to do it. A man who wants to lead an army of millions has to have acquired the capacity for it. And he must have proved his ability along the various levels of hard military service. What has happened since Hitler took over the high command himself in the winter of 1941/42? The armed forces have been put into situations that experts warned against. Heavy sacrifices resulted—avoidable sacrifices. They were caused by stubbornness, incompetence, and extravagant demands. Consider the ruin of the 6th army at Stalingrad, the collapse of the poorly thought-out enterprise in North Africa, and the vain sacrifices in Sicily. All were due solely to an incapable, unscrupulous leadership. Hundreds of thousands of good soldiers paid with their well-being, their freedom or their lives, all for the presumption and vanity of a single man. This leadership has been merciless and cold. It has brought unspeakable harm—avoidable harm—that has struck into countless families. Many higher commanders have already resigned, some have ended their lives, because they did not want to bear the responsibility for such a conscienceless and incompetent leadership. Others have been removed because they had the courage to sound a warning: a warning that precious blood should be saved and not wasted. Universal conscription and the loyalty of soldiers are great concepts. Both concepts have been misused by your leadership—to a degree that has never been known before in German history.

You know that Göring made bold to boast that he would protect German cities. While you have been fighting away from home, many of these cities have gone down in rubble and ashes. Irreplaceable cultural values have been destroyed. So have innumerable places of work, hundreds of thousands of homes. Countless families of brave soldiers are no more. Never before has something so terrible happened to the German fatherland.

Soldiers! It may not go on like this. Your return home must not bring you back to a field of ruins. You do not want the youth, deprived of the education you have had, to lose still more: not only their homeland, not only their parental home, but even their souls. For if the ruins of war continue to spread, material wants may drive out all feeling for honor, freedom, and fellow man. Do you want morals and decency in your homeland to surrender to wrongdoing and evil? Do you want the younger generation growing up at home to blame you because we were not brave enough to save the fatherland? Perhaps we have already hesitated too long; but it is certain that we may not wait any longer. For now the most dishonorable move of all is being prepared. It is a move to make the leaders of the armed forces responsible for the whole misery. Most of all, we have to act because—and that weighs heaviest—crimes have been committed behind your back that besmirch the shield of honor of the German people and befoul the good reputation that Germany has acquired in the world. Self-created personages sitting in the highest positions have permitted these crimes, or have even committed them. They have used the war to enrich themselves shamelessly at the expense of our own and foreign peoples. They have profited from the hardship of the poor and from human unhappiness. These men have not hesitated to feather their caps with the fame you have won.

They boast even though they have never personally experienced war in their lives. You will learn the details. We shall take strict measures against these offenders, and the proceedings will be public. The worst is that the shameless goings-on have been ordered or tolerated by Adolf Hitler. You can call such a leadership either mad or fully responsible for its acts. In either case, it has forfeited any claim to your loyalty, whether based on your duty to God or on your duty to humankind. For this leadership itself has broken the oath it once swore to the fatherland. Like every other citizen, your leaders owe obedience to that oath. By breaking it, they have trampled on the faithfulness that they pledged to others who took the oath. Such a leadership could do nothing any more except lead us toward a final catastrophe. That we are firmly determined to avoid. We swear this before God. For this same purpose we call on your sworn loyalty. In agreement with your most senior soldierly leaders and my colleagues, I have taken over political and military leadership. I am sure of your confidence. Outstanding men from all walks of German life have agreed, and have pledged unselfish dedication. I shall take steps to safeguard the government leadership through men of expert knowledge and blameless character.

Soldiers! The hour has not yet come to give ourselves to thoughts of peace. We must fight on, in order to defend what is dear to us, until we can achieve an honorable end to the war. But I can already make you four promises.

First: Only limited sacrifices will be asked of you. Only those will be asked which are shown after a conscientious examination to be absolutely necessary in order to defend ourselves and to bring the war to a good outcome.

Second: Trustworthy German men with expert knowledge will do their best to come to a permanent settlement with all peoples: one that safeguards our future.

Third: Behind your back, and under your protection, there will be a decent order at home again. Justice and cleanliness, decisions by experts, and unselfish attention to duty will again be the order of the day.

Fourth: After the war, all the strength of the people will be employed to create living quarters, household effects, food, and a truly social way of living together. We will have quiet, dedicated work as our goal in life. We will all have to work hard and to live simply. But in exchange for doing that, we shall find strength and spiritual riches once more.

I trust that at the front and at home all will continue to do their duty. Our unity can be our strength framed in humility before God, for honor and freedom, for people and fatherland.

German soldiers!

More than four years of courageous struggle lie behind you! Millions of our comrades have fallen on the battlefields of Europe and Africa, in the air and on the seas. Hitler's dishonorable leadership has sacrificed whole armies. They have gone down, taking with them the flower of our youth, in Russia and on the Mediterranean—for the sake of fantastic ideas about boundless conquests. There is an example that throws a harsh light on the cruel truth. It is the example of the irresponsible engagement of the 6th army at Stalingrad, and its meaningless sacrifice. Competent officers who opposed this mad business were removed. The general staff was brushed aside. Hitler's pretended strategic genius pushes us, in spite of your heroic actions, towards a fatal ending. At home, more and more places of family life and of work are being destroyed; 6 million Germans are already without a home. Behind your back, corruption and crime tolerated or even ordered by Hitler are taking an unheard-of toll. In this hour of highest distress and danger, German men have done their duty before God and the people. They have provided Germany with an experienced, responsible leadership.

There is a man who warned us where we were headed, in due time. As chief of the general staff, he stood up determinedly against this war. For doing so, he was dismissed by Hitler. This man, . . . has taken over the provisional leadership of the German Reich and the top command within the German armed forces. The government is composed of experienced men who have proved themselves—men from all walks of life, all parts of our fatherland. This government has taken up its tasks. I have been entrusted with the supreme command of the combined armed forces. The commanders-in-chief on all fronts have placed themselves at my disposal. The German armed forces now follow my order.

Soldiers! What is at stake is a just peace. We seek a peace that makes possible a life in freedom for the German people. We want voluntary and productive cooperation among all the peoples. I guarantee you that from now on only those sacrifices will be asked of you that are necessary to reach this goal. The entire strength of the people will be engaged in this task from now on. There will be an end to the meaningless dissipation of the nation's strength, and to the half-decisions, the delayed decisions, that have cost so much blood.

Wherever you are stationed, at the front or in the occupied regions, I bind you in loyalty to the laws of absolute obedience, soldierly bearing, and honorable attitude. Whoever offends against these laws will face the consequences. At home we are also fighting for justice and freedom, for decency and cleanliness. I expect that everyone among you will continue to do his duty faithfully and bravely. On that depends the future of our fatherland, our own future and that of our children.

Soldiers! The existence and the honor of our fatherland are at stake: the true community within our own borders and a community with the peoples of the world.

[von Witzleben]

Appendix V

DRAFT OF A GOVERNMENT DECLARATION

The following text is the third version of a policy statement distilled from contributions over the years by civilian and military conspirators. It probably would have been broadcast by the chancellor-designate, Carl Friedrich Goerdler, once the Nazis were overthrown.

1. The first task is the restoration of the full majesty of the law. The government itself must avoid every arbitrary act. Accordingly, it must subject itself to an orderly control by the people. During the war, this control can only be applied in a provisional manner. For the time being, men of honesty and expert knowledge, from all walks of life and all areas of Germany, will be called into the Reich Council. The government will report to this Reich Council and take its advice. Once we were proud of the lawfulness and honesty of our people, and of the sureness and dependability of the German administration of justice. The more must be the pain of all of us, as we see that this system of justice is well-nigh in ruins.

RESTORATION OF JUSTICE

No human society can exist without law. No one, including the person who thinks that he despises law, can do without it. There comes an hour for everyone in which he calls for justice. God has given us the necessity for law in his ordering of the universe, in his act of creation, in his commandments. He has endowed us with insight and with strength to make our worldly establishments secure in their framework of law. In this spirit, it is necessary to restore the independence of the judiciary. We are well aware that many judges have acted only under pressure of the outer terror. Even so, we will rigorously examine whether judges have gone beyond that, and are guilty of miscarriage of justice. The guilty ones will be removed. In order to restore public confidence in the administration of justice, laymen will be part of the proceedings, as a matter of principle, in criminal trials. This also applies to the provisionally appointed courts-martial.

Justice will be restored. It is not the business of the judge to create new law; he is to apply the law, and most precisely. Justice shall not be the rigid letter of the law, but on the other hand it must be firm and clear. It was a crime against the people and against the judges themselves to give the latter only vague concepts, and an alleged philosophy of life, as their guiding line. It is unbearable that human beings are sentenced who could not have known that their deed was punishable. Insofar as the state has exempted actions of its own organs from punishment after the fact, those exemptions will be cancelled, as being incompatible with justice; and those responsible for the exemptions will be held to account. The law will be enforced against everyone who has violated it. Lawbreakers will receive their deserved punishment.

Both individuals and property will be protected from arbitrary actions. Only the judge, and then only according to law, may interfere with those personal rights of the individual that are indispensable for the continued existence of the state and for human well-being. The concentration camps will be broken up as soon as possible, the innocent inmates dismissed, and the guilty ones brought to court under orderly procedures.

But we also expect no one to attempt mob justice. If we are going to restore the majesty of justice, we have to expend every effort to prevent the taking of personal revenge. Such revenge is only too understandable, viewed against the widespread suffering from injustice, the widespread damage to the human personality. Whoever has a grievance may file a claim with any public authority he chooses. His charge will be forwarded to the appropriate authority. The guilty will receive sure punishment. But the charge must be founded. The making of unfounded charges will be punished, and anonymous accusations will be thrown into the wastepaper basket.

AN END TO CORRUPTION

2. We want to restore the foundations of the moral society, and to do that in every sector of private and public life.

Such outright corruption has been practiced among our people, by such high personiges of the Nazi régime, as has never before been perpetrated on our people. While our soldiers fight, bleed, and die in action at the fronts, men like Göring, Goebbels, Ley, and their comrades have been leading a life of luxury; have robbed; have filled their cellars and attics; have called on the people to hold firm, and have personally slunk away from facing the sacrifices being made out there. All wrongdoers will be brought to account, with the whole rigor of the law. Their ill-gotten goods will be confiscated and returned to those who suffered the loss. But in addition the principal culprits shall suffer personal and economic penalties. Their total property, and that which they have illicitly handed over to relatives, will be confiscated. The draft-exempt positions that were created on a political basis are abolished. Every able-bodied man can prove at the front what he is and what kind of will to hold firm he has. We will not tolerate armchair heros any longer.

Part of the task of restoring right and justice involves the decent treatment of every human being. The persecution of the Jews, which has been pursued in the most inhuman, merciless, and degrading forms, which can never be atoned for, is stopped at once. Whoever thought he could enrich himself with Jewish property will learn that it is a disgrace for any German to seek such evil gains. The German people will not put up with marauders and hyenas among the creatures created by God.

We feel it as a deep dishonor to the German name that crimes of all sorts have been committed in the occupied areas behind the combat troops, and misusing their protection. These wicked acts besmirch the honor of our men who have died in battle. Here we will work toward atonement.

Whoever used the war situation out there in those areas to fill his pockets, or in some other way has defected from the course of honor, will be severely taken to account.

A MORAL FAMILY LIFE

One of our principal tasks is to mold the family once more as the nucleus of the national community. To do this, we need the influence of the parental home itself, plus the strength of religion and the cooperation of the churches. A clean and wholesome family life can be built up only on a serious and responsible evaluation of the life-community of marriage. We have to fight the double standard if our children are not to become debauched. For how can parents demand wholesome patterns of living from their children, if the parents do not observe propriety themselves, and set their children the best example? The life of our people will only become healthy again if our families become healthy again. We do not want to split our people asunder. We know that many entered the ranks of the party from idealism, in bitterness over the dictatorial treaty of Versailles and its consequences, in resentment over national indignities. We know that others joined the party under outer compulsion—economic or other pressures. The people must not break up along party and nonparty lines. All Germans belong together who feel and act German. The only line that has to be drawn is one separating crime and unscrupulousness on one side from decency and cleanliness on the other side. Using this as our basis, we want to dedicate our strength to the internal reconciliation of our people. For only if we remain united on the basis of justice and decency can we come off honorably in the battle of our destiny to which God has committed us.

FIGHT AGAINST LIES

3. We declare war on lies. The sun of truth shall disperse their dense mist which hangs over our land. Our people has been shamelessly lied to, about its economic, financial, and political—as well as its military—situation. The facts will be established and made public, so that every single person can check them. It is a huge mistake for a government to assume that it is permitted to lie in order to line up the people for its aims. God knows no double standard of truth in his order.

Moreover, the lies turned loose by governments have short wings, and are always borne on cowardice or lust for power. Success in maintaining a national position, the happiness of a people, and the individual's peace of soul can only be built on truth. Realities are often hard; but a people that cannot stand them any longer is lost in any case. The individual can only put forward the appropriate amount of strength if he sees the situation as it is. The mountain-climber who underestimates the height of the mountain-top to be attained, the swimmer who does not correctly estimate the stretch to be negotiated, will use up his strength prematurely. All false propaganda therefore brings about its own end; and that is true above all for the Reich propaganda ministry. Moreover, the misuse of the propaganda units of the armed forces must stop. No propaganda is required to embellish the life and the death of our soldiers; those realities are engraved on the hearts of every German woman and mother—yes, on the heart of every German here at home.

4. The vanished freedom of intellect, of conscience, of faith, and of opinion is restored. The churches are once more entitled to function freely according to their confession. In the future, they will exist in complete separation from the state. They can do full justice to their task only in a condition of independence, avoiding all political activity. The state itself will be based on the Christian attitude in word and in deed. For we owe to Christianity the evolution of the white peoples, and our capacity to contend with the bad instincts within us. No state or nation can dispense with this self-mastery by the individual. But genuine Christianity also demands tolerance towards persons of another faith and towards freethinkers. The state will allow the churches full leeway once more to be active in the sense of true Christianity, in particular in the fields of public welfare and education.

The press shall be free again. During the war it will have to subject itself to the restrictions that are indispensable in any nation in any war. Everybody who reads a newspaper, however, will know who stands behind that newspaper. The press will not be permitted to spread untruth, deliberately or through negligence. Under a strict code of honor, the editors will ensure that the press, too, observes the laws of decency and of duty towards the fatherland.

5. It is above all the German youth that calls out for the truth. If a proof of the divine nature of human beings were needed, here one is. Even children have a natural recognition of truth and lies. They turn away ashamed and disgusted from the untrue mental attitudes and words that are expected of them. Probably the meanest crime of all was to disregard and misuse the young people's sense of truth, and with it their idealism. We will protect and strengthen this youthful heritage.

One of our main tasks, in fact, is the care of the youth and its education. This education will be relinquished, first and foremost, to the parents and the schools. All schools will impart elementary basic knowledge to the children, simply, honestly, and undeviatingly. Once again, education must be of that general sort which captures the heart and mind. It must have its roots in the people, so that there is no spiritual gap between educated and noneducated.

Once more education will be placed on Christian-spiritual foundations—without, however, violating the Christian laws of complete tolerance toward those of other beliefs. From this basis, the educational system must evolve again, quietly and steadily. It must be protected against constant basic changes and upheavals.

COURAGE TO TAKE RESPONSIBILITY

6. The administration of state must be ordered anew. Nothing will be revoked that has stood the test. But we will have to restore clear lines of responsibility immediately, and also the freedom for independent decisions. Our formerly proud administrative system has been reduced to a jumble of senselessly turning machines and little machines. Nobody dares any longer to make an independent and honest decision. But we shall expect the opposite of our officials. With a minimum of writing, they shall do the right thing in the simplest way.

Once more the official must set an example, in his whole conduct of his office and his life; for the people have entrusted him with the public authority. The career of official shall lie open only to a man who is decent, who has acquired expert knowledge, who has shown strength of character, and ability for accomplishment. There will be an end to the party-book official. Once again our officials shall obey only the law and their consciences. The official must show himself aware of the privilege that the community bestows on him: a secure way of life while others have to struggle for bare essentials. The official, protected in his reputation and his rights, shall be absorbed in the aspiration to use his special position to do justice.

In order to make possible this impeccable performance, and to save the people from unworthy persons in public positions, all appointments and promotions since January 1933 are declared to be provisional. Each individual official will be examined as soon as possible to learn whether he has offended against justice, against the law, or against the decent standard required of an official. If misconduct is ascertained, appropriate action will be taken, by punishment, dismissal, transfer, etc. Courts of honor of the officials will assist in this procedure. Provisional officials whose accomplishments do not meet the requirements of their office will be transferred to positions for which they are adequate, or if this is impossible, will be dismissed.

Luxury has no place in public offices; the place for comfort is in the private dwelling. Accordingly, office chiefs are instructed to take the

APPENDIX V

necessary steps immediately. Superfluous articles of furniture will be assigned to persons who have suffered damage in air raids.

THE CONSTITUTIONAL QUESTION

7. Orderly administration plus equitable distribution and execution of community responsibilities are possible only on the basis of a constitution. A permanent constitution can only be created after the end of the war, by agreement of the people. For the frontline soldiers have a special claim to take part in this task. Therefore we all must be content for the time being with a provisional constitution, which is being proclaimed simultaneously. It, too, is binding on us.

Prussia will be dissolved. The Prussian provinces as well as the other German Länder will be reorganized as Reichsgau areas. The individual Reichsgau will have a constitutional life of their own within the nation. To a large extent, they will enjoy self-government. To the self-government of the Reichsgau, of the districts, and of the communities will be entrusted those public responsibilities that are compatible with the unity of the Reich and its purposeful leadership.

In each Reichsgau, administration will be exercised in the name of the Reich by the Reichsstatthalter, who is shortly to be appointed. These top officials will grant as free a hand as possible to the local organs of self-government, while at the same time ensuring the unity of the Reich. Elected bodies will ensure a link between the government and the people.

8. During the war, the economy will have to be controlled, with price supervision. Everyone will understand that a free economy is not possible so long as there is a scarcity of vitally important goods. Not, that is, unless one were willing to get on with the day's affairs by coldly ignoring the needs of the less well-to-do classes. We know quite well how disgusting our present economic set-up is. It lends itself to corruption, and it does not serve, as it so often pretended, the true interests of the consumer. For the time being, we can only simplify it and free it from inner confusions, from tangled lines of responsibility—and from a lack of responsibility. We shall cancel all measures that have interfered too deeply with the freedom of the individual. We shall also get rid of ill-considered measures that have needlessly dried up supplies of essential goods in commerce, handicraft, trade, industry, and agriculture.

Nor may state interference be allowed unnecessarily to disturb economic processes, the joy of endeavor and creation, and the potentialities of inventiveness. (The law should do no more than set limits on economic freedom, insisting on fair competition and a decent attitude.) In view of the fatherland's shortages of raw materials and the fact that we cannot support ourselves from our soil alone, any goal of economic autarchy is a cowardly renunciation of the chance to share in the goods and services of the whole world through trade.

SOCIAL-ECONOMIC ORDER

The goal of our economic order is that each worker, employee, and entrepreneur shall share our economic goods. The question is not merely how to foster the initiative of the enterpriser, and how to require him to compete in efficient production. No, the German worker also must and shall have the opportunity to take part creatively in the responsibility for the economy. Of course, he, like other members of society, must live within the natural laws that rule the economy.

Property is the foundation of all economic and cultural progress; without it, the human being gradually sinks to the level of the animal. Property, therefore, is protected—not only in the hands of the great property-owner, but also in the hands of the small owner who calls only household effects his own. The misuse of property will be fought as determinedly as an unhealthy concentration of capital that increases human dependency.

The economic order will be built upon individual responsibility. The heretofore practiced system of regimentation from above must be abandoned. The object is to restore to the economy the beneficent effects of independence of action and personal responsibility. The aim is to win the confidence of all, including the workers, in the fairness of the economic order.

ARRIVING AT A FAIR SOCIAL DISTRIBUTION

9. From the above, we can arrive at the social policy of the state. It shall protect those who are weak and who through no fault of their own become indigent; it shall give them the opportunity to find shelter against the adversities of life. The government's social policy shall also come into play where the motive of preserving savings (capital) conflicts with the motive of securing the working power of those now living. Such conflicts of interest can arise in times of great political and economic tension. It would be frivolous to solve them in such a way as to use up the capital, that is, the savings. The small saver

would like that development as little as it would serve the interest of the community if, for instance, all farms and all industrial enterprises were to be suddenly without machines. On the other hand, all these capital goods are valueless if they cannot be used to maintain the people who are alive today. Thus the question is how to find a fair balance or equalization. There must be a feeling of responsibility, with every individual aware at the start that he, like everyone else, must make sacrifices.

Insofar as the resources of the various branches of the professions and the business community do not suffice to bring about such equalizations between future needs of the community and immediate individual human needs, the state and the individual citizen must enter the picture. If necessary, the state will have to levy the cost of an equalization on the shoulders of the people as a whole, on everyone who is part of the economic community. As for social establishments, insofar as they concern workers, the workers have full rights of self-administration.

But we must bear in mind that the state has no inexhaustible means. It lives only by what its citizens accomplish and make available to it. It cannot give out to individual citizens more than it has available from the productive power of these citizens. Therefore we refuse to make promises of economic well-being. We all know that the man who has squandered his savings has to accomplish a great deal if he wants to regain the standard of living that he is used to. So it is with the family, with every association, and with the state. Any other conception makes no sense. Cheap promises that the state can do everything are unscrupulous demagogy. The state is you, with your resources and strength. We and the organs of the state are merely your trustees. Everyone must commit his strength in the times ahead. It is obvious that after the enormous destruction of this war, our productive power must be especially high, if we are to produce replacements of clothing, homes, household effects, and workshops. And finally, we want to make a better life possible for our children. But we are convinced that we can do all this if only we can get to work again in a climate of law, decency, and freedom.

ACHIEVING A STABLE CURRENCY

10. A basic prerequisite of a healthy economy is a sound public budget. Expenses must stay within the limits of real income that the state and its regions draw from the citizens. To reestablish such a sound fiscal

order will require effort, will-power, renunciation, and struggle. Yet that fiscal order is the most important, the one indispensable, basis of a sound currency and of all economic life. On a sound currency depends the value of all savings. Without it, moreover, we would not have the foreign trade on which we have depended for hundreds of years.

Taxes are going to be considerable; but the more carefully, then, we will see to it that tax money is spent thriftily. It is more important that we leave the citizen the necessities of life than that the state administrations supply themselves with fine equipment, or set off on tasks that are not consonant with the simple mode of living of individuals.

We demand a similar awareness from the business community. It must become aware once more that high administrative expenses— the kind of thing that serves merely the comfort or the self-assertion of some individuals—have to be borne by all, in the form of higher prices, or by the workers, as lower wages. The abolition of the enormous outlays by the National Socialist party alone will begin the curative process.

Since 1933, the basis of orderly public budgets has been abandoned, with continuous and unscrupulous waste of assets, and by mounting indebtedness. It was easy to juggle the idea before the public that wastefulness could raise the general standard of living. In actuality, this method was miserable, for it consisted simply of the uninhibited piling up of debts. Therefore, particularly during this war, which forces every government to make enormous expenditures, we will establish the utmost simplicity and economy of operation in all public service. A real balancing of the budget can only be approached after the end of the war.

We perceive an immense danger in the growing burden of debts of governments everywhere, combatant and neutral alike. These debts imperil the soundness of the currencies. After the war every government will be confronted by an extraordinarily difficult task. We hope that a basis of peaceful cooperation can be achieved among the nations, so that we can find solutions for the problem of amortizing debts.

11. For the present, however, we are at war. While the war continues, all our work, sacrifice, and devotion are due to the men defending the fatherland at the front. For their sakes we must contribute everything possible in mental and material resources. We stand with them.

But all may know that from now on only those sacrifices are demanded that are necessary for the defense of the fatherland—no longer those that serve a madman's greediness for conquest and craving for prestige. We can be sure now that we will pursue this war to the attainment of a just peace, with the honesty that distinguishes each true soldier. From now on our full dedication is to those who up to now have been victims of the war.

In our concern for the front, we must do what is necessary and do it with the greatest clarity and simplicity. We will put an end to the back-and-forth traffic in bombastic and unfulfillable orders. No longer will the economy be asked to produce impossible numbers of tanks today, of planes tomorrow, and the day after tomorrow of other weapons and equipment. Only what can be achieved will be demanded. As an about-face from the despotic tyranny we have known up to now, we expect everyone in the war effort from now on to point out mistakes and inconsistencies—in good time, and on his own initiative.

THE VOICE OF THE TRUE GERMANY

12. We have warned against this war that has brought so much suffering to all mankind, so now we may talk frankly. Although we must refrain just now from making bitter accusations, for the sake of the national dignity, nevertheless those responsible for the war will be brought to account. Yet, as essential as this is, it is still more important that we strive towards an early peace. We know that we alone are not masters over war and peace; in the final outcome, we are dependent on the other peoples as well. For now, we must hold firm. But right now, we also want to invoke, once and for all, the voice of the true Germany.

We are deeply convinced that the world faces one of the most serious decisions that has ever confronted populations and their leaders. God himself imposes on us the question whether we want to conform to his order of justice, whether or not we want to follow his commandments, to respect freedom and human dignity—and to help each other.

In this hour we have to advise our people that it is our own highest duty to wash clean the German name, which has been soiled many times over. We Germans alone can and shall do the job, bravely and patiently. We must do it seriously, honestly, relentlessly, for our future depends upon it. For God is not here to be called upon on each

266

cheap occasion as "Providence"; He also demands that his order and his commandments be respected. To assume that the future could be built on the unhappiness of other peoples, built on the suppression of human dignity, was a terrible error, whose roots go back to the unfortunate and dictatorial treaty of Versailles.

None of us wants to encroach on other peoples' sense of honor. What we ask for ourselves, we must grant, want to grant, to others. We believe it is in the interest of all peoples that the peace be a lasting one. For that, international confidence in the new Germany is necessary. Moreover, that confidence cannot be forced, nor attained by talking. But whatever the future may bring, this is sure: We despise the churlish policy of casting brickbats at the enemy. We are convinced that all leaders of states want not only the best for their people but also an end of this conflict, with some constructive prospects for the future. We believe those leaders will be ready to join us soon in ameliorating the human suffering that has come to peoples everywhere in the backwash of this senseless total war.

Let us tread the road of decency and mutual respect once more! That is the spirit in which all of us want to fulfill our obligations.

Let us be guided in everything we do by God's commandments, which have been written upon our consciences. Let us follow these commandments even when to do so seems hard. Let us do all we can to heal wounded spirits and to repair the damage that has been done. Then alone will we be able to lay the basis for a secure future. Then we will be able to consider our people as a member of a family of peoples, united once again in confidence, wholesome work, and constructive goals. We owe this to our soldiers who have fallen in action, whose love of fatherland, whose courage to sacrifice have been grossly misused. Those soldiers who realized how their idealism was being taken advantage of continued to do their duty only under the most severe conflicts of conscience. And meanwhile, see how much glowing human happiness has been extinguished, the world around!

May God give us insight and strength to mold the meaning of these sacrifices into a blessing for generations to come!

Selected Bibliography

Abshagen, Karl H. *Canaris*. London, 1956.
Allen, William S. *The Nazi Seizure of Power*. Chicago, 1965.
Amort, C., and Jedlicka, M. *The Canaris File*. London, 1970.
Andreas, Friedrich R. *Berlin Underground 1938–1945*. New York, 1945.
Balfour, Michael, and Frisby, Julian. *Helmuth von Moltke: A Leader Against Hitler*. London, 1972.
Bartz, Kurt. *The Downfall of the German Secret Service*. London, 1956.
Baumont, Fried, and Baumont, Vermeil, eds. *The Third Reich*. New York, 1955.
Bauer, Hans. *Hitler's Pilot*. London, 1958.
Beneš, Eduard. *Memoirs of Dr. Eduard Benes*. London, 1954.
Bernadotte, Folke. *The Curtain Falls*. New York, 1945.
Best, S. Payne. *The Venlo Incident*. London, 1950.
Bethge, Eberhard. *Dietrich Bonhoefer*. London, 1970.
Bezymenski, Lev. *The Death of Adolf Hitler*. New York, 1968.
Blond, Georges. *The Death of Hitler's Germany*. New York, 1954.
Blumentritt, General Günther. *Von Rundstedt*. London, 1952.
Boehm, Eric H., ed. *We Survived: The Stories of Fourteen of the Hidden and Hunted of Nazi Germany*. New Haven, Conn., 1949.
Boldt, Gerhard. *Hitler: The Last Ten Days*. New York, 1973.
Bonhoefer, Dietrich. *Letters and Papers from Prison*. New York, 1967.
Boveri, Margaret. *Treason in the 20th Century*. New York, 1963.
Brook-Shepherd, Gordon. *The Anschluss*. New York, 1963.
Brown, Anthony Cave. *Bodyguard of Lies*. New York, 1973.
Bullock, Alan. *Hitler, A Study in Tyranny*. New York, 1961.

Selected Bibliography

Cadogan, Sir Alexander. *The Diaries of Sir Alexander Cadogan 1938–1945*. New York, 1972.

Carell, Paul. *Hitler Moves East: 1941–1942*. New York, 1966.

Colvin, Ian. *Chief of Intelligence*. London, 1951.

Conway, John S. *The Nazi Persecution of the Churches 1933–1945*. London, 1968.

Cookridge, E. H. *Inside S.O.E.* London, 1966.

Delarue, Jacques. *The Gestapo*. New York, 1964.

De Launay, J., ed. *European Resistance Movements*. 2 vols. London, 1960, 1964.

Deull, Wallace. *People under Hitler*. New York, 1953.

Deutsch, Harold C. *The Conspiracy against Hitler in the Twilight War*. Bloomington, Minn., 1968.

Dietrich, Otto. *Hitler*. Chicago, 1955.

Dönitz, Admiral Karl. *Memoirs*. London, 1958.

Dulles, Alan W. *Germany's Underground*. New York, 1947.

Eden, Anthony. *Facing the Dictators*. London, 1962.

Fest, Joachim C *Hitler*. New York, 1974.

Fitzgibbon, Constantine. *The Shirt of Nessus*. New York, 1957.

François-Poncet, André. *The Fateful Years*. London, 1949.

Gallo, Max. *The Night of Long Knives*. New York, 1972.

Gehlen, Reinhard. *The Service*. New York, 1972.

Gilbert, Felix. *Hitler Directs His War*. New York, 1950.

Gisevius, Hans B. *To the Bitter End*. Boston, 1947.

Gollwitzer, H. *Dying We Live: The Final Messages of the Resistance*. New York, 1956.

Gordon, Harold J. *Hitler and the Beer Hall Putsch*. Princeton, N.J., 1972.

Görlitz, Walter. *The German General Staff*. New York, 1959.

Grunberger, Richard. *The Twelve-Year Reich*. New York, 1971.

Guderian, General Heinz. *Panzer Leader*. New York, 1952.

Halder, General Franz. *Hitler as Warlord*. London, 1950.

Hassell, Ulrich von. *The Von Hassell Diaries*. New York, 1947.

Harris, Whitney R. *Tyranny on Trial—The Evidence at Nuremburg*. Dallas, Texas, 1954.

Henderson, Neville. *Failure of a Mission*. New York, 1940.

Hitler, Adolf. *Mein Kampf*. Boston, 1945.

——. *Hitler's Secret Conversations*. New York, 1961.

Hoffmann, Heinrich. *Hitler Was My Friend*. London, 1955.

Hoffmann, Peter C. *The History of the German Resistance 1933–1945*. Cambridge, Mass., 1976.

SELECTED BIBLIOGRAPHY

Höhne, Heinz. *The Order of the Death's Head*. New York, 1970.

Irving, David. *Hitler's War*. New York, 1977.

John, Otto. *Twice through the Lines*. London, 1972.

Keitel, Field Marshal Wilhelm. *Memoirs*. London, 1956.

Kesselring, Field Marshal Albert. *A Soldier's Record*. New York, 1954.

Klein, B. H. *Germany's Economic Preparations for War*. Cambridge, Mass., 1959.

Koch, H. W. *The Hitler Youth*. New York, 1976.

Kogen, Eugen. *The Theory and Practice of Hell*. New York, 1961.

Kramary, Joachim. *Stauffenberg*. New York, 1967.

Krausnick, Helmut, *Anatomy of the SS State*. New York, 1968.

Leber, Annadore., ed. *Conscience in Revolt*. London, 1957.

Liddell-Hart, Basil H. *The German Generals Talk*. New York, 1948.

Ludecke, Kurt. *I Knew Hitler: The Story of a Nazi Who Escaped the Blood Purge*. New York, 1937.

Manvell, Roger, and Fraenkel, Heinrich. *The July Bomb Plot*. London, 1964.

——. *The Canaris Conspiracy*. New York, 1970.

Maser, Werner. *Hitler's Letters and Notes*. New York, 1974.

Moltke, H. J. von. *A German of the Resistance*. London, 1947.

Mosse, George., ed. *Police Forces in History*. London, 1975.

Nicholson, Harold. *The War Years 1939–1945*. New York, 1966.

Noakes, Jeremy, and Pridham, Geoffery. *Documents on Nazism 1919–1945*. New York, 1975.

Nogueres, Henri. *Munich*. New York, 1965.

O'Neill, Robert. *The German Army and the Nazi Party*. New York, 1966.

Papen, Franz von. *Memoirs*. New York, 1952.

Payne, Robert. *The Life and Death of Adolf Hitler*. New York, 1973.

Pope, Ernest. *Munich Playground*. New York, 1941.

Prittie, Terrence. *Germans against Hitler*. London, 1964.

Reitlinger, Gerald. *The SS—Alibi of a Nation*. New York, 1957.

Ribbentrop, Joachim von. *Ribbentrop Memoirs*. London, 1962.

Ritter, Gerhard. *The German Resistance: Carl Goerdler's Struggle against Tyranny*. London, 1958.

Rommel, Erwin. *The Rommel Papers*. New York, 1953.

Rothfels, Hans. *The German Opposition to Hitler*. London, 1961.

Schacht, Hjalmar. *Account Settled*. London, 1948.

Schellenberg, Walter. *Hitler's Secret Service*. New York, 1958.

Schlabrendorff, Fabian von. *The Secret War against Hitler*. New York, 1965.

Selected Bibliography

Schmidt, Paul. *Hitler's Interpreter*. London, 1951.

Scholl, Inge. *The White Rose*. London, 1956.

Schramm, Percy. *Hitler: The Man and the Military Leader*. Chicago, 1971.

Schramm, Wilhelm Ritter von. *Conspiracy among Generals*. New York, 1957.

Schussnigg, Kurt von. *Austrian Requiem*. New York, 1946.

Seaburg, Paul. *The Wilhelmstrasse*. Berkeley, Calif., 1954.

Shirer, William L. *Berlin Diary*. New York, 1941.

——. *The Rise and Fall of the Third Reich*. New York, 1960.

Smith, R. Harris. *O.S.S.: The Secret History of America's First Central Intelligence Agency*. Berkeley, Calif., 1972.

Speer, Albert. *Inside the Third Reich*. New York, 1970.

Speidel, General Hans. *Invasion 1944*. New York, 1950.

Sykes, Christopher. *Troubled Loyalty: A Biography of Adam Trott zu Solz*. London, 1968.

Taylor, Telford. *Sword and Swastika*. New York, 1952.

Toland, John. *Adolf Hitler*. New York, 1976.

Trevor-Roper, Hugh R. *The Last Days of Hitler*. New York, 1947.

——. *Hitler's Table Talk*. London, 1953.

——, ed. *Hitler's War Directives*. New York, 1965.

Walimont, General Walter. *Inside Hitler's Headquarters*. Washington, D.C., 1964.

Weiner, Jan. *The Assassination of Heydrich*. New York, 1969.

Weisäcker, Ernst von. *Memoirs*. London, 1951.

Werth, Alexander. *Russia at War 1941–1945*. New York, 1964.

Westphal, General Siegfried. *The German Army in the West*. London, 1951.

Wheeler-Bennett, John. *The Nemesis of Power*. New York, 1967.

Young, Desmond. *Rommel, the Desert Fox*. New York, 1950.

Zeller, Eberhard. *The Flame of Freedom*. Coral Gables, Fla., 1969.

Zimmermann, Erich, and Jacobsen, Hans-Adolf, eds. *Germans against Hitler*. Bonn, West Germany: Federal Press and Information Office, 1960.

Sources

For complete names, titles, and publication data,
see the Bibliography.

Part I: THE HUNTED

Chapter 1—Executive Action

National Archives, microfilm publication T-175. National Archives (Göring statement of July 9, 1934). Munich Provincial Court, records. International Military Tribunal, Nuremberg (IMT), vol. 7.

Baynes, *Speeches*. Gallo, *Night*. Höhne, *Order*. Gisevius, *Bitter*. Toland, *Hitler*. Shirer, *Rise*. Wheeler-Bennett, *Nemesis*. Ludecke, *Escaped*.

Chapter 2—Betrayal in Berlin

IMT, vol. 27. National Archives, T-84 (includes transcript of Gestapo interrogation of Fritsch et al.). National Archives (U.S. Embassy report, Berlin, July 2, 1934).

O'Neill, *German Army*. Fest, *Hitler*. Schellenberg, *Secret Service*. Bullock, *Study*. Shirer, *Rise*. Gisevius, *Bitter*.

Part II: THE HUNTERS

Chapter 3—The Oster Plan

Documents on British Foreign Policy, 3. IMT, vol. 9. IMT, supplement B. *The Times*, London, August 6, 1969. Documents on German Foreign Policy, vol. 2.

Sources

Beneš, *Memoirs.* Rothfels, *German Opposition to Hitler.* Halder, *Hitler.* Weisacker, *Memoirs.* Deutsch, *Conspiracy.* François-Poncet, *Fateful.* Guderian, *Panzer.* Henderson, *Failure.* Hassell, *Diaries.* Ritter, *Goerdler.* Colvin, *Secret Enemy.* Brook-Shepard, *Anschluss.* Jedlicka, *Canaris.* Nogueres, *Munich.*

Chapter 4—Alone against the Führer

German Foreign Ministry Archives, Koblenz. Hoover Institute Library, G-321.

Hoffman, *Maurice Bavaud's Attempt* (in *Police Forces*). Speer, *Inside.* Trevor-Roper, *Hitler's Table Talk.* Irving, *Hitler's War.*

Chapter 5—Clandestine Missions

Documents on German Foreign Policy, vols. 4, 6, 7. IMT, vols. 34, 37.

Ritter, *Goerdler.* Zeller, *Flame.* Weisacker, *Memoirs.* Höhne, *Order.* Schacht, *Account.* Schmidt, *Hitler's Interpreter.* Colvin, *Secret Enemy.* Balfour, *von Moltke.* Schlabrendorff, *Secret War.* Rothfels, *German Opposition to Hitler.* Brown, *Bodyguard.*

Chapter 6—The Craftsman

Institute for Contemporary History, Munich, Quarterly #17, 1969 (Dr Anton Hoch). Bundesarchiv, Koblenz, file R/22/3100 (Gestapo interrogation). National Archives, T-175. *Der Stern,* May 10, 1966 (Elser interrogation).

Best, *Venlo.* Schellenberg, *Secret Service.* Höhne, *Order.* Irving, *Hitler's War.* Hoffmann, *German Resistance.*

Chapter 7—The Traitor-Patriots

National Archives, record groups 226, 338. IMT, vols. 10, 12, 20, 24. Documents on German Foreign Policy, D, 8.

Grunberger, *Reich.* Klein, *Economic Preparations.* Halder, *Hitler.* Warlimont, *Headquarters.* Deutsch, *Conspiracy.* Ritter, *Goerdler.* John, *Twice through.* Dulles, *Underground.* Reitlinger, *Alibi.* Abshagen, *Canaris.* Hoffmann, *German Resistance.* Jedlicka, *Canaris.* Zimmermann, *Germans against Hitler.* Höhne, *Order.* Boveri, *Treason.* Reitlinger, *Final Solution.* Gilbert, *Hitler Directs.* Prittie, *Germans against Hitler.* Colvin, *Secret Enemy.*

SOURCES

Chapter 8—Revolt in Munich

Landsarchiv, Berlin, transcripts IH 47/43, I II 101/43, 6J 24/43 (indictments and sentencing of the Scholls, Huber, and others before the People's Court).

Leber, *Conscience*. Koch, *Hitler Youth*. School, *White Rose*. Conway, *Nazi Persecution*. Carell, *Hitler Moves*. Dulles, *Underground*. Zeller, *Flame*. Rothfels, *Resistance*.

Chapter 9—Flight from Smolensk

National Archives, T-175. National Archives, MS A-855 (monograph by Baron von Gersdorff). Letter to author from Dr. Frank H. Panton, M.B.E., director, Propellants, Explosives and Rocket Motor Establishment, Ministry of Defence, Waltham Abbey, Essex.

Cookridge, *Inside S.O.E.* Bauer, *Hitler's Pilot*. Irving, *Hitler's War*. Schlabrendorff, *Secret War*. Schellenberg, *Secret Service*. Gisevius, *Bitter*. Jedlicka, *Canaris*. Weiner, *Heydrich*. Reitlinger, *Alibi*. Höhne, *Order*.

Chapter 10—Silent Pistol, Silent Bomb

National Archives, T-175. IMT, vol. 31 (von dem Bussche).

Bethge, *Bonhoefer*. Werth, *Russia*. Hoffmann, *German Resistance*. Toland, *Hitler*. Ritter, *Goerdler*. Zeller, *Flame*. Gisevius, *Bitter*. Dulles, *Underground*. Kesselring, *Record*. Keitel, *Memoirs*. Fest, *Hitler*.

Chapter 11—Finis Initium

National Archives, T-78, T-311, ML-125, ML-690. National Archives, MS B-344. IMT, vol. 33. Interview with Dr. Hubertus Strughold.

Kramery, *Stauffenberg*. Warlimont, *Headquarters*. Boveri, *Treason*. Gisevius, *Bitter*. Zeller, *Flame*. Prittie, *Germans against Hitler*. Young, *Desert Fox*. Hoffmann, *German Resistance*. Ritter, *Goerdler*. Schlabrendorff, *Secret War*. Zimmermann, *Germans against Hitler*.

Chapter 12—Explosion at Rastenburg

IMT, vol. 33. National Archives, T-38, T-78, T-84 (includes Kaltenbrunner Report). National Archives, record group 238.

Sources

National Archives, MS B-272 (Blumentritt), MS B-499 (Soden-stern).

Fitzgibbon, *Nessus*. Kramery, *Stauffenberg*. Hoffmann, *German Resistance*. Keitel, *Memoirs*. Speer, *Inside*. Zeller, *Flame*. Irving, *Hitler's War*. Trevor-Roper, *Hitler's Table Talk*. Warlimont, *Headquarters*.

Chapter 13—Fateful Hours

National Archives, MS B-272. Kaltenbrunner Report. National Archives, record group 338 (includes Remer account). IMT, vol. 33.

Zimmermann, *Germans against Hitler*. Schramm, W., *Conspiracy*. Gisevius, *Bitter*. Hoffmann, *German Resistance*. Zeller, *Flame*. Schellenberg, *Secret Service*. Rothfels, *Resistance*. Boveri, *Treason*.

PART III: CALVARY

Chapter 14—Vengeance

National Archives, R-60,67. National Archives, T-120. National Archives, record group 226. IMT, vols. 16, 33.

Boldt, *Ten Days*. Schlabrendorff, *Secret War*. Leber, *Conscience*. Jedlicka, *Canaris*. Bernadotte, *Curtain Falls*. Zimmermann, *Germans against Hitler*. Irving, *Hitler's War*. Abshagen, *Canaris*. Boehm, *We Survived*. Young, *Desert Fox*. Donitz, *Memoirs*. Grunberger, *Reich*. Blond, *Death*. Bethge, *Bonhoefer*. Colvin, *Secret Enemy*. Toland, *100 Days*. Bezymenski, *Death of Hitler*.

Index

276

INDEX

Index

Müller-Hillebrand, Burkhart, 167
Munich, 10–13, 64–66, 91–103, 116–35, 160
Munich conference (1938), 54–57, 72
Munich putsch (1923), 64–66
Mussolini, Benito, 57, 152, 185, 190–91, 199, 237

National Socialist party, x–xi, xvi, xxi, 4, 6–8, 17–18, 23, 32, 35–36, 38–40, 43, 45, 47n, 60, 90–91, 118, 122, 131–32, 169, 175, 183, 203, 207, 221–22, 226, 237
National Socialist Teachers' League, 60
Nebe, Arthur, 48
Netherlands, 42, 84–85, 103–4, 107, 111–12, 228
Neurath, Constantin von, 21–22, 27
Normandy, 171–74, 179–80, 198, 200–201, 215, 227
North Africa, xix, 136, 158, 163–66
Norway, 42, 110–12
Nuremberg, 53
Nuremberg war trials, xviii–xix

Oberg, Carl-Albrecht, 210, 215–16
Office of Strategic Services (OSS), 151
OKH, see Army High Command
OKW, see Wehrmacht High Command
Olbricht, Friedrich, xviii, 138, 142, 153, 168–70, 177, 183, 194–96, 200, 202, 204, 208–9, 211–14
Osborne, Francis d'Arcy, 109
Osborne, Walter Dodd, 158n–159n
OSS (Office of Strategic Services), 151
Oster, Hans, xviii, 39, 42–43, 48, 51–54, 56, 58, 78, 84–86, 106–8, 111–13, 138–39, 148–50, 175, 228, 232

People's Court, xvi–xvii, 70, 132, 221–22, 228, 230, 233
Piffrader, Humbert, 196
Pius XII, 109–10
Poland, ix, 42, 72–74, 76–79, 81–83, 110, 167, 232
Polish corridor, 73
Probst, Christoph, 119, 124–25, 131–34
Prussia, see East Prussia
Prussian militarists, ix–x, 8, 19

Raeder, Erich, 21
Rastenburg, see Wolf's Lair
Rath, Ernst vom, 67
Reichenau, Walther von, 9, 44
Reich Labor Service for Young Women, 120
Reich Main Security Office (RSHA), xvii

Reich Military Court, 149
Reichsbank, 27, 41, 73
Reichs Defense Council, 20
Reichstag, 4, 16–18
Reichswehr, 6, 8–10, 12, 14, 16, 79
Remer, Otto Ernst, xix, 183, 205–9
Ribbentrop, Joachim von, xix, 20, 27, 42, 80, 84–85, 191–92
Roeder, Manfred, 149–50
Röhm, Ernst, xix, 4–5, 8–11, 13–15, 36, 38, 40, 45
Rommel, Erwin, xix, 136, 139, 164, 174–77, 179–80, 197–98, 231
Roosevelt, Eleanor, 134
Roosevelt, Franklin, 76
Rösler, Ernst, 114
Rote Kapelle, 124–25
RSHA (Reich Main Security Office), xvii
Rumania, 74, 156
Rundstedt, Gerd von, xix, 31–32, 83, 174
Russia, ix, xv, 20, 41–42, 61, 73, 75, 78, 81, 113–15, 123–24, 134–35, 137, 139, 153–54, 156, 168, 172, 176, 184, 203–4, 232, 234–37

SA, see Sturmabteilung
Sas, Gisjbertus, 111–12
Schacht, Hjalmar, xix, 27, 41, 58, 73–74, 78, 232
Schady, Werner, 213
Schairer, Reinhold, 74
Schellenberg, Walter, xix, 26–29, 103–4, 159
Schlabrendorff, Fabian von, xix–xx, 75–76, 79–80, 137–43, 145, 220–21, 229–32, 238–39
Schlee, Rudolf, 208–9, 212–13
Schleicher, Kurt von, xx, 3–7, 13, 16
Schmid, Wilhelm, 11, 13
Schmid, Wilhelm Eduard, 12
Schmidhuber, Wilhelm, 148
Schmidt, Otto, 25–26, 30–31
Schmitt, Ludwig Wilhelm, 12
Schmorell, Alexander, 119–21, 124–28, 131, 135n
Schmundt, Rudolf, 144–45, 189n
Schneiderhuber, August, 11, 13
Scholl, Hans, xx, 117–34
Scholl, Sophia, xx, 119–22, 125–34
Scholl, Werner, 124
Schulz, Paul, 13–14
Schutzstaffel (SS), xvii–xviii, 8–13, 15–16, 19, 24–26, 28–29, 48–51, 53, 60, 62–63, 67, 79–80, 82–83, 85, 87, 91, 103–5, 107, 114–15, 122, 129–30, 137–38, 145, 150–51, 154, 159, 161–62, 169,

INDEX

Schutzstaffel (SS) (*continued*)
175, 179, 183, 186, 191, 196–98,
200–201, 203, 208–11, 215, 219, 221,
227–28, 233, 235–36, 238
Schwaerzel, Helene, 226
Schwerin, Gerhard von, 76–77
SD, *see Sicherheitsdienst*
Sicherheitsdienst (SD), 27, 39, 48, 50, 83, 87,
103, 126–27, 145
Siegfried line, 47, 107
Simpson, William, 234
Sippenhaft, 222
Smolensk, 136–47
Sodenstern, Georg von, x–xi
Spain, 21
Speer, Albert, 62
Speidel, Hans, 198–201
SS, *see Schutzstaffel*
Stalin, Josef, 75
Stang, Ulrich, 111–12
Stauffenberg, Claus Schenk von, xx, 163–73,
175–87, 189, 191, 193–99, 202–5,
211–15, 222, 250
Steiner, Felix, 235
Stevens, S. Payne, 103–5
Stieff, Helmuth, xx, 142–43, 153, 158, 170,
178, 189, 201, 222
Stinnes, Hugo, 108
Stoll, Erich, 223
Streicher, Julius, x
Strünck, Elisabeth, 49
Stülpnagel, Karl Heinrich von, xx, 43,
175–76, 180, 197–99, 201–2, 209–10,
214–16, 219–20
Sturmabteilung (SA), xix, 4, 7–13, 15–16, 35,
45, 66–67
Sudetenland, 40*n*, 42, 53–55, 57, 61, 169
Sweden, 42, 110, 134, 150, 159, 226–27
Switzerland, 42, 60–61, 73, 134, 148,
150–51, 159

Terboven, Josef, 7, 9
Teuchert, Friedrich von, 210–11
Thiele, Fritz, 189
Third Reich, *see* Germany
Thomas, Georg, xx, 43, 77–78, 107, 110
Todt, Fritz, 115
Treskow, Henning von, xx, 136–45, 147,
153, 160, 162, 168, 172–73, 220–21,
230

Treviranus, Gottfried Reinhold, 13–14
Tunisia, 163–66
Turkey, 155

Ukraine, 42, 74, 154
United States, 41, 77, 113, 136, 151–53, 155,
164–66, 170–73, 180, 232–35, 238

"Valkyrie" plan, 169–216, 222
V rockets, 156, 171, 200
Vansittart, Robert, 45, 76
Vatican, 109–10, 148, 228
Vermehren, Erich, 159
Versailles treaty, x, 4, 18–20
Volkssturm (Home Guard), 236
Vollmer, Georg, 93, 105

Wagner, Eduard, 197
Wallenberg, Jakob, 226
Weber, Christian, 100
Wehrmacht, xix–xxi, 18–20, 26–28, 32,
39–41, 43, 50, 52, 55, 57, 59–61, 73,
75, 77–79, 81–85, 90, 101, 103, 106,
109, 111, 113–15, 119–20, 135, 140,
144, 150, 152, 155, 159–60, 162,
167–72, 175, 180, 183, 186, 197–98,
201, 203, 205–8, 210–11, 213, 219,
221, 223–24, 227, 229, 235–36, 251
Wehrmacht High Command (OKW), 77,
110, 112–13, 143, 150
Weimar Republic, *see* Germany
Weisse Rose, Die (The White Rose), 120–22,
125, 131, 135, 222
Weizmann, Chaim, 226
Weizsäcker, Ernst von, 43, 80
Wenck, Walther, 235–36
Wessel, Horst, x, 100
Westphal, Siegfried, 78
Wiedemann, Fritz, 42
Witzleben, Erwin von, xxi, 50–53, 56–58,
195, 198, 200, 202–4, 222–24, 247,
255
Wolf's Lair (Rastenburg), 155, 157, 159–60,
170, 177–78, 180, 182–94, 196–204,
207–8, 214, 221, 225, 227, 231, 237
Woyrsch, Udo von, 83

Zipfel, Friedrich, 163–64

HITLER'S EUROPE
ON
JULY 20, 1944

Frontlines

Nazi Dominated Lands

Enemy Countries

Liberated Areas

Neutral Countries

NORWAY

DENMARK

NORTH SEA

IRELAND

ENGLAND

London

Amsterdam

HOLLAND

BELGIUM

Brussels

GERMAN
REICH

ENGLISH CHANNEL

ARMY GROUP B

Paris

Dacha

FRANCE

SWITZERLAND

Berch

BAY
OF
BISCAY

ARMY GROUP

ITA

SPAIN

0   100   200 miles

0   100   200   300 kilometers

CORSICA